COVER TO COVER

A JOURNEY THROUGH THE SCRIPTURES

DEAN HILL

DREAM WORD BOOKS
AURORA, COLORADO

© 2007 by Dean Hill

All rights reserved. No part of this publication may be reproduced, stored in a retrieval system, or transmitted in any form or by any means, electronic, mechanical, photocopy, recording or otherwise, without written permission from the publisher.

Dream Word Books
479 S. Kingston Circle
Aurora, CO 80012
303-548-5441

Editor: Mara G. Gaiser
Cover and interior design: Alan Bernhard, Argent
Produced by Dianne Howie, Backscratcher Books LLC

First Edition

ISBN 978-0-9792354-0-5

Printed in Canada

IN MEMORY OF BECCA BINGHAM

Becca was tragically taken from this life, along with her two children, Macie and Garrison, when this book was being published. A devoted follower of Jesus, Becca participated enthusiastically in our congregation's first devotional journey through the Bible. I am forever in her debt for encouraging me to develop this journey into a printed book.

Special Thanks

- To Allen Huth, whose passion for daily Bible reading challenged and inspired our congregation and whose Bible reading plan we followed.

- To Paul Dunne, who gave me the idea of a daily e-mail devotion.

- To those who originally received these devotions by e-mail and progressed all the way through the Bible in 2005.

- To those of this group who encouraged me toward getting the devotions into book form.

- To Stephanie Staley, for providing replacements for the e-mails that mysteriously disappeared from my computer.

- To Camille Yax, for compiling the devotions into an orderly format for the publisher.

- To Liz, Jake, and Isaac, my home team, for releasing me over and above the already full slate of demands of pastoral ministry, so I could pursue this project daily throughout the year.

- To the Christopher J. McCandless Memorial Trust Fund, and to its administrators, Walt and Billie McCandless, for financially supporting this project. (This trust was begun with proceeds from the book *Into the Wild*, by John Krakauer, the story of Christopher's adventures and disappearance.) Also, thanks to Walt for the firm encouragement to walk forward with the book.

- To Hap and Judi Lundquist, this printing's other major donors, for their magnificent generosity and belief in me and in this work.

ACKNOWLEDGMENTS

The Bible reading plan followed in *Cover to Cover* comes from:
Allen J. Huth, *Bible Reading Journal: Hearing from God Daily* (Denver, Colorado: The EZRA Project, 2002)

Unless otherwise indicated, scripture quotations and references are from:
International Bible Society, *The Holy Bible: New International Version* (Grand Rapids, Michigan: Zondervan Bible Publishers, 1973, 1978, 1984)

FOREWORD

For many years I tried unsuccessfully to read the Bible from cover to cover. Instead, like many folks, I settled for a select few favorite books and familiar passages, all the while looking yearningly at what I perceived to be the daunting task of tackling more formidable sections of the Bible, including much of the Old Testament.

All of this changed when two important events happened. Dean Hill challenged the congregation at Cherry Creek Community Church in Denver, Colorado, to participate in the Ezra Project, which is designed to guide folks through the Bible with daily readings in sensible portions arranged in a chronological order—not as they appear sequentially in the "Good Book." Surprise! The daunting task gets much easier when one follows the Ezra formulation, which makes each daily reading part of an exciting progression. Important eras and events are looked at in different ways by many authors, and as a result, the Bible comes alive and the reader is immersed in the evolving strands of time in the history of God's people. The most important catalyst, though, was still to come.

Pastor Dean inspired me to accept the Ezra Project challenge when he offered to provide our congregation commentary and prayer for each of the daily readings. Dean's e-mail missive came right on schedule each day, and I for one wanted to keep pace by reading the Ezra Project selection for the day before logging on to the Internet to retrieve Dean's message. I saved each e-mail in a special file, and as the year progressed, found myself thinking about how to preserve this wonderful experience for others. It is a blessing to have made the journey through the Bible and to see the same opportunity given to others through this book.

Thanks, Dean.

Walt McCandless

INTRODUCTION

The Bible is more than just a book. It is God's written word to the human race. It contains all the truth we need to know God and walk with him through this life. It reveals the story of redemptive history (the creation, man's fall, and God's pursuit of reconciliation with the human race he loves – first through the nation of Israel, then through his Son, Jesus). Further, it chronicles the spread of the Gospel of Christ throughout the known world, and it provides a prophetic account of the end of history as we know it and the triumph of the kingdom of Christ. Along the way, the scriptures provide us with a multifaceted picture of God's character, principles to live by, human examples to follow (and some *not* to follow), and glimpses into the kingdom of heaven. Most importantly, it shows us the path by which we can personally access the grace of God, the most awesome power in the universe!

Unfortunately, statistics show us that even among "Bible-believing" followers of Christ, this marvelous book is woefully under read. This fact led me to ask Allen Huth of the Ezra Project to come to Cherry Creek Community Church—where I am the senior pastor—on the last Sunday of 2004 to share the importance of reading the word of God daily.

Allen challenged our congregation to read through the whole Bible during the upcoming year. In consideration of this challenge, the worship director at Cherry Creek Community Church, Paul Dunne, approached me and said, "Dean, you really ought to consider doing a daily e-mail devotion to accompany our folks' reading through the Bible."

I laughed it off at first, but the more I thought about it, the more the idea appealed to me. I ended up embracing it as my "project of the year," and it truly became a blessing for me and, it seems, for many who received it. The book you have in your hands is the compilation of that year of e-mail devotions. The Bible reading plan contained within was put forth by the

Ezra Project. When faithfully followed, it will take you through the whole Bible in a year. It can be started at any time during the year, as the readings are not dated, but numbered.

The devotional thoughts and prayers are not meant to substitute for your direct interaction with the biblical text. They are only meant to serve as a companion as you journey through the Bible, hopefully helping you to identify and focus with greater clarity on that to which God is directing you. As I told our congregation, however, if God is leading you in a different direction through the scripture reading on a particular day, *please* disregard my focus and pursue what he is saying to you!

May you be blessed as you partake of God's word in the coming year!

Peace to you,

Dean Hill
Denver, 2007

DAY 1

He Who Made Us Is For Us

SCRIPTURE READING: GENESIS 1–3

Throughout this passage, notice all the ways God blesses Adam and Eve (and, consequently, humanity in general). He creates a wonderfully balanced world, perfectly equipped to provide for Adam's and Eve's needs. He makes them and breathes life into them, places them in a beautiful, lush garden, and gives them to each other as companions. Even after they sin, He lovingly clothes them and gives the first foreshadowing of redemption through Christ (3:15). Ponder today God's heart toward you personally. Even though sometimes we are tempted to think that God is out to get us, it is clear that God desires what is good for us and wants to bless us! He is for us! Praise him today!

PRAYER STARTER

Lord, please deepen my awareness of your heart toward me. Guard my heart and my head from the lie that you are out to get me. Help me walk in the awareness of your love and your desire to bring blessings, not curses, into my life.

DAY 2

The Sickness of Sin

SCRIPTURE READING: GENESIS 4:1–6:8

We see in today's reading the rapid expansion of both the human race and sin upon the earth. In only one generation, sin "progressed" from disobedience of a simple, but direct command all the way to the murder of a brother. Within a mere nine generations, humankind had become so wicked that the Lord was grieved to the point of erasing it from the earth. Realize today the cancerous nature of sin and its ability to corrupt quickly and comprehensively. Ask the Lord to keep you sensitive to sin in your life and quick to flee from its grasp, so you will bring joy to God's heart rather than grief.

[handwritten note: slippery slope down]

PRAYER STARTER

Heighten my sensitivity to sin's seriousness, Lord. Forgive me the times when I have acted as if sin has no consequence. Help me to consistently turn away from sin and toward you in my life.

DAY 3

Believing Enough to Obey

SCRIPTURE READING: GENESIS 6:9–9:29

ONE OF THE MOST AMAZING VERSES in all of scripture is Genesis 7:5, "And Noah did all that the Lord commanded him." When I look in the preceding verses at all the Lord commanded Noah to do and think about the faith of this man, I am constantly amazed. Although Noah had never seen rain, he built an *enormous* vessel! He gathered a pair of each of the animals and loaded them on the ark, all in response to *what God had said!* The Bible says that God found him righteous in that generation. I believe the righteousness God saw in Noah was, in addition to moral behavior, the fact that *he believed God enough to obey him,* even when it didn't make sense. Pray for that kind of faith today, in your life and in the lives of those you love!

PRAYER STARTER

> LORD, IT IS SO EASY FOR ME TO HOLD BACK from obeying you at "full speed" because I lack faith. Please build my faith and trust in you, so that I may consistently and without hesitation obey you, even when I don't understand everything.

DAY 4

The Spirit of Babel

SCRIPTURE READING: GENESIS 10–11

THE CLASH BETWEEN MAN'S PRIDE and God's sovereignty is seen again at Babel and is summed up in the phrase, "Let us make a name for ourselves." We humans always seem to have a bent toward self-glorification, to want to be gods unto ourselves. Remember that this was the original sin of Satan and that God takes it most seriously.

PRAYER STARTER

LORD, BY THE POWER OF YOUR HOLY SPIRIT, please quell today this desire within me to be a god, to live for my own glory. Help me to submit to you, forsake the pride with which I so often approach this life, and live truly for your glory. Tame my selfishness; crucify the ugly spirit of Babel within me!

DAY 5

Becoming a Blessable Blessing

SCRIPTURE READING: GENESIS 12–14

Abram, like Noah before him, was chosen to be an instrument of salvation and blessing in God's plan. What does it take to stand out like this in God's sight? These two men seem to have two distinguishing marks: great faith and great obedience. Abram believed God and obeyed him. It's not that great people of faith never fail—even morally at times, as these two also prove—but that they resiliently keep seeking to obey and please God. I believe God sees Abram's heart, his willingness, and his potential as a "blessable blessing." Pray today that God finds great faith in you and willingness to obey him, and that he will bless you and make you a blessing, just as he promised to Abram!

PRAYER STARTER

Help me, Lord, to trust and obey. I know that through growth in these two areas, I can become more and more of what you want me to be, and thereby be used in greater and greater ways by you.

DAY 6

Made Right by Faith

SCRIPTURE READING: GENESIS 15–17

Genesis 15:6 is one of the most important verses in the Bible. God credited the faith that Abram demonstrated as righteousness. It is significant that God attributed Abram's belief as righteousness before the law was given (at Sinai through Moses) and before the ritual of circumcision was commanded (in Chapter 17). Because the New Testament assures us that this principle applies to us as well (see Romans 3:21–22, 4:18–25 and Galatians 3:14–18), this means that neither law nor ritual of any kind, but simply *belief* and *faith,* make us right with God. True faith always leads to obedience, but obedience to a set of laws is never the starting point or what makes us right with him. Praise God today that we don't have to perform to earn his love, and again ask him to build a great faith in you like that of Abram!

PRAYER STARTER

> Thank you, Lord, that I am considered righteous in your sight based on my faith, not my performance. Continue to save me from the legalistic tendency to try to win your favor. Teach me what it means to be given favor and to live from this position.

DAY 7

In the World, Not of the World

SCRIPTURE READING: GENESIS 18–19

Both Lot (19:8) and his daughters (19:30–38) display shocking moral compromise. Could it be that they were influenced by the value system of Sodom because of their immersion into its culture? Today we must be careful of this very same danger. We are not called to be separatists from society, but to infiltrate it with the living gospel of Christ. The challenge is to engage with the people of this world in appropriate, constructive, and loving ways and meet them where they are—not by being legalistic, judgmental, or condemning "extremists." At the same time, we are called to stand out and be distinctly devoted to Christ as evidenced by our attitudes, conduct of life, speech, habits, and so forth. We are to be "thermostats" that influence the culture around us, not "thermometers" that simply register the moral and religious climate of society. We are to listen to his voice more strongly than the voice of this culture about relationships, sexuality, truth telling, contentment, humility, decision making, values, and so forth. Ask him to help you down this path today.

PRAYER STARTER

Lord, help me to be a thermostat that influences the culture around me on behalf of you, rather than a thermometer that merely reflects the "temperature" of the culture around me.

DAY 8

The Courage to Be Truthful

SCRIPTURE READING: GENESIS 20–22

This is the second time Abraham has pulled this trick of lying about Sarah. It all stems from living in fear rather than living in faith. Abraham thinks he has to deceive Abimelech for two reasons. Abraham doesn't trust that God will care for him or work in the king's life and he doesn't believe strongly enough in the intrinsic value of truth—that it is always better to tell the truth and suffer the consequences than live in deception. The beauty of this reading is that Abraham seems to have learned his lesson, at least about God's devotion, because we see Abraham in Chapter 22 exhibit perhaps the ultimate act of faith in the entire Old Testament—willingness to sacrifice his son because of his faith in God.

PRAYER STARTER

Lord, give me a faith that doesn't allow me to assume you will not act when a situation is difficult, but that allows me to be courageous, honest, and forthright as I walk out my faith.

DAY 9
Servanthood, Above and Beyond

SCRIPTURE READING: GENESIS 23–24

Notice that Abraham's servant was looking beyond physical beauty in his search for Isaac's wife. He was looking for a woman who would perform an "over and above" act of servanthood. He was looking for character. In the customs of that day, women were required to offer water to weary travelers, but to water all the camels was way above and beyond expectations! We live in a world that often encourages us to do or give the bare minimum. When was the last time you went above and beyond in loving, serving, giving, working, praying, and so forth, for the good of the kingdom or another person? May God make us like Rebekah—selfless enough to go above and beyond!

PRAYER STARTER

Lord, I want to be an "over and above" believer, willing to go the extra mile, to do the tough thing. I want to be more selfless and more like you than anyone tells me I have to be. I trust in your power to make this a reality!

DAY 10

The Price of Immediate Gratification

SCRIPTURE READING: GENESIS 25–26

ESAU IS THE VERY PICTURE of the impulsiveness and greed that have seemingly engulfed this culture in so many ways. He trades the greatest blessing a son could have, his birthright—a double portion of the inheritance and eventual leadership of the family—for the immediate gratification of food! He pays dearly for his choice, as do his descendents. We are quite susceptible to the same temptation—trading that which is important and lasting for that which is trivial and temporary. May our values and actions increasingly reflect what is truly enduring!

PRAYER STARTER

GOD, PLEASE PROTECT ME from living according to impulse and appetite, from ignoring future consequences and eventualities, and from blindness to what is truly valuable in my life today.

DAY 11
Ungodly Shortcuts

SCRIPTURE READING: GENESIS 27–28

It is now Jacob and Rebekah who act out of fear and presumption rather than faith. Although the blessing and the birthright are bound together, and although Isaac's blessing is needed to make binding the birthright sold earlier to Jacob, God *has already promised* Rebekah that Jacob will become the leader of the family (25:23). Rebekah and Jacob take matters into their own hands by deceiving Isaac, and they end up suffering drastic consequences. Some of the consequences for Jacob are: Esau wants to kill him, he never sees his mother again, the family is divided, Esau becomes the founder of an enemy nation, and Jacob spends years in exile from his family. Pray today for the wisdom, courage, and discipline to live God's way and not take dishonest or ungodly shortcuts, even toward what you think are good ends.

PRAYER STARTER

Lord, I truly want to live in faith and I realize that my attempts to do things my way instead of yours are sinful. Enable me to turn from reacting in fear and trying to make my own way when circumstances frighten me. Give me the kind of faith that results in steadfast obedience to you!

DAY 12

Rebounding When Wounded

SCRIPTURE READING: GENESIS 29–30

THE SAME JACOB who has sought destructive shortcuts earlier now agrees to work for seven years to earn Rachel as his wife. You may rightly say he doesn't really have anywhere else to go at the moment. But consider also that he agrees to seven more years even after being tricked into marrying Leah! In this reading, Jacob exhibits the kind of perseverance and determination that God can work into a person's life. Although this kind of faithfulness is really its own reward in many ways, God also clearly honors it when it is demonstrated in a life.

PRAYER STARTER

LORD, GIVE ME A FAITHFULNESS that will not yield to self-pity when I am wounded, but will allow me to "press on" with my eyes on the prize, today and always!

DAY 13

Giving Fear to God

SCRIPTURE READING: GENESIS 31–32

When seized with fear about meeting his brother for the first time in twenty years, Jacob prays. The content of his prayer is instructive for us. He offers humble thanks and praise to God and then simply confesses his fear and asks for deliverance. He ends by recounting the promises of God to him. Being a person of faith does not mean never being afraid, but it does mean expressing that fear to God and releasing it to him in prayer, so that you can walk on in faith.

PRAYER STARTER

Today, walk through the prayer model above with whatever it is that brings you fear.

DAY 14

Struggling With God

SCRIPTURE READING: GENESIS 33-35

Jacob is reminded in 35:10 of his new name, Israel, "he struggles with God." This name not only characterizes the wrestling match at the end of Chapter 32, but in a sense Jacob's whole life. Jacob's life is riddled with trials, disappointments, and difficulties. Yet he maintains a desire to engage with God and stay close to him, even though sometimes that means struggling mightily. God would so much rather we engage with him rather than turn our backs on him! Sometimes, when life gets tough and easy answers are scarce, our instinct is to walk away from him or nurse our pain alone. God invites us to bring our troubles to him and struggle with him, not away from him. The very name "Israel" is a tribute to Jacob's desire to do this very thing. Let's join Jacob; after all, we who are in Christ are called the "new Israel"!

PRAYER STARTER

In many ways I, too, am one who struggles, Lord, and sometimes that struggle is with you. Help me never be afraid to engage with you. Thank you that you can handle my pain, questions, and struggles as well as my joy, certainty, and victories.

DAY 15

Bragging and Jealousy

SCRIPTURE READING: GENESIS 36–37

TWO OF THE MOST COMMON CHARACTERISTICS of human interaction, and their consequences, are exposed in Genesis 37: boastfulness and jealousy. Joseph's boasting about his dreams aggravates his already strained relationship with his brothers. Our way in this world is never made easier by boasting and bragging. The jealousy of Joseph's brothers proves even more destructive than his boasting, to the point that they are enraged enough to abandon what is right. When jealousy grips us, our justification and resulting actions begin to make sense to us. We must cultivate thankful hearts of contentment that will not stoop to a scorekeeping mentality in life. Ask for God's help to keep your tongue from boasting and your eyes from envy. They both are dead end streets!

PRAYER STARTER

LORD, PLEASE GIVE ME ENOUGH SECURITY IN YOU that I don't feel the need to boast to validate myself in others' eyes. Help me be content enough with the ways you've chosen to bless me that I don't give myself over to envy.

DAY 16

A Clinic in Character

SCRIPTURE READING: GENESIS 38–40

Many painful "bad breaks" come Joseph's way in rather rapid succession. He has been sold by his brothers and taken as chattel to a foreign land. Now he is falsely accused, stripped of the position he has attained, and thrown into prison. Despite these misfortunes, Joseph continues doing his best and using his gifts at every step, rapidly rising to leadership status in prison and then serving two prisoners by interpreting their dreams. He really gives us a workshop in character! How do you respond when trouble comes your way? Pray today for the strength of character to carry on like Joseph and not give in to discouragement.

PRAYER STARTER

I realize, Father, that I need your help if I am to conquer discouragement the way Joseph did. When things do get hard in my life, give me the character to be persistent and the empowering of your Spirit to be victorious.

DAY 17

The Path of Preparation

SCRIPTURE READING: GENESIS 41–42

THE PROGRESS JOSEPH MAKES developing his leadership skills is instructive for us. He first rose to leadership in Potiphar's house. Then the warden put Joseph in charge of the prison in which he found himself. In this reading, Pharaoh appoints Joseph to direct the whole nation of Egypt! We have to believe that the earlier instances were divinely ordained preparation for governing the most populous nation in the known world. What if Joseph had given up when he was thrown into prison? In much the same way, it is probable that God uses the trials we currently face to prepare you and me for something significant. Take heart! Choose the path of faithfulness, just as Joseph did, and who knows what God will do with and through you in the future!

PRAYER STARTER

> LORD, SOMETIMES IT SEEMS MY TRIALS are without purpose and that all the effort I put into developing my character and skills is just a big waste. Please keep my eyes on the prize, that I might honor you all along the way to whatever the future holds!

DAY 18

The Perspective of Providence

SCRIPTURE READING: GENESIS 43–45

Joseph displays remarkable insight in Genesis 45:4–8 when he refuses to blame his brothers for their treatment of him, seeing instead the hand of God engineering the entire circumstance for his purposes. We desperately need such a vision of God's sovereignty in our lives today! (By the way, it is often much easier to have this kind of perspective on someone else's situation than our own, isn't it?) May you begin to glimpse the good he wants to work, even amid your life's darkest and most painful moments. Spend some time now considering the good he has accomplished thus far in your life through specific painful events and seasons. Thank him, and then ask him for more of Joseph's perspective today in your own life.

PRAYER STARTER

Thank you, God, that you do bring good out of bad situations. Help me to avoid living as a "blamer," and let me see your hand at work above and beyond the circumstances and people that have hurt me.

DAY 19

Investing in Future Fruit

SCRIPTURE READING: GENESIS 46–47

THE WALK OF FAITH that Joseph has been on for the last twenty years or so results now in blessings, not only for Joseph himself, but also for his father, brothers, and entire family. They are delivered from famine and receive the opportunity to live in the best part of Egypt because of the character Joseph has displayed through the years. Over time, his outlook, determination, morality, and giftedness have forged his solid character, led to his honored position in Egypt, and established him as one to whom God can entrust great blessings and responsibilities. It is our nature to often wish to rush to the fruit gathering, to the blessing. But we cannot know all the implications for the future that are wrapped up in today's choices, attitudes, and actions! May we not cut off the future blessings God wants to give to others through us by being selfish, petty, immoral, impatient, foolish, or lazy today.

PRAYER STARTER

LORD, HELP ME BE FAITHFUL TODAY so that I can be a greater blessing tomorrow!

DAY 20

Life Lessons from Joseph

SCRIPTURE READING: GENESIS 48–50

As the life of Jacob draws to a close, we are reminded of three "life lessons" in 50:15–25. All three represent a mind-set that is foreign to this world's way of thinking, but should be normal among people of faith. Meditate on each on of these lessons, and how they apply to your life right now:

1. To truly forgive others is to release forever and completely any desire for retaliation and revenge (vv. 15–21).

2. God really does bring good out of evil for those who trust in him (v. 20).

3. We can face death with complete trust in God, both for our own future and for those we leave behind—if we spend a lifetime demonstrating and developing our faith as Joseph did (vv. 24–25).

PRAYER STARTER

God, please help me practice true, deep, total forgiveness to others, just as you have to me. Please help me continually see the good you are working amid the evil and hurtful events of my life. Please help me to walk in faith every day I have left on this earth, that I may face my death with complete trust in you!

DAY 21

Beyond Our Control

SCRIPTURE READING: JOB 1–3

Modern humans want to believe that we can shape our own destiny and completely control our own circumstances; if we just make all the right choices, life's events will go well for us. This would make the converse proposition true as well: "If things don't go well, I am responsible and have somehow brought it on myself by mismanagement, bad decisions, moral compromise, or poor performance."

This section of Job shatters that paradigm. It makes it clear that many outcomes are beyond our control, and that forces are at work that are far above our agendas and "life plans." Sometimes we don't even realize the arrogance with which we operate! The Bible does teach the principles of sowing and reaping, natural consequences for actions, and even God's direct discipline for wrongdoing. These principles, however, clearly do not apply to Job's suffering. He could not have done anything to avoid his losses. The issue at hand in God's eyes was his response to the suffering. This was the challenge issued by Satan, and this was the primary purpose for which God allowed Job to suffer.

PRAYER STARTER

God, forgive me for thinking that I can control every outcome in my life. Free me from taking too much or too little responsibility for what befalls me. Help me live wisely so as not to cause unnecessary consequences; help me also to be humble enough to believe I can't fix every present problem or avoid every potential problem. Free me from that way of thinking so that I can respond in faith to whatever comes, just as your servant Job did.

DAY 22

Believing the Best About Others

SCRIPTURE READING: JOB 4–7

ELIPHAZ IS THE FIRST OF THREE "FRIENDS" to make the same judgment about Job—that he must have done something wrong or he wouldn't be suffering. Consider today the relational dynamics of Eliphaz's approach. He starts giving advice based on incorrect conclusions about Job's actions, Job's spirituality, and Job's real needs. Have you ever been too quick to criticize, judge, and/or advise someone else without truly understanding their situation? Ever had it happen to you? Surely there are times for sharing wisdom with others to help them with problem solving, decision making, and even accountability. But we really need a healthy dose of restraint when it comes to presuming another person's responsibility for their hardships before we know the whole story. Pray today that God works in you a heart of grace toward others, and make the effort today to err toward believing the best about others until you have reason to believe otherwise. Give advice with the utmost humility to avoid having the judgmental spirit of Eliphaz. You might find others even more open to your input if you adopt this approach!

PRAYER STARTER

LORD, MAKE ME WISE in the way I offer advice to others. Start with my heart, keeping me from judging them or seeing myself as superior. Also touch the words of my mouth, so that they would always be helpful, not hurtful.

DAY 23

Rightly Handling Truth

SCRIPTURE READING: JOB 8–11

ALL THREE OF THE MEN that speak in this section express some truth but ultimately mishandle it by applying it poorly. Bildad and Zophar continue Eliphaz's earlier proposition that Job just needs to "repent and prosper." They are correct when they observe that God ultimately punishes the wicked and that those who trust in things other than God will be disappointed. They are, however, clearly mistaken in their blanket judgment of Job's situation and their "prosperity gospel" claims of untold wealth and success for all who follow God.

Job, for his part, is correct in his appraisal of God's almightiness and humankind's inability to challenge him (9:3–4), but he is badly mistaken when he implies that God is capricious and unjust (9:21–24). We must constantly guard ourselves against allowing our experiences, our preferences, and other people's opinions to shape our view of God. Instead, we need to rely on the totality of the biblical revelation to shape our understanding of both God's character and his dealings with people.

PRAYER STARTER

GOD, HELP ME KNOW YOU BETTER TODAY. Help me discern and courageously reject unbiblical ideas about you, whatever their source may be.

DAY 24

Hope Beyond This Life

SCRIPTURE READING: JOB 12–15

AMID HIS CONTINUED COMPLAINTS about his suffering, Job makes a couple of profound statements. These statements display the kind of transcendent mind-set God wants each of us to embrace. In 13:15, Job essentially says he will continue to hope in God until and even beyond physical death; and in 14:13–17, he expresses a degree of hope in the resurrection of the dead. The reality of eternal life with God is important for us to grasp as we grapple with the book of Job. His story forces us to ponder such issues as the suffering of the righteous and the unfairness that is inherent in this life. But believers in Christ have an awesome perspective from which to process the painful issues of life—Christ is Lord over all of them, including death itself, and we will ultimately share in his victory! The promise that there is a glorious life beyond this one is perhaps the only truth that can really sustain us and give us hope as we ponder or experience suffering like Job experienced. Ask God to give you a more eternal, victorious perspective when suffering finds you, no matter its scope or magnitude.

PRAYER STARTER

> LORD, HELP ME TO REST in your absolute lordship when suffering visits me or those I love. Just knowing that you transcend every limitation and hardship in this life, even death itself, frees me to respond with courage instead of complaint.

DAY 25

A Friend in Need

SCRIPTURE READING: JOB 16–19

*J*OB CALLS HIS FRIENDS "miserable comforters" (16:2) because they continue to wrongly blame his suffering on his sin. Job says that if the roles were reversed, he would use words to give them encouragement, comfort, and relief (16:5). He is basically telling them exactly what he needs from them as friends, and yet they still don't get it!

What kind of friend are you in such circumstances? Sure, sometimes friends need to deliver a hard word of truth, and maybe encouragement is just "not your gift," but there is a good chance your friends need and want far more comfort, encouragement, and relief from you than correction and confrontation. You at least owe it to them to be sure before you offer the latter. May God make us all better friends today!

PRAYER STARTER

LORD, SHOW ME HOW TO BE AN ENCOURAGER to those around me who struggle. Even amid my own struggles, give me some way to build someone else up today.

DAY 26

The Prosperity of the Wicked

SCRIPTURE READING: JOB 20–22

Although Job continues to proclaim his personal innocence, he now takes on the argument of his friends that wicked people never end up prosperous. Job is frustrated because this is certainly not what he has observed. He has seen wicked men thumb their noses at God and yet continue to prosper all the way to the end of their lives.

What about you? Does the prosperity of the wicked ever cause you confusion, anger, and even jealousy? It is important to remember that material prosperity and poverty are not accurate indicators of God's favor. Both conditions, even if they last the entirety of this life, are strictly temporary. No one truly "gets away with" wickedness, as Job wrongly assumes. We must remember that this life is short, and that a future judgment is coming. The Bible is clear that the real "bottom line" is not what we often think of as the bottom line. It is not what you have, but what you become and who you serve that determines success in God's eyes.

PRAYER STARTER

> **GOD, PLEASE KEEP ME FAITHFUL TO YOU** through either poverty or prosperity, and keep my prime focus on pursuing and pleasing you today. Let me become everything you have in mind for me to be.

DAY 27

The Mystery of God's Wisdom

SCRIPTURE READING: JOB 23–28

IN THIS READING, Job begins the longest discourse (six chapters) in the entire book by agreeing with his friends about God's power and about the fruitlessness of a wicked life. But then in Chapter 28 he adds an appeal about the mystery of God's wisdom. He argues that there are limits on what we can understand and that our starting point for wisdom is not our own observations or those of our ancestors, but simply the fear of God and the pursuit of righteousness (28:28). Ask the Lord to give you deeper respect and reverence for him, even as you seek to find meaning in the events of your life. He created us and therefore knows how we function best, so his insights and guidelines form the wisest path for us! Keep your focus on submitting to him and obeying him because that is the ultimate demonstration of wisdom in anyone's life.

PRAYER STARTER

LORD, PLEASE GIVE ME A CONSTANT AWARENESS of the limitations of my own intellect. I know that your wisdom is infinitely beyond mine, so bring me to the place of humility in which I am totally committed to knowing and following your plans for me above all else!

DAY 28

The Good Old Days

SCRIPTURE READING: JOB 29–31

No one can blame Job for looking back wistfully at his former situation. Anyone having lost all he did in such a short time would go through periods of grieving what had been lost. This does, however, point to a very real danger for us. If we aren't careful, we can waste a lot of time and energy in our lives looking back at how things used to be. We should certainly cherish our good memories and learn from our bad ones, but we must avoid functioning in the mind-set Job expresses in this section: "How I long for the months gone by." We can be overly distracted or even paralyzed if we fixate on the past at the expense of the present and future. Ask God to help you find balance in this area.

PRAYER STARTER

Lord, set me free from idealizing the past. Give me as much excitement about the opportunities of the present and the possibilities of the future as about the blessings of the past.

DAY 29

The Fruit of Suffering

SCRIPTURE READING: JOB 32–34

Far more than the other three men, Elihu attacks Job's response to his suffering and accuses Job of perpetuating his suffering by complaining against God. He comes closer to being helpful than the others have, although he still assumes suffering is always tied to sin (34:11).

Elihu points out one of the purposes of suffering in 33:19–30, although he is wrong in assuming it applies to Job in this instance. He speaks of suffering not so much as direct punishment for sin, but as a corrective measure to keep us on the right path. There is a truth here for us. While we would not want to oversimplify any particular case of suffering and pinpoint a needed correction as the reason—as Elihu seems to do—we need to be aware that God can use painful events in our lives to help us regain perspective and restore our commitment to following him fully. Whether it is a near-death experience, a loss, a bout with pain, or a hard time in an area of life, such as finances or relationships, God can use struggles to give us renewed humility and attentiveness to him. Are you going through a struggle of any kind right now? Will you turn toward God in humility and dependence in the midst of that struggle and allow him to renew the importance of your walk with him?

PRAYER STARTER

Lord, I know that somehow you are at work in and around all my sufferings. Help me persevere with your divine help, that I might emerge from pains and struggles even closer to you.

DAY 30

Questioning God

SCRIPTURE READING: JOB 35–37

Remember that God never fully condemns Elihu's words as he condemns the words of Eliphaz, Bildad, Zophar, and even Job. At times Elihu drifts toward the same mistaken grid for interpreting suffering as Job's three friends, but he does interject the concept of mystery into the discussion by saying simply that we don't and can't understand all God's ways and reasons. This perspective is indispensable when interpreting the problem of human suffering.

Elihu also rightly points out the hard truth that God is under no obligation to respond to those who question his doings. Our evaluation of the "fairness" of what God allows does not detract from his glory in the least. We are not qualified to evaluate him! When we accuse him or presume to hold him accountable, we are forgetting our place and crossing over a line into pride. This is not helpful either for our wholeness or for our relationship with God. We will have the opportunity to explore this further tomorrow, as God answers Job. For today, thank God that he doesn't mind us expressing our feelings and even our frustrations to him. Ask him to help you never to cross over into the realm of accusation against him.

PRAYER STARTER

> Lord, thank you that you can handle all my frustrations and questions about why things are as they are. Help me to express myself freely to you, and yet always to be respectful of you and know my place.

DAY 31

Absolute Sovereignty

SCRIPTURE READING: JOB 38–42

The saga of Job concludes with a dramatic encounter in which the Lord reiterates his identity as the almighty king of the universe in response to Job's accusations. Like Job, when we are in a season of questioning God's ways, we often experience a fresh realization of his sovereignty, which stops us in our tracks. When God does this to those whose hearts are not completely hardened against him, they always seems to get back to the same place as Job: "Surely I spoke of things I did not understand, things too wonderful for me to know."

God can handle it when we struggle with pain, confusion, and questions about the losses of this life. We must, however, always be careful not to judge him according to our own very limited understanding. We need to always remember who he is and who we are.

PRAYER STARTER

Dear Lord, I know that your wisdom is far above my understanding. Forgive me for times when I have questioned you in a spirit of pride. Thanks for being patient with me and reminding me of your absolute sovereignty!

DAY 32

Beyond Our Limitations

SCRIPTURE READING: EXODUS 1–4

As God speaks to Moses and appoints him to a great task, Moses shifts into excuse-making overdrive (3:11–4:14). You can undoubtedly relate to many of the feelings Moses is wrestling with here. No one knows all the core issues behind his "who am I's" and "what if's." Whatever the causes of his feelings of inadequacy, Moses needs to believe that God can work beyond and in spite of his personal limitations. Oh, how we each need this same realization in the things God calls us to do for him! Even if we are right about our inadequacies, we need to have two beliefs: God is not content to leave us as we are, but desires to equip us and make us more than we are right now. More importantly, our limitations do not cancel God's power. Rather, he delights in working great things through improbable people! Notice that God does not try to assure Moses, "You're a great guy," but instead, "I will be with you." God still promises his presence to those who trust him and obediently step up. Allow him to overcome your excuse making. Ask him to shore up your faith and then to use you mightily!

PRAYER STARTER

Lord, help me not to hide behind excuses when it comes to stepping out in faith to serve you. Thank you for not being limited by my inadequacies. Glorify yourself by working through me today!

DAY 33

When a Heart Is Hardened

SCRIPTURE READING: EXODUS 5–8

Hardness of heart is a funny thing. Notice that Pharaoh's only "softening" occurs when he and his people suffer severe plagues and then quickly subsides when relief comes. How could the king of the mightiest nation on earth be so fickle and shallow? Don't kid yourself—each one of us has the potential to behave exactly the same way when we have turned away from or against the Lord. We can easily be influenced by external pressures to acquiesce with our lips and yet hold out on him in our hearts. The Bible is clear in multiple passages that God at times uses our experiences of pain and loss to get our attention and to work repentance within us. The next time he gets your attention, make sure you continue to focus on him after your pain subsides!

PRAYER STARTER

Oh, Lord, please give me a soft heart that will not harden when I am at ease, but will continually see my need of you and seek you intently.

DAY 34

Obeying Without "Results"

SCRIPTURE READING: EXODUS 9–11

COULD IT BE THAT WE ARE TOO RESULTS ORIENTED as Christ followers? Consider Moses for a moment. God promises him ultimate victory and deliverance, but also tells him forthrightly that Pharoah's heart will remain hard throughout all the miracles until the very end. Even though God himself has said it will be futile, Moses goes to Pharaoh ten times out of sheer obedience to God—*knowing*, mind you, that Pharaoh's heart will be hard. In contrast, sometimes we operate too much on a success/failure model that calls for instant, tangible results and victories. Some questions to consider are:

> Whatever happened to the intrinsic value of obeying God?
>
> Can we shift to finding joy in simple obedience and then "let the chips fall where they may"?
>
> How would such a paradigm shift affect your sharing of the gospel?
>
> How would it affect your everyday obedience to God?
>
> Had Moses been a twenty-first century Christian, which visit to Pharaoh do you think would have been his last?

PRAYER STARTER

LORD, GIVE ME A HEART that will find great joy in obeying you today, regardless of the immediate results.

DAY 35

Remembering His Graces

SCRIPTURE READING: EXODUS 12–13

GOD PLACES A HIGH VALUE ON REMEMBERING. Even before he executes the Passover, he begins to tell the Israelites how to commemorate it in years to come. The precision with which the ceremony is described, however, is not commanded because technically correct religious rituals have some intrinsic spiritual power, but to prevent the meaning of the festival from becoming diluted over time. Remembering the deliverance from Egypt is the main thing, not the intricacies of the observance. God wants his action in human history to be indelibly stamped on the hearts of his people!

The Lord has provided the greatest of deliverances to those of us who are in Christ. Spend time today remembering his sacrifice on the cross and the ways he worked in your life to bring you to salvation. Thank him for other deliverances he has worked in your life, and allow these memories to encourage you about whatever trials you are currently facing. Let the joy of remembering give you strength for today. He is still the same God!

PRAYER STARTER

LET ME LIVE MY LIFE as one who remembers you constantly, Lord. As I recall the victories of the past, may it strengthen me for the challenges of today and tomorrow.

DAY 36

Faith When We're Trapped

SCRIPTURE READING: EXODUS 14–15

God allows the Israelites to be in a trapped situation for a bit, and their faith seemingly vanishes. Although they have just seen a great miracle leading to their deliverance—ten miracles, actually—they exhibit shallow faith and are too ready to panic. In 14:13, thankfully, Moses shows tremendous growth as a leader by his strong encouragement.

Of course, it is easy for us to criticize the Israelites' attitude from the safe distance of three millennia away, but they were facing a certain death without God's direct intervention, so their reaction was certainly within the realm of normal. The catch is that God does not call his people to respond in normal, natural ways, but with supernatural perspective! When you are caught in a problem and see no immediate way out, will you respond like Moses or like his followers?

PRAYER STARTER

God, please grow my faith today so that I will have a reservoir from which to draw during tomorrow's crises.

DAY 37

Fresh Manna for Today

SCRIPTURE READING: EXODUS 16–18

THE SENDING OF MANNA as daily provision is a wonderful step in building of the Israelites' faith. The fact that it has to be gathered every day increases their sense of daily dependence on God. Yesterday's manna will not do! It must be gathered fresh every morning, or else it rots and fills with maggots.

Likewise, our spiritual walk with God needs to grow into the "daily dependence" stage. We need to engage with him daily in prayer and scripture reading, as well as move toward moment-by-moment consciousness of his presence. Just as yesterday's manna would not last to sustain them physically, our past experiences of intimacy with God and what he has illuminated of his word will not remain fresh for us without this daily seeking. Ask him today for freshness in your walk with him and for a persistent heart that seeks him with regularity. Then your faith and dependence on him can grow as he wants.

PRAYER STARTER

> WHILE I THANK YOU for all the victories of the past, Lord, I know that I cannot afford to live on them today. You have new works you want to do in and through me, and I don't want to block these works because I am so busy looking backward.

DAY 38

The Holy "Other"

SCRIPTURE READING: EXODUS 19–21

Notice that in this passage about the setting for giving the law, reference is repeatedly made to the Israelites keeping their distance from the mountain. They tremble at the thunder, lightning, and smoke and are warned of destruction if they come too near to the Lord. God's holiness, transcendence, and power are so absolute that all humans, even his people, are absolutely unworthy to stand in his presence.

Remember that his holiness and "otherness" is just as absolute today, and that it is only through Jesus that we can boldly come into his presence without fear. Knowing all that Jesus accomplished for us in clearing the way for a relationship with God, we are tempted to forget his awesomeness at times. We can sometimes approach our relationship with him and how we live our lives with flippancy and irreverence about who he is and who we are. Ask God to give you balance between a holy fear of him and the joyful freedom of unfettered access to his grace and his presence in your life. We desperately need both realities in our lives.

PRAYER STARTER

Lord, I revere you today. Please establish a holy fear and respect for you in my heart. I never want to disrespect you or treat you flippantly. Show me any ways I have done this so I may turn from them and walk in reverence as well as intimacy with you.

DAY 39

It's Not a Jungle Out There

SCRIPTURE READING: EXODUS 22–24

In most of the laws given in Chapter 22 of Exodus, the emphasis is on protecting personal property and individual well-being. The concept of restitution—that a person must make amends for any personal injury he causes and pay back what he has stolen, damaged, or destroyed—is presented again and again. Interestingly, the mind-set of many today is "If I can get away with it, it must be okay." We see by the severity of the punishments prescribed how seriously God regards the matter of taking advantage of other people. We live in a world where often the "law of the jungle" still rules, and where the craftiest, cruelest, and underhanded often seem to get ahead and get away with their ruthlessness. Rest assured that in God's economy, which is the only one that eternally matters, such actions and attitudes are not overlooked, and we do not need to fear that wicked people will ultimately end up ahead or that evil will win.

PRAYER STARTER

God, please examine my heart and show me any areas in which I have taken advantage of others that need to be made right. Please protect me from the temptation to hurt others when it arises and give me a heart of love for others that will go beyond not hurting them, but will yearn to actively bless others.

DAY 40

The Dwelling Place of God

SCRIPTURE READING: EXODUS 25–27

As we progress through the description of the tabernacle (the tent in which the Israelites were to worship the Lord, and in which his presence was manifest), it is important to understand that the tabernacle and its contents are for us a type (a visible, physical representation) of some spiritual truths that actually occur in the New Testament. We will be looking at a few of these the next couple of days, and it will hopefully become a great point of worship for you as we consider these truths.

Today, consider the tabernacle itself. It is a type of the church (not the building, but the entire body of Christ-followers collectively) because God inhabits his church through the Spirit (Ephesians 2:19–22). It is a type of the individual believer because God inhabits each person who accepts Christ as Lord and Savior by faith (2 Corinthians 6:16). It is finally a type of heaven, where God actually sits on his throne in the holy of holies (Hebrews 9:23–24).

PRAYER STARTER

> Thank you, God, for the incomprehensible realities represented by the tabernacle. Let me fully embrace the truth that your church is your habitation; that as a follower of Christ I have you, the awesome God of the universe, living in me; and that you even now reign in glory and are high and lifted up on your throne. I worship you for your might, power, and splendor; and also for the nearness and intimacy of you in my heart.

DAY 41
The Price of Sin

SCRIPTURE READING: EXODUS 28–29

ONGRATULATIONS FOR MAKING IT THIS FAR in your reading! Hang in there. In the coming readings we will walk through some very common "bog down" points for folks intending to read through the whole Bible. However, there are some important lessons and applications for our lives in the next few books, so do not let the admitted monotony of some of this material discourage and defeat you. Keep your eyes on the prize!

In today's reading, we find the beginning of the sacrificial system in Israel. Contemplate that the daily sacrifices are, in fact, types of Christ—they are the literal and terrible penalties for sin and the dramatic measures that had to be taken to remove its stain. Thank God today that Jesus became the final and all-sufficient sacrifice, paying the price for our sins by his slaughter on the cross. Draw near to God in prayer today. Jesus died so you could.

PRAYER STARTER

FATHER, THANK YOU FOR SENDING JESUS to die on the cross for my sins. The fact that you wanted a relationship with me that badly still moves me. When I am tempted today, help me remember the terrible price of my sin.

DAY 42

The Aroma of Worship

SCRIPTURE READING: EXODUS 30–31

THE INCENSE THAT IS PRESCRIBED throughout these descriptions serves as a type (remember, a "type" in theology means a visible, physical representation of a spiritual reality) of worship. Just as incense smoke has a pleasing aroma, true worship from our hearts is pleasing to God as it wafts into his presence. Spend some time today just worshipping God—tell him how wonderful, awesome, glorious, mighty, righteous, kind, wise, etc. he is. When it comes from our hearts, this kind of worship is a pleasing aroma to him. Get joy and renewal today from pleasing God with your worship.

PRAYER STARTER

LORD, TEACH ME TO WORSHIP YOU from my heart. Give me the perseverance to continue to practice active praise as I learn more and more about how to praise you better.

DAY 43

The God We Can't Control

SCRIPTURE READING: EXODUS 32–34

What an outrageous and bewildering act on the part of the Israelites! What are they thinking? A mere three months or so after leaving Egypt, they turn to outright paganism because they are frustrated with the length of time Moses spends on the mountain with God, and with God's transcendence of the physical realm. They want gods that operate according to their time frames, who are at their beck and call, and also gods that are visible and touchable.

Unfortunately, these same instincts can lead us today into a sort of idolatry. Don't look for or create a god you can control, like the Israelites did. Instead, continually submit to the God of the Bible, realizing that he is in some ways mysteriously beyond us, and also that he sometimes has a time frame that does not fit our preferences. Once we accept these realities and embrace them, we can live in joyful trust that he is in control, even if we can't understand everything and even when he says, "Wait in faith, child!"

PRAYER STARTER

God, help me never to try to control you, or to desert you for lesser gods that I believe might serve me more. Remove me from the throne of my life, that I may fully follow the living God!

DAY 44

Generosity and Servanthood: The Kingdom's Currency

SCRIPTURE READING: EXODUS 35–36

The Israelites are hard to figure out. Even after their apostasy with the golden calf, once they decide to give themselves to the Lord, they again become a positive example for us of how the kingdom is supposed to work. Notice two points that today's passage tells us about them. First, they all gave generously to the work of advancing God's purposes, to the extent that the craftsmen had to tell them to stop bringing their offerings (36:5–7)! Have you ever heard of a church in this predicament? Second, a number of people stepped up and used their gifts and talents to advance the purposes of God when they were needed.

This poses two questions to ponder before the Lord today: First, am I being generous, doing my part, for God's kingdom with the financial resources he has brought my way? And second, am I joyfully and regularly serving him with the talents and gifts he has given me? These are two questions that *cannot* be left out of any serious discussion of what it means to follow Jesus today. Lay these two questions out before the Lord today and allow him to show you where growth may be needed.

PRAYER STARTER

Lord, help me be a generous financial supporter of your work on earth today, specifically through the local church. Help me further find ways to use my gifts and talents to serve you on a regular basis.

DAY 45

The God Who Goes With Us

SCRIPTURE READING: EXODUS 37–38

Have you ever considered why the Ark of the Covenant, which was the sovereign center of God's earthly presence during this dispensation, had poles for carrying it that remained in the rings on the sides at all times; and why the tabernacle where it was housed had to be a tent? It was because God chose to be on the move with his people! As long as they were not settled, but traveling, he was committed to going everywhere they went. He would not confine himself to a permanent dwelling while his people were on a journey.

Meditate today on the fact that God does not merely sit in heaven with his "feet up," but is here with us every day of our lives. In this age, he even dwells within his followers by his Holy Spirit. He is in every circumstance with us, just as he was back then!

PRAYER STARTER

Thank you, God of all creation, for your presence in my life. Help me today to be more aware of you than ever before. Teach me how to hold your hand and be in fellowship with you throughout my day. Help me to be your "tabernacle" today, your fullness and power dwelling in me, in order to bring you maximum glory.

DAY 46

Clothed in His Righteousness

SCRIPTURE READING: EXODUS 39–40

Think today about the special garments worn by the high priest as he ministered before the Lord. All the finery and symbolism of the ephod, the breastpiece, the robe, the tunic, the turban, and the sash were not for the aggrandizement of Aaron, the first high priest, but rather to symbolize the nation of Israel set apart to the Lord. As the priest ministered before the Lord, he represented the entire nation of Israel. Likewise, he was only permitted into the Lord's presence fully clothed in the holy garments. He was allowed to do so for the specific functions of the office of priest and nothing else. In a sense, the garments he wore imparted him with righteousness and holiness required for standing in the Lord's presence. To fail to wear them properly could result in death (Ex. 28:35, 38)

Those who are in Christ now have been clothed in his salvation and righteousness. We can come before God's throne, not because we are good enough and not because he has relaxed his standards one bit, but because we are clothed with Christ. Christ is the only high priest worthy to enter the presence of the Father *on his own merit* and he has imputed that merit to all who are his. This is humbling indeed, but let it embolden you today to pray confidently and boldly to the Father.

PRAYER STARTER

Lord, thank you for desiring personal fellowship with me. Thank you for dealing with my sin so that this fellowship is possible. Teach me to draw close, Lord, in spite of my unworthiness and your abject holiness. Let me be confident, and yet filled with awe, every time I come before you in prayer.

DAY 47
Offerings

SCRIPTURE READING: LEVITICUS 1:1–5:13

Today's reading speaks a lot about offerings and details the procedures for bringing various types of offerings to the Lord under the system of sacrifice in the Old Testament. Consider the whole idea of offerings for a bit today. Granted, we are not under the same type of system at all, in which offerings are made for sin, guilt, peace, and so forth, but the idea of offerings to the Lord should still be a central focus of our personal worship. Do you regularly "offer up" anything to the Lord? In some ways, this is what it's all about. He desires and requires that his followers offer up our worship, our service, our monetary and material gifts, and even our very lives unto him. What do you need to offer today?

PRAYER STARTER

LORD, HELP ME TO OFFER FREELY TO YOU the things that I should. Help me not hold back my time, my talents, my treasure, or my affections from you.

DAY 48

Sin's Perpetual Cost

SCRIPTURE READING: LEVITICUS 5:14–7:38

Within these further guidelines for the performance of various kinds of offerings, notice what we learn about the seriousness of sin. Sin is such a serious matter that in the Old Testament, even one sin requires the shedding of blood for forgiveness. It is so serious that even unintentional sins require a sacrifice and restitution. As believers of Christ, we often need reminders of sin's seriousness. This is because we know that Christ has provided a once and for all sacrifice for sin, and as believers, we know we have forgiveness for all our sins as a free gift from God. This makes it easy for us to think it doesn't matter in a situation whether we choose the right or the wrong. Nothing could be further from the truth! And as believers in Christ, we still need to say "no" to sin. When we know what is right and choose to do wrong anyway, we cheapen Christ's sacrifice, grieve the heart of God, and sabotage our effectiveness and power (among other things). Without the powerful visual reminder that the daily slaughter of the sacrificial system provided for Israel, we need to meditate regularly on sin's cost and seriousness to keep our perspective clear.

PRAYER STARTER

> Lord, I need to see sin the way you do. I know that sin is real, and it's just as costly today as it was back then. May the fact that Jesus has paid in full for my sin never cause me to take it flippantly or to rush into sin with a feeling of license. Instead, let me exercise even more restraint and desire to keep myself free from it.

DAY 49

Every Believer a Priest

SCRIPTURE READING: LEVITICUS 8–10

Let me encourage you once again to hang in through Leviticus. It can be challenging reading, but still contains treasure to be found! In today's reading, notice the concept of the priesthood. In the Old Testament, individuals were needed to be set apart as representatives of the people before God. They "stood in the gap" between God and humanity, making sacrifices and securing forgiveness for the people. This system was necessary because of the inability of people to relate to God personally (or collectively) because of sin.

The beauty of the situation for those who are in Christ today is that he himself has become our high priest, transforming this old system into an entirely new one. Now, all believers can approach God through Christ, without another human mediator. This doctrine is called the "priesthood of the believer," but is far more than mere doctrine. It means that there is no longer a need for a priestly order, but that you and I have full access to God. It means that our sins are dealt with directly by the grace of Christ, without the need for another human being to "bestow" forgiveness on us. And it means that we each can be as close to God as anyone else when we pursue him through growth in Christ.

PRAYER STARTER

Thank you, Father God, for granting access into your presence to a sinner like me through the finished work of Christ on the cross. Help me draw near today, to hear your voice, to respond to you in obedience and faith, and to be in fellowship with you continuously throughout this day.

DAY 50

Set Apart for God

SCRIPTURE READING: LEVITICUS 11–12

Focus on 11:44–45 today. Notice that God calls his people to reflect his holiness in their lives. What does holiness mean? Does it mean perfection? No, but it does mean being "set apart." Just as God is separate from the created order and not subject to its laws or its impurities, the Israelites were to live holy lives, separate from citizens of the pagan nations around them and that did not reflect their patterns of life. This expectation extended even to the diet they were to eat. The Lord was serious about his people being like him—and he still is. Peter quoted these same verses to challenge Christian believers to live pure lives in 1 Peter 1:15–16.

Meditate today on ways God may want you to reflect his holiness in your life more fully. Does an area of your life look more like the unbelievers' lives around you than the God you love and serve? Offer that area up to him in prayer.

PRAYER STARTER

Lord, show me how I can better reflect your holiness in my life. Help me be more serious about really being like you in every way—that others may see you through me.

DAY 51

Caring for My Body

SCRIPTURE READING: LEVITICUS 13–14

We serve a God of intense practicality! These regulations about disease and mildew, and even a lot of the dietary laws that we will see more of later, have profound health implications, especially considering the relatively primitive understandings of disease that existed in the cultures of that day. A significant spiritual and religious element is certainly apparent in the regulations, as disease and mildew signify uncleanness and sin and result from the falleness of the created order. It is unfortunate that these guidelines were ultimately interpreted to mean that anyone with a debilitating sickness somehow brought it on himself or herself through personal disobedience (as we have witnessed in the book of Job).

However, the greater truth we need to glean from today's reading, I believe, is that God was and is concerned about the physical health of his people. He desires that we be stewards of our physical bodies and trust him for our physical needs. How is your stewardship in this area?

PRAYER STARTER

God, thank you for loving me in practical ways that extend even to the care of my physical body. Please make me wise in my choices concerning exercise, rest, diet, and so forth, and help me trust you in sickness and health as the ultimate shepherd of my body as well as my soul.

DAY 52

Access to the Holy Place

SCRIPTURE READING: LEVITICUS 15–17

The Day of Atonement came only once per year. It was the one time all year that the high priest went beyond the curtain separating the Holy Place from the Most Holy Place. He would sprinkle blood on the altar in the Most Holy Place as a sin offering, as described in Chapter 16. This curtain's function was to separate all the people, even priests, from the presence of God. The message was that man was separated from God because of sin and could approach him only through blood. The priest even had to offer incense prior to the offerings so he would not die in the presence of the Lord.

When Jesus died on the cross, the curtain in the temple was torn in two, proclaiming in a powerful way that all believers now continually have access to God's presence. This is because as our ultimate high priest, he went into the actual Most Holy Place, the presence of God, and made atonement for us by his own blood.

We all need to treasure more the tearing of this curtain. It is only through reading passages such as this one in Leviticus that we begin to fully appreciate the access that Jesus purchased for us.

PRAYER STARTER

Holy God, thank you that I have a privilege that used to be reserved for one man, once per year! I can be in your presence daily, with my sin and guilt paid for by the precious blood of Jesus. I can pursue a relationship with you based on love and obedience, not distance and terror. I desire to be faithful in this pursuit, for the highest glory for my soul is to be in your presence!

DAY 53

Sexual Responsibility

SCRIPTURE READING: LEVITICUS 18–20

WE CONSIDER TODAY A LONG LIST OF FORBIDDEN PRACTICES, a few of which were rituals uniquely identified with the Israelite people and their unique role and identity (e.g., "Do not wear clothing woven of two kinds of material," "Do not cut the hair at the sides of your head or clip off the edges of your beard"), but most of which reflect principles of morality and godly living that still are relevant today.

A large number of these commands apply to sexual sins. We live in a society that takes such practices lightly, and even condones some of them. Many today find a lot of these practices acceptable, but God takes sexual sin very seriously. It disrupts family life and society, weakens or shatters the commitment of marriage partners, threatens mental and emotional well-being, spreads disease, and defiles individuals in the sight of God. Moreover, it reveals a low self-worth and a low regard for the value of others. Spend time today surrendering your own sexuality to the Lord, and commit its use to follow the guidelines in God's word. Also pray for a "stemming of the tide" in regard to the sexual perversion and promiscuity in our nation and world.

PRAYER STARTER

> GOD, MAY THE THINGS THAT DISGUST YOU disgust me! I commit the use of my sexuality to you, and I ask that you turn back the darkness of perversion that seems to have such a foothold in today's society.

DAY 54

Offering Up My Best

SCRIPTURE READING: LEVITICUS 21–23

The phrase "without defect or blemish" is used often when describing the sacrifices that were to be offered to the Lord. This is because the sacrifice was to represent God's holy nature and foreshadow the perfect sacrifice of Jesus on the cross for sin.

We learn some great lessons from this for our own lives. We learn to give our best to God rather than giving him leftovers. We learn not to offer anything that is tarnished and common but only what honors God. True worship acknowledges and proclaims God's supreme worth! Offerings of lame or blemished animals were not adequate back then, and neither are halfhearted offerings and insincere worship expressions today.

PRAYER STARTER

God, help me consistently offer up my best to you—in my prayer life, my service, my giving, and my worship.

How do I continually give my best to God? Every area of my life needs to be penetrated with the truth that God deserves my best... always. My prayer life... needs a more "wholehearted" effort.

DAY 55

God's Ownership

SCRIPTURE READING: LEVITICUS 24–25

The idea of a Year of Jubilee may sound quite inequitable to us, with our modern ideas about property ownership. Returning all land every fifty years back to the family to whom it was originally assigned seems to cancel any purchases of property made in the previous 49 years. However, the whole point of this exercise is made clear in 25:23: "The land must not be sold permanently, because the land is mine and you are but aliens and my tenants."

The Year of Jubilee upheld the principle of God's ultimate ownership of the land. Think about this for a moment. How strongly do you and I believe that God owns it all? It is easy to say this, but of course our actions validate our words. Many today tend to think that giving ten percent to the Lord, which is the biblical standard, seems rather steep. But we have this principle in part to accomplish the same as the Year of Jubilee, to cement in our hearts that God is the true owner of all our wealth. Whether you currently tithe or not, check your heart today on this issue. Do you really believe that God owns it all, as the Bible teaches?

PRAYER STARTER

Lord, this day help me to hold loosely enough the treasures that I "own" that I am free to walk with you.

How can I become more of a giver... + demonstrate that God owns it all? Humility is an important part of this I think. And, remembering that God owns 100% of what I have. If I give 10% to him... he's letting me keep 90% which is quite generous!

DAY 56

The Need for Extreme Makeover

SCRIPTURE READING: LEVITICUS 26–27

CONGRATULATIONS! You have now made it through Leviticus, a book that, because of its unique make-up as a book of laws, detailed rules, and procedures, is a common bog-down point for those wishing to read through the entire Bible.

It is true that many of these laws will be changed in the New Testament, but a passionate lesson is underlying this book. God is determined to give the nation of Israel an "extreme makeover," to create a distinct people worthy of carrying his identity and fulfilling his purpose of redemption in the world. The Old Covenant is an attempt to accomplish this makeover by law. Unfortunately, it turns out the law is powerless to truly change the heart of man. It ultimately only magnifies his fallenness.

Now, with the church, God is still about the business of "extreme makeover." He still wants to produce an obedient people who can be his vessel of redemption to the world. He now does this by the transforming work of his Spirit in the life of the believer, producing in us Christ-like qualities such as love, joyfulness, peacefulness, and so forth. Thank God today for his work of transforming your life by the power of his Spirit. Consciously submit to his working in you today, and ask him to keep honing your character to be more and more like Jesus!

PRAYER STARTER

LORD, I HUNGER TO BE TRANSFORMED to be like you. I know you have worked some things into me and out of me since I came to you. I truly desire more!

I need to strive to let God continue to transform my heart. The change in me needs to be God's work in my heart, rather than me trying to follow a set of rules.

DAY 57

Finding God in Our Wanderings

SCRIPTURE READING: NUMBERS 1–2

Hopefully you're ready to gear up for some exciting stories and lessons in the book of Numbers. It will be quite a change from Leviticus, but not quite yet. The book of Numbers opens with an account of the census and the arrangement of tribal camps of the Israelites. There is, however, an important spiritual lesson here. Notice that the Israelites, although they ended up wandering in the desert for a period of forty years, did not do so as an unorganized mob. They had a set pattern for their camp, each tribe having its place to occupy. And at the center of the camp was always the tent of meeting (the tabernacle). Each time they pitched their tents, it served as a visual reminder to them, of what should be at the center of their lives.

The lesson for us should be obvious. No matter what wanderings we may go through, and no matter how frustrated, unsure, or confused we may become, we must always remember to do two things based on what the Israelites did: find and pursue the order that the Lord desires in the conduct of our lives and remember to keep God himself in the very center of our attention and affection. If we could accomplish these two things, our lives could be filled with his grace and useful for his purposes, even when we are "wandering" without all the answers and direction we might desire.

PRAYER STARTER

Oh Lord, help me not to distance myself from you in my wanderings. Help me walk in your ways and set my heart on you continuously and consistently.

DAY 58

Using What I Have for His Glory

SCRIPTURE READING: NUMBERS 3–4

THE ASSIGNMENT OF CERTAIN TASKS to three distinct groups of Levites in Chapter 4 is interesting as well as instructive for us. If you were born into the Kohathite clan, you were involved in caring for the "most holy things." If you were born a Gershonite, you were involved in carrying the coverings, curtains, and the like from which the tabernacle was assembled. The Merarites were responsible for carrying the structural framework of the tabernacle. The work of the Lord is still intended to be divided among the priests, and as we learned back in Leviticus, *we are all priests!*

Of course, the complication with this now is that we are not assigned tasks in the Lord's work based on our lineage, but on our spiritual giftedness, abilities, burdens of heart, personality, and experiences. Sometimes this takes a measure of thought, effort, and time to discern, and even some trial and error. The fact remains that everyone who is in Christ has a vital ministry to perform in the kingdom. Have you found yours? Are you developing and pursuing it vigorously? No task that furthers the work of the church and advances the kingdom—by exalting God and encouraging his people) is insignificant! We have a whole chapter here devoted to what might be considered fairly menial tasks. But they were *essential* to the spiritual well-being of the nation!

PRAYER STARTER

LORD, LET ME BE FAITHFUL as I discern and pursue the ministries to which you would have me give myself.

What is my vital ministry? How can God use me? Am I allowing God to develop + use my gifts/talents for his glory?

DAY 59

Holiness and Purity

SCRIPTURE READING: NUMBERS 5–6

THE NAZIRITES WERE ORDINARY LAYPEOPLE who dedicated themselves to an extra regimen of purity, usually for a specified period of time. During this time, they drank no wine and let their hair grow long. They were set apart as a visual reminder of purity and holiness. Holiness and purity are themes that run throughout the book of Numbers. The gulf that separates God and humankind because of sin is emphasized consistently through the book, just as it is in the two chapters of today's reading. In approaching God, the Israelites had to use great care.

By showing so graphically and consistently just how great this gulf was between people and God, the book of Numbers helps us appreciate all that Jesus did in bridging that gulf. It provides an important background to what the New Testament tells us is possible about the nature of our relationship with God: a friendship, being able to approach him any time, and a heavenly Father who is interested in the personal details of our individual lives.

PRAYER STARTER

OH LORD, PLEASE MAKE ME AWARE again today of the profound change Jesus' death on the cross brings to the relationship between you and humanity. Help me never take lightly your holiness and purity. Let me walk and live in that holiness and purity even as I draw closer and closer to you as my Father and friend.

Sometimes I take for granted the freedom I have in approaching Christ + my relationship = him. I have never known otherwise, but Numbers is teaching me how blessed I am to have a personal relationship c Christ.

DAY 60

Participating in His Purposes

SCRIPTURE READING: NUMBERS 7

As THE EXTRAVAGANT OFFERINGS are brought from each of the twelve tribes at the dedication of the tabernacle, it is all about *participation*. Each tribe brings a gift, and each member of each tribe thus participates in the celebration.

The kingdom of God is still about participation. Participation does not always require a tangible, physical gift, but it always requires something of us. It might require the time and attention of interacting with someone else. It might require the effort to perform an act of service. It might require the engagement of our hearts and minds in authentic worship. It might require giving a "cup of cold water" to someone who hurts. It might involve offering forgiveness, again, to someone who has hurt you. You get the point. To truly participate in the Christian life, we must cross over to that place where we are not simply consumers anymore, but contributors. If we expect our friends, our parents, our spouses, our church, or even God himself to continually pump us full of blessings, inspiration, and so forth,, just so that we can stay "fat and happy," we have quite missed the point! Scripture screams this message on nearly every page! Participation is truly an issue of the heart before it becomes an external expression of the life. So what is the attitude of your heart today?

PRAYER STARTER

LORD, TODAY HELP ME participate with you by offering something.

Consumer vs. contributer ← I need more of that.

→ it comes down to service and putting others' needs before my own. I need to give of myself more in relationships/friendships. More encouragement, kindness, joy, love...

DAY 61

Moving at His Impulse

SCRIPTURE READING: NUMBERS 8–10

CONSIDER THE PATTERN the Israelites followed in 9:15–23 concerning the cloud above the tabernacle that indicated the presence of the Lord. They were determined to move only when he moved, and rest when he rested. They would remain encamped until the cloud moved, whether that meant a day, a week, or a year. But when the cloud moved, they immediately would set out again on their journey.

The Israelites' focus on the cloud represents the sensitivity we as believers are to have to God. We should only and always wish to move at his impulse and command. If he is not leading in a given direction, it is folly to go there. If he is leading in a certain way, it is folly to hesitate. This is true of everyday obedience to him as well as major life decisions. As the song says, "I don't want to go somewhere if I know that you're not there." But how do we attain such sensitivity, so that we know where he is and is not leading today? We don't have a visible cloud, as did the Israelites. Many books have been written and sermons preached on this matter of hearing God, but central to *all* of them worth their salt is that God speaks to us through a love relationship that is real and personal. So, logically, the more diligently we pursue and attain that relationship, the more clearly we will consistently hear from him. We may want something more dramatic or easier, but pursuing this relationship through the disciplines of Bible reading and prayer, and through other auxiliary disciplines, such as journaling, group worship, fasting, solitude, and so forth, is the surest path to the kind of sensitivity to his Spirit that we crave.

PRAYER STARTER

GOD, I AM SO FAR FROM HAVING THE SENSITIVITY to your Spirit that you wish me to have. Make me humble enough and hungry enough to seek you more fervently. Let me move more and more according to your impulse, not my own.

DAY 62

Comparison and Complaint

SCRIPTURE READING: NUMBERS 11–13

Today's reading provides a stern reminder of how seriously the Lord takes two attitudes that are fairly commonplace in our world today: grumbling and jealousy. In the same way that the Israelites began again to grumble about their diet, it is always easy for us to find things to complain about and blame on others. But if God's people are constantly in a state of discontent and complaint, what does that say about our faith? What does it say to the world about our God? I'm sure you can see how this dynamic can seriously impede the progress of the kingdom of God.

Closely related to this spirit of complaining is the attitude of jealousy. The jealousy that Miriam and Aaron display toward Moses is also easy for us to adopt. Again, it is always easy to spot someone who has an "easier" life than you, has more power than you, has more money than you, and so forth. But one of the most wonderful comforts of a true, dynamic faith in God is the ability to see him as sufficient and to give him thanks for the blessings that are ours, without a constant need to compare and complain!

PRAYER STARTER

Lord, today give me the faith of contentment and not complaint. Help me find joy in you and the blessings you've brought my way. Still the ache for more and better and most and best that seems to always live within me.

I need to have God work in my ♡ so instead of complaining or comparing how someone is better than me... become the person God wants me to become. He wants to work in my ♡!

DAY 63

Arrested by the Obstacles?

SCRIPTURE READING: NUMBERS 14–15

Why did the Israelites ultimately have to wander for forty years in the desert? Unbelief! But they only did the "reasonable" thing. The ten negative spies, and the grumbling community who believed their report, merely responded naturally to what they observed. They saw the obstacles in their way—the enemies in the land—and they got scared and panicked. Surely there is nothing morally wrong with this, is there?

But you see, that is not how people of faith act! People of faith act like Joshua and Caleb who said, "...do not be afraid of the people of the land, because we will swallow them up. Their protection is gone, but the Lord is with us. Do not be afraid of them." Of course, the faithless then wanted to stone them, but the real issue was not what the faithless could do to the faithful, but what God would do with the unfaithful.

Who do you fear today, God or other people? And in what arena do you have the opportunity to show yourself a person of faith instead of a faithless grumbler and rebel?

PRAYER STARTER

Lord, help me to see my circumstances through the eyes of faith. Help me clearly see your mission for me, and embrace it fully, believing that you will empower me to deal with any and every obstacle in my path.

DAY 64

Repeat Offenses

SCRIPTURE READING: NUMBERS 16–18

It seems as if there is no end to the opposition Moses must face from within the Israelites' community. The rebellion of Korah and the others comes fairly soon after the ten spies' demise because of nonbelief and rebellion back in Chapter 14. As we read this, it is easy for us to say, "What's wrong with those guys? God has just acted in judgment once again on those who opposed Moses, and here is another group ignorantly rebelling against him, and in actuality, against God."

However, we need to remember that just as these Israelites have a hard time really learning the lesson that whoever opposes Moses opposes God, we ourselves have a hard time learning many lessons. As a result, we sometimes keep going over the same old ground again and again, stuck in the same destructive patterns. Do you know of a repetitive sin pattern in your life that you need to ask God to break and to strengthen you against? Are you able to see the destructiveness of sin in others' lives and thereby strengthen your resolve to live for God?

PRAYER STARTER

Forgive me, Lord, for my lack of spiritual progress, and especially in the areas in which I am a "repeat offender." Give me strength and grace to walk forward in these areas, that you might claim victory in my life.

DAY 65

The Uncleanness of Death

SCRIPTURE READING: NUMBERS 19–21

CONSIDER TODAY THE LINK between death and uncleanness. Numerous times in the ceremonial law, including this instance in Chapter 19, the Israelites are told that coming into contact with a dead person or animal will make them unclean. Of course, the practical side to this command is that disease can be spread through improper handling of dead things. But consider today the symbolic impact of this command. What all these commands about dead things being unclean reinforced for the Israelites was the idea that sin, death, and uncleanness all somehow belong together and that life, cleanness, and righteousness all belong together. Sin leads to spiritual uncleanness, death, disease, and decay. So in our day-to-day lives, we have the choice to walk in the ways of sin, death, and dirtiness or the ways of life, cleanliness, and righteousness. Choose life today!

PRAYER STARTER

LORD, PLEASE HELP ME IN EVERY INSTANCE to walk in the ways of life, not death. When sin and compromise look attractive, help me realize the cost of such choices, and that in the end, their result is death. Guard me continually from the stench of the unclean. Let the fragrance of my life be pleasing to you today.

DAY 66

Unwilling Instruments

SCRIPTURE READING: NUMBERS 22–24

The story of Balaam is one of the most bizarre in all of scripture. An apparent "prophet for hire," he is unable to deliver the curses against the Israelites for which Balak retains him. Instead he blesses them and prophesies good things for them. The larger themes here are God's favoring of the Israelites and his superiority and dominion over the pagan sorcery of other nations. But God's use of Balaam for his purposes is the focus of our meditation today. According to Numbers 31:8 and numerous New Testament references, still God used Balaam in a dramatic way to accomplish his purposes—even though this man enters the story with wholly selfish motives, is a pagan sorcerer, is clearly a reluctant prophet for the Lord, and although he proves to be only a temporary "convert" to the Lord. It is awesome to serve such an almighty God! People may think they are in control of their own destinies, but God himself is ultimately in charge of human history, and he is able to use it all for his ultimate glory. It is both comforting and freeing for us as believers to realize just how "in control" God really is. Thank him for this today.

PRAYER STARTER

God, you can use even the most unwilling and rebellious person as an instrument to accomplish your will. Help me to be a willing instrument, so that I may share in the blessings of your advancing kingdom!

DAY 67

Seduced Into Compromise

SCRIPTURE READING: NUMBERS 25–26

Numbers 25 is a tragic tale of the seduction of a number of the Israelites into false pagan worship. In this case, the seduction took place through sexual immorality. The women of Moab first got the men to indulge in illicit sex, and then used the pleasure and false intimacy that resulted to lure them into joining in the worship of their false gods, which was a further abomination before the Lord.

What can we learn from this passage? Certainly none of us have idol worshippers next door seeking to entrap us in exactly this same way; however, this passage contains real truth to bless and help us. The lesson for us is twofold. First, we should realize the insidiousness of sexual compromise; it has the same potential to darken our hearts and open us to forsaking the Lord. Second, we must be wary of the influence of those around us and the potential for us to be led astray into attitudes, practices, and lifestyles that do not honor the Lord. Although the following words of caution should be self-evident in today's social and spiritual climate, they bear repeating: *just because someone I know—and perhaps even like—does something, says something, or believes something, does not make it right!*

PRAYER STARTER

Lord, help me first to guard my sexuality, that its expression may honor you, and also to live by conviction in every area, that the pressures of others may not cause compromise in me.

DAY 68
Faithfully Preparing

SCRIPTURE READING: NUMBERS 27–29

When Joshua is commissioned to succeed Moses in Chapter 27, it is a remarkable event in which God's caring control over the fortunes of Israel is again shown vividly. Moses asks God to "... appoint a man over this community, to go out and come in before them, one who will lead them out and bring them in, so the Lord's people will not be like sheep without a shepherd." God has already been preparing the next leader of Israel as Moses' assistant for the last several years, and Joshua is now called "a man in whom is the spirit" (v. 18).

Many times we do not know for what future role the Lord is preparing us; but we can be certain that whether he leaves us on this earth another five, ten, or fifty years, we are preparing now for the opportunities, challenges, and assignments that will eventually come our way. Joshua was faithful as Moses' assistant and then as a spy of Canaan, and all these experiences prepared him to be effective as Israel's leader. This role was far less about the position than it was about the mission. It was not a reward for faithfulness so much as it was the next opportunity to be used by God in greater measure and with greater responsibility.

Be faithful today in the role in which he's placed you. Be fully present in the moment, not daydreaming about the future to the point of being ineffective in the present. But also realize that today is the training ground for tomorrow, and your usefulness to him tomorrow will be determined largely by your faithfulness today!

PRAYER STARTER

Lord, grant me the heart of Joshua, so that I might be fully prepared for whatever you ask of me in the future, whether it is "great" or "small."

DAY 69

Truth Over Convenience

SCRIPTURE READING: NUMBERS 30–31

This reading dedicates a lot of space to the matter of vows made before the Lord. Although in the new covenant we are no longer bound to the details and intricacies of the law, this passage imparts a principle that we need to take to heart in today's world, and that is the importance of speaking the truth and fulfilling the promises we make. It is so easy to get careless with our speech in the fast-paced world in which we live. We move at such break-neck speeds today between work, family, friends, recreation, and church that sometimes we can fall into saying what is convenient rather than what is true. Ask the Lord to show you any patterns in your speech that are deceptive and help you faithfully keep the promises you make, both to people and to him!

PRAYER STARTER

Father, I know that you desire truth in my innermost being. Show me my deceptions and deliver me from them, so that I can truly reflect your honest and authentic nature.

DAY 70

The Price of Cowardice and Sloth

SCRIPTURE READING: NUMBERS 32–33

In today's reading, the tribes of Reuben and Gad display yet another attitude that the Lord finds displeasing. They want to stay on the east side of the Jordan, remain uninvolved in the conquest, and take it easy while their countrymen go to war. They get rebuked for discouraging others with their lazy attitudes and are even compared to the nonbelieving spies who discouraged the rest of the Israelites. They are then commanded to help in the conquest of Canaan before they come back across.

Can you think of ways this attitude manifests itself today? At times we all have an impulse to rest, take it easy, let someone else do the hard work, and just enjoy our inheritance. But that is not what we are called to do! And that's not the attitude God blesses and empowers for greatness. Join the battle today!

PRAYER STARTER

Lord, help me to not be the one who hangs back and lets others "take the land." Help me to never discourage others with an unwillingness to get involved and "get my hands dirty" when you are calling me to do your work.

DAY 71

My Spiritual Heritage

SCRIPTURE READING: NUMBERS 34–36

The focus of both chapters 34 and 36 is the preservation of the inheritance for posterity. Although the apportionment of the land is an act of faith at this time because the land is not yet possessed, it is meant to be perennial—to last for all time, from generation to generation. The Gileadites' concerns about the land of Zelophad are also about the proper passing down of his land within their clan. This was a matter of immense importance in Israel. Each tribe, clan, and family was ultimately meant to retain the land parceled out to them for all time. These two chapters, as well as a significant part of the commands about the Year of Jubilee, center on passing on the inheritance.

We each need to remember that we are responsible for the spiritual heritage we pass down. Whether or not we have natural children, we are all passing down spirituality to future generations. Not only that, we are also responsible for what we pass down. The only way to ensure that what we pass on is worthwhile is to pursue the Lord with all our hearts and be continually mindful of our influence on all those who come after us.

PRAYER STARTER

I know that far more important than my possessions, passions, or positions is the impact my life makes on future generations. Lord, help me pass on good things spiritually to those who come after me.

DAY 72

Retracing My Steps

SCRIPTURE READING: DEUTERONOMY 1–2

The Book of Deuteronomy contains Moses' recap of the occurrences from the Exodus to the Israelites' current situation, poised on the edge of the promised land, about to enter and claim it. He details the laws that God has given them. As we explore this book, we will recognize many more valuable insights to apply to our own spiritual pilgrimages and lives.

In these first two chapters, Moses begins to recall the recent history of Israel while hearing all the people. This activity has the value of helping the Israelites remember how they got to where they are. Sometimes it is valuable for us to conduct a similar exercise and ask the question, "How did I get to this place in my life?" If we have made mistakes along the way, we can recall them and learn alternate ways of handling such matters in the future. As we recall the good things that have befallen us and resulted from our lives, we can praise God as we remember his faithfulness to us, and we can draw closer to him in worship.

PRAYER STARTER

Just like the Israelites of old, Lord, I need to examine my recent steps. Where they have been foolish or sinful, please forgive me and give me a new walk. Where they have been pleasing to you, please solidify and multiply such occasions in my life. And where they have been graced by your blessing, thank you for your faithfulness and love!

DAY 73

God's Greatness and Nearness

SCRIPTURE READING: DEUTERONOMY 3–4

Moses' encouragement to the Israelites in Chapter 4 encourages us as well. Two themes are prominent throughout the chapter. First of all, he repeatedly urges them not to forget who God is and the great things he has done for them. He reminds them that no other nation has experienced the same miracles and deliverance as Israel has. They must always remember that "the Lord is God; besides him there is no other." They are told to take this truth to heart—to hold onto it and allow it to shape their understanding of all of life.

Second, Moses emphasizes the intimacy of God's relationship with his people. He refers to God's nearness, his mercy, and even his jealousy, all of which indicate that he is very attentive *and* very personally involved in their lives.

May you truly grasp both of these truths in a powerful way today. They have the potential to change your life!

PRAYER STARTER

Lord, let me never forget that you are the one true God. Help me recognize you as God in the depths of my heart and in the expressions of my life. Let me grasp your nearness and involvement in my life, that I may more fully experience you.

DAY 74

Updating the Covenant

SCRIPTURE READING: DEUTERONOMY 5–7

Before Moses recites the Ten Commandments for the nation, and before he goes on in Chapter 6 to give them what Jesus called the greatest commandment ("Love the Lord your God with all your heart, with all your soul, and with all your strength"), he first reminds them in 5:3 that the covenant relationship springing from those commands is a *present-day* reality. He is in essence updating or extending the covenant to the present generation. In other words, he is not just reciting words from the past, but words that are meant to define the relationship that the current generation has with the Lord.

It is easy at times for us, just like the Israelites during this period, to miss out on the abundant life God has planned for us because we need to "update the covenant." We need to realize, in the same way, that it was not just previous generations that Christ died for, and it was not just our mothers and fathers or grandparents in the faith that were called to walk faithfully with the Lord, but it is *this* generation as well! May we never believe we have a part in his kingdom because we are born into a certain family or country or race or denomination! It is always and only as we personally respond to him and walk with him by faith that we fulfill his purposes for our lives and reap the blessings of a genuinely redeemed life. Just as he called the Israelites to a fresh faith in every generation, so he calls us today.

PRAYER STARTER

Lord, let my heart be renewed today in the intimacy of relationship with you. Let me never be content with the mere label, "Christian." Help me see that this race of living as your disciple was never more important than it is at this moment in history, that the stakes have never been higher.

DAY 75

Depending on God

SCRIPTURE READING: DEUTERONOMY 8–10

THE ISSUES OF PRIDE AND HUMILITY take center stage in this reading. We learn that the wanderings in the desert were needed for the Israelites to learn humility and dependence on God. Because of his fatherly love, he graciously fed them with manna and kept their clothes from wearing out, but they had to learn that they needed God more than any material provision they could ever possess. Moses further warns the Israelites against pride and forgetting the Lord when prosperity comes their way. He assures them that it is not their righteousness that has merited them the inheritance of the Promised Land.

Unpopular as this kind of talk is, we desperately need these words today! As you meditate on the matters of pride and humility, ask the Lord to teach you the lessons of dependence on him that so often are the hardest to learn. Let him use your hardships to break your pride and independence. Ask his protection against pride in times of prosperity.

PRAYER STARTER

Lord, teach me what you worked so hard to teach the Israelites: you are truly the One I need above all else in this world, and I am completely dependent on you for everything, from my material provisions to righteousness itself.

DAY 76

Dealing with Threats to My Devotion

SCRIPTURE READING: DEUTERONOMY 11–13

Today's reading concerns the intensity of love and devotion the Lord desires from his people. He wants his people to truly dedicate their lives to trusting and obeying him. They are to centralize their worship to one location to safeguard it against becoming corrupted with the abominable practices of the nations surrounding them. They are to be ruthless about ridding themselves of people who try to entice them into turning away from the Lord, whether it is a prophet, their own brother or wife, or even a whole town.

Do you need more of such seriousness about the Lord's calling in your life today? We should exhibit this same ruthlessness about being faithful and obedient to God. Although our tactics might need to be modified from those of the Israelites, we, too, should rid ourselves of those things that continually influence us toward compromise or rebellion against God. Find ways to proactively increase the intensity of your devotion to God.

PRAYER STARTER

My Father, please grant that I would have a heart of steadfast commitment and white-hot passion for you. Show me the things in my life that threaten that commitment, and then show me how you would have me deal with them.

DAY 77

Kingdom Leadership

SCRIPTURE READING: DEUTERONOMY 14–17

*I*N THE DESCRIPTION OF THE KING in Chapter 17, we see leadership in God's kingdom graphically contrasted with the leadership values of this world. The Israelites are told directly that their king is not to acquire many horses, many wives, or large amounts of silver and gold. We all know enough about ancient kingship to know that these things were usually inseparable from the office of king. The more of these possessions a king had, the greater his kingship. But the distinguishing mark of Israel's king is to know and obey the laws of God. He is not to put himself above the other citizens of the kingdom. How different from the picture of leadership this world embraces!

Think about your own concept of leadership. Is it defined by the accumulation of material goods? Is it about attaining a position of superiority? Do these accomplishments make someone a leader? Is your goal to be a "king" in this world's eyes or in the invisible kingdom that turns this world's values upside-down?

PRAYER STARTER

LORD, HELP ME TAKE STEPS toward greatness today—not greatness as this world defines it, but the true greatness of serving you. If this involves "power, position, or possessions," let me not be ensnared by such influences, but let my heart remain true to you. If it does not, teach me to recognize and rejoice at the true greatness you are working into my life.

DAY 78

Rejecting the Detestable Ways

SCRIPTURE READING: DEUTERONOMY 18–21

We read today (18:9–13) some of the "detestable ways" of the nations of Canaan that the Israelites will encounter as they settle in the land. The Lord has made it clear to the Israelites that their conquering of these peoples will be a form of punishment on Canaanites for doing such things. But the commands to the Israelites to maintain separation from these people and their practices warrant further consideration. You see, it was not for an ideal of racial purity that the Israelites were told not to intermarry with these peoples, but because of the danger that they would adopt their detestable practices and turn from the Lord. Whenever they did so in the years to come, they began to lose their identity as the Lord's special people and their fulfillment of his mission for them.

In the same way, we need to ask ourselves periodically, "In my life, who is influencing whom?" We are constantly among people who engage in the "detestable ways" of today's world, and it is just as essential to God's purposes today that his people be distinct from such things in order to accomplish his purposes. Of course, our conquest is not a military campaign to execute judgment and conquer a physical piece of property, but to win men, women, boys, and girls to the Savior, and thereby advance his kingdom. What are the "detestable ways" that most threaten to undo you?

PRAYER STARTER

Lord, I want to be all I can for you. Forgive me for when I've lost sight of that goal, and help me to be stronger in recognizing and rejecting ways of life, speech, attitudes, and thoughts that do not please and glorify you. Make me a light to those trapped in the detestable ways of this age!

DAY 79

People or Money?

SCRIPTURE READING: DEUTERONOMY 22–25

Notice the number of provisions in the law, especially here in Chapter 24, for treating other people with dignity, no matter their station in life. An Israelite is not to take a man's means for making a living as a pledge on his debt (v. 6). A lender is not to go into a debtor's house to get his pledge (vv. 10–11). He may not even keep a poor man's pledge overnight when he might have need of it (vv. 12–13). An employer is to pay a poor man promptly (vv. 14–15). When harvesting, all are to find ways to leave some for the poor (vv. 19–22).

Numerous such conditions are scattered throughout the law, but instead of focusing on any single one today, let's consider the overarching message their presence in the law teaches. They show us the importance of respecting people more than we respect money! What a valuable lesson this could be for today's society. Have you learned it?

PRAYER STARTER

Lord, please give me a heart that is not engrossed in the materialism of our day, but truly values other people more than mere money. This is a hard thing, Lord, and it requires a kind of death within me. But I know that the life beyond that death is more abundant and free, so I ask you to get me there.

DAY 80

The Optimism Grace Brings

SCRIPTURE READING: DEUTERONOMY 26–28

Moses, true to the form of many treaties of that day, uses the third of his great speeches (chapters 27–33) to summarize curses that will happen if the covenant is not kept and blessings that will happen if it is kept. He seems to have a rather pessimistic tone in these verses, spending much more space on the consequences of disobedience than on the blessings of obedience. We might interpret his negativity as a reflection on the harshness of God as revealed in the Old Testament, but perhaps it would give us more insight just to reflect a bit on Moses' state of mind. He has led this people for forty years and has seen their fickleness time and time again. If they aren't complaining about their conditions and longing for Egypt, they are turning to false Gods and pitifully debasing themselves. Perhaps the emphasis on the curses is just Moses' pessimism about the people he has struggled to lead. It turns out that his pessimism is well warranted, for the Israelites indeed failed to keep this covenant and were dispersed among the nations (28:36–37) on at least three major occasions in the years to come.

So, you might ask, what is the lesson for us? We who are in Christ are under a different covenant in relationship to God. Moses was right in being pessimistic because we now know that it is *impossible* for men to keep the law with their own strength. The good news is that we can live with true *optimism*, because Christ has already fulfilled the law for us and has given his righteousness to us if we are in him. So, while our actions still have consequences, both good and bad, we can rest in the truth that our relationship with God is secure and is not based on our performance. What a relief! I don't know about you, but sometimes my performance isn't so good!

PRAYER STARTER

Lord, I know I cannot be good enough to earn your favor. Help me drink deeply of your grace, that I may truly be transformed by love, not law. Teach me what this means.

DAY 81

From the Heart

SCRIPTURE READING: DEUTERONOMY 29:1–31:29

Go back and count the number of times the word "heart" is used in chapters 29 and 30, as Moses reiterates the importance of the Israelites remaining faithful to the Lord amid the temptation to turn away to other gods. A leading theme of this whole section is the status of their *hearts*. Even in an age of law, the Lord was not just after their external obedience to a list of decrees. He has always been primarily after the hearts of his people!

Today, God is still far more interested in our hearts than in any external ritual or act of obedience. Offer him your heart today and set your affection on him above what this world offers for you to love. Obedience will follow true heart devotion to God!

PRAYER STARTER

Lord, change my heart's coldness and indifference to you. Help me set my affections on you. Give me a mind that understands and eyes that see and ears that hear you.

DAY 82

Finishing Well

SCRIPTURE READING: DEUTERONOMY 31:30–34:12

Moses' experience of looking over into the Promised Land had to be the ultimate time of bittersweetness for him. He had led these people for forty years, through trials and joys, defeats and victories, frustrations and satisfactions. And now, although he sees the land he has led them to, he is not able to lead them into it.

We don't know, of course, all the details of Moses' thought processes, or what he shared with those closest to him as he contemplated this situation. However, in what we have recorded in scripture, there is a conspicuous absence of complaining and moaning about the situation. We don't find Moses wasting a lot of time on "what if's," "should haves," and "might have beens." Instead, he spends his last days encouraging the Israelites and giving them the laws they are to follow so their future will bring glory to God. He could have easily heaped blame on the Israelites for his plight, for if they had acted in faith 38 years prior, he would have spent the last 38 years in the land. Furthermore, they were the ones who provoked him to strike the rock at Meribah, which led to him being barred from the land. But Moses does not lose himself in blaming the Israelites or himself. Instead, he does his part to prepare them for the future, he receives the blessing of seeing the land, and then he dies in peace and with honor.

Too many times, we are hindered from this kind of response because we allow ourselves to be caught up in regret and condemnation for our failures, or we become embittered with blame for others or harbor anger because of missed blessings and opportunities. No matter our age, we should learn from Moses the art of finishing well. May you finish well, starting today.

PRAYER STARTER

Lord, make me a better person than I currently am. Free me from the weight of regret, blame, and anger, so that I may finish well for you.

DAY 83

Strong and Courageous

SCRIPTURE READING: JOSHUA 1–4

Consider today the act of faith performed by the priests who carried the ark in Chapter 3. They were called upon to step into the Jordan River at flood stage so the presence of the ark would stop the water from flowing. Hence, all the Israelites could walk over on dry ground. It is important to note that the priests had to take that step *before* the water stopped flowing. This act is a picture of faith for us. In numerous situations throughout life, God calls on us as his followers to take a step of faith *before* we see his deliverance. This calling is not about living recklessly and taking risks just for the thrill involved; rather, the point is to live with a mind-set of abandonment to God. Sometimes the step is a large one, like a life-altering decision or change of direction; sometimes it is smaller, like the "risk" of saying something about your faith to a friend, giving regularly to the Lord's work, or confessing a wrong done to another. Whatever the step is, we can be assured that the God who stopped a river for his people will never desert us when we step out in faith for him!

To what step of faith is he leading you? Will you embrace it for God's glory, your good, and others' blessing, as did the priests, or will you stand safe on the shore, looking over into a Promised Land from which your fear has barred you from entering?

PRAYER STARTER

Lord, help me to be strong and courageous like Joshua. Grant me a willingness to step out in obedience to you, trusting you for the outcome!

DAY 84

Holding Back the Kingdom

SCRIPTURE READING: JOSHUA 5–8

Notice that the initial defeat of the Israelites at Ai was brought about by the disobedience of only one man, Achan. The whole nation suffered because he was unfaithful and greedy. Although God's dealings with us today are usually not quite as severe, this episode holds a spiritual truth for us. When it takes hold in the life of one of God's family, hardness of heart and sinful rebellion, can adversely affect the progress of the whole body. Each of us should be in the habit of examining ourselves, lest we impede the progress of the kingdom and hurt the whole body because of our disobedience. Today, ask the Lord to make you sensitive to any areas of disobedience in your life, and turn them over to him in repentance. Doing so may have effects far beyond your own life!

PRAYER STARTER

Guard me, oh Lord, from the spirit of Achan. Let me not hold back your kingdom's advance, but help it onward.

DAY 85

Open to His Lead

SCRIPTURE READING: JOSHUA 9–11

It is always a mistake to live our lives without consulting the Lord for wisdom when making decisions. Do not pass over the little phrase in 9:14, "The men of Israel sampled their provisions but did not inquire of the Lord." Israel makes a treaty under Joshua's leadership, and all the assembly leaders ratify it, all without seeking the Lord and asking him whether it is the right thing to do. They end up getting duped into an alliance they neither want nor need. Many in our world today see asking the Lord about such things as foolishness and a waste of time. But as people of biblical faith, we have to realize that living life by our own wisdom inevitably ends in the same kind of foolish decision making as the Israelites fell into—with the same kind of result.

Sometimes we don't ask the Lord's advice because we have already made up our minds. We are afraid he will tell us something we don't want to hear or that the way he directs us will be more difficult. Do not let this fear hold you back from wholeheartedly seeking him. His way is always best! What decisions lie before you today, next week, and next month? Commit now to seeking the Lord's wisdom by asking him to show you the right path and give you the courage to take that path.

PRAYER STARTER

Lord, please show me your ways. I will seek your will in my decisions because I really do know your way is best. Give me the resolve to follow through on this, even when I am apprehensive about where you might lead.

DAY 86

Faith to Grasp the Future

SCRIPTURE READING: JOSHUA 12–14

Caleb finally receives what was promised to him forty years ago, when he was one of two faithful spies who urged the Israelites to go in and take the land at that time. We learn a couple of things from this episode. The first and most obvious lesson is that God ultimately rewards obedience, even though at times that reward might be significantly delayed from our viewpoint. The second lesson could be more easily missed—Joshua officially grants Caleb the land of Hebron before it has even been conquered! This tells us something about the level of faith at which these men were operating. Caleb, although eighty years old, never has any doubt that Israel will possess Hebron; he just wants to be assured of the privilege of conquering and then possessing it personally, as he has been promised. Joshua, as well, never has a moment's doubt about the conquering of Hebron. He never even wishes Caleb well in the conquest. He considers the conquest as good as done.

Let us ask God for such faith in what he has called us to do and what he has promised us. We can be just as sure that our obedience will not go unrewarded, and that the things God promises are as good as done. May we live like we believe it!

PRAYER STARTER

Increase my faith, oh Lord. Let me never lapse into the belief that my obedience and labor for you is in vain, just because I do not presently see the full reward. Let me move with the confidence and courage of Joshua and Caleb, who trusted your words absolutely and acted upon them.

DAY 87

Hearing His Call to Action

SCRIPTURE READING: JOSHUA 15–17

The people of Joseph exhibit an attitude common in American culture today. When Joshua adds the hill country to their allotment, they respond with two complaints: the hill country is not big enough and the Canaanites within their allotment are too strong for them to conquer. Joshua handles this masterfully, basically telling them that since they are big and strong enough to need an extra allotment, they are surely able to clear enough of the hill country to inhabit and conquer even the Canaanites with iron chariots. He pretty much tells them that at this point it is up to them to improve their situation!

How often we display this same attitude. God blesses us in some way, great or small, and still we can find reasons to complain and wish life were easier. Sometimes we need to hear the words of Joshua and realize that sometimes blessings are not just handed to us "on a silver platter." Sometimes we have to work hard, sacrifice, and even suffer on our way to receiving the blessings of God. Take heart today, and don't dwell on what is wrong, inadequate, or less than perfect in your life. Instead find a way to be more content, at peace, and thankful for the blessings that are present. You'll end up far happier and more effective every time you make this choice.

PRAYER STARTER

Lord, forgive me for wanting a perfect life just handed to me with no effort required on my part. Help me clearly know what is your responsibility and what is mine, but never to sit back and whine when you are calling me to action.

DAY 88

Seeking His Light

SCRIPTURE READING: JOSHUA 18–19

Picture this: three men from each of the remaining seven tribes come together with Joshua to divide up the remaining 8,000 square miles of real estate, and they decide the matter of who gets which land by ... casting lots! Don't let it trouble you that often in Old Testament times, the Lord chose to reveal his will through a ritual that resembled our modern practice of flipping a coin! God is sovereign and chose this method to reveal his mind to the leaders of his covenant community in Old Testament times, before the completion of scripture and before an intimate, personal relationship through the indwelling Holy Spirit were realities for his people.

The point of this passage is not that God blesses games of chance and reveals himself through them, but that God loved his people enough back then to make his will in major matters crystal clear. How much more does he wish to make himself and his will known to his followers in this age of grace! He has defined for us the path to knowing his will. The knowledge of his will comes to us through a love relationship that is real and personal. We pursue this relationship through taking his word into our lives, through daily renewing our minds, through walking in obedience to him, and through developing a continuous prayer conversation with him. We are blessed that we have a definitively more intimate and personal process with God than the one God's people had long ago.

PRAYER STARTER

Lord, reveal yourself to me as I seek you. I need your light on my path, so give me a heart that continually seeks closeness with you above all else.

DAY 89

Ask Before Attacking

SCRIPTURE READING: JOSHUA 20–22

Consider today the principle of asking before attacking. The Israelites were alarmed when they learned of the altar the trans-Jordan tribes had built, because they were concerned these tribes might be starting a new religion and turning away from God. By sending Phinehas and his delegation to them to ask about the altar, they learned their brothers' intentions were pure and honorable. In their initial rage, they could have lashed out prematurely, being "gathered . . . to go to war against them." Instead, they took the step of clarifying things so that knowing only part of the story, they would not act rashly..

Think of how much pain and conflict this one step would save in today's world. We sometimes assume the worst about others. When we act on those assumptions without asking questions to make sure our conclusions are right, we can bring a lot of unnecessary hurt onto ourselves and others and we can impede God's kingdom from spreading.

PRAYER STARTER

Lord, help me always to ask before I attack. Even when I'm not attacking others in blatant ways, help me to restrain myself from judging them in hurtful ways, so that I might bring glory to you.

DAY 90

Choosing God Without Reservation

SCRIPTURE READING: JOSHUA 23; JUDGES 1

Joshua takes a strong stand in the closing days of his life, challenging the Israelites to continue to be obedient, much like Moses had done before they entered the Promised Land. In a way, it is disheartening to read that some were still struggling with the presence of false gods and secretly worshipping them (24:14, 23), even after all the Israelites had suffered and endured. But we know from experience that this is the way sin operates—it never gives up tempting and teasing us, either. That is why Joshua's words in 24:15 can so strongly encourage us in the choices we will make today: "...choose for yourselves this day whom you will serve, whether the gods your forefathers served beyond the River, or the gods of the Amorites, in whose land you are living. But as for me and my household, we will serve the Lord."

Dare to make such a proclamation today, even if just in the recesses of your own heart. Get off the fence and serve him wholeheartedly, regardless of the choices of others!

PRAYER STARTER

Lord, give me the same courage you gave Joshua, to serve you without reservation. I will not be swayed by the choices of others around me; as for me and my house, we will serve the Lord!

DAY 91

Responding to Tests

SCRIPTURE READING: JUDGES 2–5

Today the basic pattern of the Book of Judges is introduced—that of Israel's rebellion, the Lord's judgment, Israel's repentance, and the Lord's deliverance through a judge. This pattern is repeated throughout this period of Israel's history.

The text states clearly that the other nations were left to test the new generations of Israelites to see if they would continue to obey the Lord's commands. Of course, they continually failed this test. The question all this raises for us is this: What if the Lord has allowed (not caused, but allowed) some of the sorrows and temptations that have come your way to test your heart? He doesn't test us to determine if we're worthy of his love, salvation, or anything like that—*none* of us would ever pass that test. But he does test us, among other reasons, reveal to us the progress of our spiritual growth. This hopefully has the effect of bringing us to more deeply recognize our dependence on him, to more strongly hunger for his righteousness, and to be sharpened spiritually in various other ways. Seek him for strength when you are tested today, so that in every circumstance your impulse is to follow his way and obey him.

PRAYER STARTER

Lord, it is hard to thank you for tests, pains, and temptations. But when you use them to draw me to you and shape me to be more like you, they are worthy of my most profound thanksgiving. Make me aware of the tests that lie in my path today, and help me respond in obedience.

DAY 92

The God of the Underdog

SCRIPTURE READING: JUDGES 6–8

Why does God command Gideon to reduce his force to less than one tenth of its size and to go against Midian with only three hundred men (7:2–7)? This may seem bizarre to us at first glance, but the text says that God knew the men would take all the credit and forget about him if the army was too large. He wanted Gideon and the army to have a mind-set of total dependence on him, and one way to ensure this humility was to drastically reduce their numbers. The apostle Paul recognizes the same truth at work in this passage when he says in 2 Corinthians 12 that God's strength is made perfect in our weakness.

We must remember this principle when we individually or collectively feel weak. We must find confidence in the God who can beat a mighty army with three hundred men! We must remember it when we are feeling strong so we don't become prideful and believe that our successes are our own doing. Let us find our strength in God today!

PRAYER STARTER

Lord of the underdog army, when I feel like an underdog, come and hold my hand. Help me see, believe, and trust in your mightiness and sufficiency, even when my situation looks hopeless and my resources look low.

DAY 93

Handling Power Well

SCRIPTURE READING: JUDGES 9

ABIMELECH IS A GREAT EXAMPLE of someone who is not able to handle power with wisdom. He eventually cannot tolerate any threat to his power, and his life is swallowed up by this hunger for control. He proves to be quite ruthless, and the power he grasps ends up controlling and destroying him. He is like all who share this particular dysfunction—obtaining power does not satisfy him; it only intensifies his desire to protect and expand his power base. Abimelech destroys his own brothers, as well as several whole cities that refuse to submit to him. His life is a dramatic lesson for us of what can happen if we let the power we hold or hunger for corrupt our judgment.

There will always be those who desire power but cannot use it wisely once they have it. The way to prevent this flaw in ourselves is by always walking in humble obedience to the Lord and seeking his glory instead of our own. Power must never be an end in itself for a follower of Christ, but only a means for achieving God's glory in a greater measure. How easy it is to cross over! May God ever guard our hearts!

PRAYER STARTER

> LORD, MAY I USE WHATEVER POWER or influence you choose to grant me for your glory and the good of others. Keep me humble in the way I handle power. And if you should choose that I be powerless, teach me how to receive this decision graciously and bring you glory through it as well.

DAY 94

Natural Disadvantages

SCRIPTURE READING: JUDGES 10–12

Jephthah is a compelling example of a man who, although plagued by significant "natural disadvantages," is greatly used by God. Think about his situation. He is the son of a prostitute, which undoubtedly carries a stigma in society. On top of this, his half brothers drive him out of the area. Neither of these circumstances resulted from anything he has done. They just happen. Yet Jephthah becomes a mighty instrument of deliverance for Israel and attains great power and honor in the process. He demonstrates advanced skill in negotiation with his enemies. He also displays exemplary restraint by not entering into conflict without first clarifying issues and seeking other solutions.

All that is accomplished through this man's life is done against the backdrop of an illegitimate birth and a devastating rejection early in life. God wants to do great things in each of our lives, as well, but we have experiences we would prefer to forget. Circumstances beyond our control often cause these experiences, but they can just as easily be the result of our own choices and actions. Regardless, God can give us the strength and resiliency of Jephthah to overcome obstacles and achieve his victory in our lives.

PRAYER STARTER

Lord, parts of my life could be defeating to your purposes; discouraging circumstances and events of my life could easily make me believe I'm disqualified from effectively contributing to your kingdom. I could even believe myself to be beyond the reach of your grace. But I ask you to help me to embrace your grace and drink of it deeply today, that you might get glory from my life as you did from your servant Jephthah.

DAY 95

Trusting the Wrong Voices

SCRIPTURE READING: JUDGES 13–16

Samson's life and struggles teach many important lessons, but for today, please consider his moral weakness in Chapter 16. How could a man confide like this in a woman who has already tried three times to trick him and give him up to the Philistines? The text says Sampson just intended to stop her from nagging and questioning his love for her. This seems utter foolishness to us! But we each have our weaknesses, the areas of our lives in which we could easily be duped into turning away from God and compromising with the enemy of our souls.

When you are tempted today to give in to compromise, whatever the temptation is, and whatever reason the enemy gives you, think about the foolishness of Samson. Be strong in the Lord, and do not let the enemy steal your strength because you trust the wrong voices.

PRAYER STARTER

Lord, please give clarity to my thinking. Help me not be swayed by the pressures of other people or by my own selfish desires. Let me see your way and choose it faithfully.

DAY 96

Doing Our Own Thing

SCRIPTURE READING: JUDGES 17–19

TODAY'S READING CONTAINS one of the most telling sentences in all of scripture and one that describes the prevailing attitude of Israel throughout the period of the judges: "In those days Israel had no king; everyone did as he saw fit" (17:6). Unfortunately, this passage describes not only Israel's history; it seems to mark the prevailing attitude of our culture as well.

Each of us has a choice to make: conform to the attitudes around us and society's low standards or make a stand for what is right, taking God's life principles seriously, even though most people still reject God's ways. The consequences of living according to our own whims and desires are profound, both for ourselves and those around us who need a ray of light and a witness of truth. May God ignite a revival of obedience among his people, inspired by love, not law. May we realize the true value of living under Christ's control, even if we could "get away with" living otherwise.

PRAYER STARTER

LORD, LET ME LIVE IN OBEDIENCE TO YOU, knowing your way is always best. Tame my selfishness and rebellion and help me to never surrender to the spirit of this age, which is to do as I see fit, without regard for you.

DAY 97

Turning to Him in Pain

SCRIPTURE READING: JUDGES 20–21

*I*T SEEMS THAT DISORDER bordering on chaos descended upon Israel during this period, so that much of the decision making in the book of Judges reveals a surprising absence of morality. However, notice the progression of Israelites in seeking the Lord during their conflict with Benjamin. Although they were defeated badly twice, they continued to seek God in more desperate ways. Then he finally granted them victory.

How do you respond to setbacks, disappointments, and outright defeats? Do you tend to give up on God or turn away in anger? The people of Israel chose to deepen their pursuit of God and their level of obedience to him. This is the way of abundant life and victory for us as well. When you are tested and even defeated, do not quit! Do not react in faithlessness and pride, turning to your own resources as the answer. Seek him *more* intensely. Obey him more fervently than ever!

PRAYER STARTER

LORD, HELP ME TURN TO YOU with all that I am during painful times. If it means repeated asking, weeping, fasting, or something else, I will not give up on you. You are life to me—where else will I go?

DAY 98

Character that Blesses Others

SCRIPTURE READING: RUTH

The Book of Ruth is really the story of three persons' faithfulness to God in a time when the society around them was disintegrating. God's grace is so evident in Naomi that it draws another to him—Ruth, Naomi's daughter-in-law. A devoted daughter-in-law and friend to Naomi, Ruth is an example of faithfulness because she turns from the gods of her homeland to the true God of Israel. Boaz is a heroic example of Christ-like love, in serving as kinsman redeemer for Naomi's property and in taking in the foreigner and blessing her with love and acceptance.

As you think about these three today, pray that God will work their virtuous qualities into your life.

PRAYER STARTER

Lord, I want to be an ebullient witness like Naomi, a faithful friend and godly servant like Ruth, and a vessel of kindness and redemption like Boaz. I know that you can walk me toward this kind of character. Help me take a step today!

DAY 99

Learning to Hear and Obey

SCRIPTURE READING: 1 SAMUEL 1–3

The way that God chooses to speak to Samuel in this famous passage is truly remarkable. Remember that these events take place during a time when "the word of the Lord was rare; there were not many visions." It would have been more expected for God to speak to and through Eli the priest, as he has the position of priest, years of service, and maturity of an adult, none of which Samuel possesses. But Samuel does possess a heart of faith and a willingness to minister before the Lord, hear him, and be a servant.

He serves as a powerful example to us of how to respond when God calls. Samuel invites God to speak to him, and then *listens* and *acts* on what God tells him. This might sound overly simplistic to us, but God speaks to us today through his word, and our response must be the same: we must invite him to speak and then listen and be ready to act on what he tells us. How easy it is to respond in another way to his word—to not listen to it, to disregard its message, to listen selectively, or to agree with his word, but not follow through with action. Determine today to be a constant listener *and* doer of the word of God!

PRAYER STARTER

As a boy, Samuel learned how to listen to you, and you spoke to and through him all his life. Help me live the same way, for your greater glory!

DAY 100

No Glory

SCRIPTURE READING: 1 SAMUEL 4–7

We have in today's reading the introduction of the term "Ichabod," meaning "no glory." This word serves as a sobering reminder to us as the Lord's present-day followers. The naming of Ichabod expressed a judgment on the spiritual life of Israel. Phinehas' wife, no doubt feeling intense emotion over the loss of Eli, Phinehas, and the ark itself, saw this as a dark time in the nation's history. Phinehas was dead because of his desecration of the tabernacle, and he had been the next in line to succeed Eli as priest. The Israelites were experiencing God's judgment, and his glory had indeed departed with the ark's capture by the Philistines.

Perhaps we live in a day when "Ichabod" could be written over the doors of many churches, and over the lives of many Christ-followers. But just as today's reading shows us that revival was right around the corner for Israel under the leadership of Samuel, we must know that God is able to do a great work in and through his church, even in a day like today. Let's examine our own lives first, and there make room for the glory of God. Then let's pray that "Ichabod " be removed and God's glory return to his church, this nation, and the world.

PRAYER STARTER

Lord, remove "Ichabod" far from my life. May I be marked by your glory living in and through me always. Remove any barriers to this happening fully today, both in me and in your body around the world.

DAY 101
Clamoring for a King

SCRIPTURE READING: 1 SAMUEL 8–10

Israel's clamoring after a king makes sense in certain ways. Samuel's sons proved unworthy to take his place as judges and the twelve tribes lacked a real unity throughout the period of the judges. The right king could help both of these situations. But God was displeased with the Israelites' desire for a king because at its heart, their desire was a rejection of his divine leadership: "... it is not you they have rejected, but they have rejected me as their king."

The Israelites wanted to be like the nations around them and run their nation through the strength of man. They wanted a human monarch in place of God. This is what made their desire evil. They made the mistake of thinking that a new government system would solve their problems. They failed to realize that their problem really was one of the heart, not just a matter of getting the right form of government or the right man as their leader. We can easily make this same mistake in our personal lives. We can believe that simply being more efficient, being more like others, forming the right alliances, or even being stronger can make all the difference in our lives, but what we really need most is what the Israelites needed—unified faith in God, true submission to him as the leader of our lives, and a dependence on his strength, not our own. Without these essentials, the other trappings of our lives matter very little.

PRAYER STARTER

Lord, help me depend on you and claim you as my King. Help me be wise enough not to trust in my own strength and accept the answers that the wisdom of this world provides, but live my life your way. Show me what this means today.

DAY 102

Hiding from His Call

SCRIPTURE READING: 1 SAMUEL 11–13

THE BEGINNING OF SAUL'S ILL-FATED REIGN as king foreshadows some of the dysfunctions that eventually lead to his rejection as Israel's leader. These foibles seal his identity as one of the most tragic figures of the Old Testament. We focus today on Saul's reaction when he was chosen to be the king: he hid among the baggage. We can safely assume that he hid because for some reason he was afraid of the responsibility of leadership. Maybe he feared failure. Maybe he was afraid of rejection or of how others would respond. Perhaps he was just unclear on how to proceed—there were no schools on how to be a good king in Israel. Or maybe he shrank back from the sacrifices he would have to make to serve as king.

It is important for us to remember these lessons from Saul's early years. Each of us is entrusted with responsibility in our job as well as in our home. The Bible teaches that we are also appointed a realm of responsibility in the kingdom, if we know Jesus as Lord and Savior. There is a capacity in which God has called us to serve him that lines up with our gifts, passion, personality, and experiences. Some of us are fitted for more visible places of leadership than others, but we can all be vulnerable to Saul's weakness. Determine today not to hold back from what God has called you to, especially not because of the fear of taking responsibility.

PRAYER STARTER

FATHER, I AM TEMPTED TO HOLD BACK FROM YOU. So often I see the cost as too high or wonder if I have what it takes to lead or serve in the role(s) to which you have called me. Please turn my eyes to your abundant provision and away from my inadequacies. Give me the confidence *and* willingness that comes from being full of your Spirit!

DAY 103

Speaking Too Freely

SCRIPTURE READING: 1 SAMUEL 14–15

Today we learn a very practical lesson from Saul about speaking rashly and impulsively. He makes an oath (14:24) binding the people from eating until his vengeance on the Philistines is complete. He obviously has not thought through the implications of this oath, because it ultimately results in: making his men too tired to fight (v. 28); pushing them toward eating meat with the blood still in it, which is contrary to the law of God (v.32); and almost causing Saul to kill his own son (vv. 42–44).

Let us be aware of the danger of rash words. Often, when we are experiencing intense emotion, be it anger, grief, fear, or even jubilation, we can exceed the bounds of propriety with our speech. It is easy to make promises we can't keep, damage relationships with needlessly hurtful words, or otherwise bind ourselves by what we say in the heat of the moment, without giving proper consideration to the possible results. None of us "bats a thousand" in this area, but we can determine to grow toward integrity with God's help. Decide to use restraint in what you promise, vow, threaten, or express, allowing the Lord's Spirit and solid discernment to guide your decisions about what to say and what not to say.

PRAYER STARTER

Lord, may the words of my mouth reflect your wisdom and bring results that glorify you.

DAY 104

Beyond the Outward Appearance

SCRIPTURE READING: 1 SAMUEL 16–17

THE REMARKABLE INTRODUCTION of David in these two chapters is magnificently inspiring. The truth we ponder today is perfectly summed up in 16:7, "But the Lord said to Samuel, '... do not consider his appearance or his height, for I have rejected him. The Lord does not look at the things man sees. Man looks at the outward appearance, but the Lord looks at the heart.'" Both these chapters encourage us in dramatic ways to *stop looking only at what is external!* First, God chooses the most unlikely of Jesse's sons because despite his youth and the physical prowess of some of his older brothers, God sees in David the *heart* He wants on the throne of Israel. Then, despite the mightiness of the Philistine giant, at which the whole army of Israel quakes, God intervenes because of the boldness of David's faith and confidence in him. A shepherd boy defeats a mighty warrior by throwing rocks!

Let these two episodes inspire your trust in God today. He can work through you, too, despite your "inadequacies." Your part is to grow in faith to the point that what you see with your eyes does not discourage your willingness to step forward for God. Consider it for a moment—if Samuel and David had let the observable phenomena determine their course, one of David's brothers would have been anointed king, and David surely would not have even thought about challenging the giant that day. Conventional wisdom says you choose the biggest, strongest, most handsome, likeliest, and even the oldest to serve as king, and also that shepherd boys don't mess with giants. But following God is all about learning to live by faith, that what we see isn't all there is—God is real, and at times he loves to confound conventional wisdom!

PRAYER STARTER

LORD, UNBIND ME from looking always at the externals. Help me see beyond the outward appearances, into what you are about in this world. Give me the faith to step forward for you when it is time.

DAY 105

Trust vs. Insecurity

SCRIPTURE READING: 1 SAMUEL 18–19; PSALM 59

Read Psalm 59 with the realization that in all likelihood it was written by David concurrent with the events in 1 Samuel 19. This puts it in a whole new light. David's expressions of dependence upon and trust in God throughout this trial stand in stark contrast to Saul's paranoid insecurity and jealousy.

We each have a choice of how to respond to trials in our lives, especially to threats from others. Either we can become frantic, jealous, suspicious, and ultimately hurtful, like Saul, *or* we can openly express our fears and frustrations to God, and then put our ultimate trust in his sovereignty, as did David: "O my strength, I sing praise to you; you, O God, are my fortress, my loving God."

PRAYER STARTER

Lord, in my afflictions, prevent me from becoming vengeful, spiteful, paranoid, or jealous toward others, put my trust in you, that you might deliver me and help me stand strong and secure as a person of faith.

DAY 106
Trusting When Afraid

SCRIPTURE READING: 1 SAMUEL 20–21; PSALMS 56; 34

During his periods of hiding from Saul, David's words in Psalm 56:3–4 are some of the most profoundly written: "When I am afraid, I will trust in you. In God, whose word I praise, in God I trust; I will not be afraid. What can mortal man do to me?"

What about you and me? How would we finish that sentence? "When I am afraid, I will...." There are a thousand ways we could fill in the blank, some fairly constructive, and others very destructive. But David supplies the only truly sufficient answer: *"I will trust in God."* We all have times of fear. David never said, *"If* I am ever afraid." He said, "when." When frightening events occur or when you have frightening thoughts, let your impulse be to trust in God. When I truly realize who he is, that is when I have a second, even more freeing realization—anything mortals can do to me has to pass through the most powerful, most in-love-with-me Person in the universe, my heavenly Father! Let this realization abide with you today. It could change your whole outlook, especially in situations in which you would normally walk in fear.

PRAYER STARTER

Lord, you love me just as much as you loved your servant David. I ask you, like he did, to be merciful to me when men are "pursuing" me. And I declare, like David, that I *will* trust in you when I'm afraid. Give me eyes to see who you are, so that I don't walk in fear.

DAY 107

Setting My Desire On God

SCRIPTURE READING: 1 SAMUEL 22–23;
1 CHRONICLES 12:8–18; PSALMS 52; 54; 63; 142

Psalm 63, in particular, is an excellent example of a man turning both his praises and his desires toward God when things are going badly. David wrote this psalm when he had fled from Keilah and gone into the desert to hide from Saul (1 Sam. 23). David was in about as much trouble as a human being can be. The king, the most powerful man in the land, was after him to wipe him out. Also, Saul had proven that his insane jealousy and paranoia had reached an all time high, to the point that he was willing to have priests of the Lord killed!

All this makes it quite remarkable for David to express his confidence in God's deliverance so emphatically. He so strongly believes God's promises to him that he is sure that "They who seek my life will be destroyed; they will go down to the depths of the earth...." He even proceeds to refer to himself as "the king" in verse 11 of Psalm 63!

The key to his confidence is revealed in the words of verse 1 of this psalm. His heart is set on God, and he has committed himself to earnestly seeking him. Go and respond to this kind of devotion and spiritual focus with your own increasing faith. Your confidence in God will be inevitable! Set your desire on God and his ways. See him as your water in a "dry and weary land."

PRAYER STARTER

I WANT MY NUMBER ONE DESIRE in this world to be you, Lord. Help me not to settle for less. When my way is hard, and when I need deliverance, help me to have trust and confidence in you, so that my walk of faith can be sustained like David's.

DAY 108

Restraint from Aggression

SCRIPTURE READING: 1 SAMUEL 24;
PSALM 57; 1 SAMUEL 25

Two examples emerge today of David's ability to restrain himself from aggression. What a wonderful quality and how rare in today's world! In one instance he stood strong, even against the urging of his men. In the second, he needed prompting from someone else (Abigail) to help him decide to back off. The same is true of us; sometimes to restrain ourselves from rash actions, we must stand against the urgings of others, sometimes even those we love and respect. At other times, we might need to listen to someone else who urges us to stop and think before acting.

Also, notice that David's ability to show restraint in both instances, with Saul and with Nabal, comes from his trust in the Lord and his desire to please him. He is able to slow down enough to consider the consequences for taking vengeance and to then place the outcome and the ultimate punishment of both these men in God's hands. Ask God to speed your growth in the area of restraint.

PRAYER STARTER

Lord, restrain me from taking justice into my own hands, especially in this area of vengeance toward others. I know you are the judge of all people and that your justice is inscrutable and eternal. Help me trust you enough to allow you to be the righter of wrongs in my life. Thank you that I don't have to be!

DAY 109

When I Don't Know the Answer

SCRIPTURE READING: 1 SAMUEL 26–29;
1 CHRONICLES 12:1–7, 19–22

WHERE DO YOU TURN when you don't know the answers, or when life's difficulties and obstacles seem too much for you? When Saul saw the Philistine army, he became afraid (28:5), and God was silent when he asked him what to do, so Saul turned to the occult for answers. God had specific reasons for not answering Saul, but we all have times in our lives when the way is not exactly clear to us. There are times when we are afraid of our opposition or of our situation. We need to make sure in these times that we go to the right sources for information. If God chooses not to give us all the answers we crave, we must not turn to anything or anyone else, but continue to seek him.

God speaks to us through the Bible, through the Holy Spirit, through other believers, and in a secondary way at times, through circumstances and events. People involved in the occult get their information from Satan and demons. That is why the law strictly forbade these practices (Deuteronomy 8:9–14, Exodus 22:18). Don't accept a substitute for God's voice in your life, especially about vital matters and life decisions!

PRAYER STARTER

LORD, SPEAK CLEARLY TO ME about the things I need to know. Give me ears to regularly hear you speaking to me through the Bible and other legitimate avenues. Help me accept when you are silent about a matter and patiently walk in obedience to you until I know more.

DAY 110

Finding God When Threatened

SCRIPTURE READING: 1 SAMUEL 30–31;
1 CHRONICLES 10; 2 SAMUEL 1

IN HIS REACTION AFTER THE DISCOVERY of Ziklag, David gives us an example of steadfast faith and trust in the Lord. His *own men* were talking of stoning him because of their intense grief. But David did not lapse into self-defense, nor did he react in fear. He "found strength in the Lord his God." Then David inquired of the Lord what he should do next.

If we could just learn this simple lesson, the effectiveness of our life and witness for the Lord would be multiplied! God stands with us as his children when we are falsely attacked or accused no less than he stood with David. We simply need to learn how to trust him and resist our fear of other people.

PRAYER STARTER

LORD, HELP ME WALK IN FAITH instead of fear when other people misunderstand and misjudge me. My strength comes from you. Teach me how to find you when I am threatened.

DAY 111

Never Out of His Control

SCRIPTURE READING: 2 SAMUEL 2–4

The war, political maneuvering, intrigue, alliance-shifting, and murders that took place in the years immediately following Saul's death can be difficult to interpret. The code of ethics these men followed is foreign to us, and it is a challenge to sort out all the mixed motivations that drove them, including family loyalty, personal advancement, revenge, and the genuine best interests of the nation of Israel. However we interpret each man's actions, one thing is certain: God was ultimately in control the whole time, orchestrating the events toward the outcome he had already determined—David eventually sitting on the unified throne of all of Israel.

It is encouraging for us today to consider the sovereignty of God in our lives. He has purposed great things for his people, the church, and he is still working in every situation for our ultimate good. Rest in this knowledge today. When you don't understand the circumstances of your life, or when you feel as though you have failed so much that you must have messed up what God wanted to do, remember this episode in David's life. Everything was in turmoil, and yet God was moving events according to his plan the whole time!

PRAYER STARTER

Help me today to trust in your power and your goodness, Lord. Help me trust your power enough to know that nothing is truly out of control, and help me trust your goodness enough to know you are always influencing things for my ultimate good and the good of your kingdom.

DAY 112

Patience Through the Wait

SCRIPTURE READING: 2 SAMUEL 5:1–6:11; 1 CHRONICLES 11:1–9; 12:23–40; 13:1–14:17

David actually became king over Judah thirteen years after his initial anointing by Samuel, and his final anointing as king of all Israel, recorded here, came another seven years later, or *twenty years* after Samuel picked him out from among Jesse's sons! He had to overcome Saul's oppression, wars with the Philistines, his best friend's death, and seven years of "partial fulfillment" before he received what God had promised.

Do you ever get impatient about God answering prayer, bringing blessings, providing deliverance, or fulfilling promises? He wants to teach us to walk faithfully with him as we await those fulfillments, whatever they may be. When things come quickly and easily to us, sometimes it is easy to take them for granted or even to dismiss God's role in bringing them about. Whatever you are waiting for today, find God sufficient in the meantime!

PRAYER STARTER

Forgive me, Lord, for always wanting life to go my way *now*, and for being disappointed, discouraged, and even resentful when it doesn't. Help me to learn patience and how to have joy in you as I wait, no matter how long it takes. I know patience is your way, but it is hard for me in my humanness. I need your strength to truly change my impatience.

DAY 113

Greatness Comes from God

SCRIPTURE READING: 2 SAMUEL 22; PSALM 18

CONSIDER ALL THE NOUNS David uses to describe God in his song of praise in 2 Samuel 22: rock, fortress, deliverer, shield, horn of salvation, stronghold, refuge, savior, support, and lamp. David had seen God act in all these ways through years of trial and oppression, as well as throughout his ascent to the throne of Israel.

Notice the commonality behind these acknowledgments of God's activity. David clearly sees that any greatness he has comes from God: "You give me your shield of victory; you stoop down to make me great. You broaden the path beneath me, so that my ankles do not turn." (vv. 36–37). We are often quick to take the credit for any small bit of excellence or accomplishment in our lives when instead we need to live more in the awareness that it is God who blesses us, opens opportunities for us, and sustains and enables us in our performance. May we acquire the heart of David—a heart that is not just eager to acknowledge God's enabling with our lips, but that senses deep within our utter dependence on him for everything!

PRAYER STARTER

I AM DEPENDENT ON YOU. Without you, there is no me. Without you, I would have no life, no redemption, no personality, no talents, no stamina, no intelligence, nothing. I thank you today for all the wonderful doors you have opened to me. You are my rock, my fortress, my deliverer, my shield, the horn of my salvation, my stronghold, my refuge, my savior, my support, and my lamp. I will walk with you today.

DAY 114

Unashamed Worship

SCRIPTURE READING: 1 CHRONICLES 15–16; 2 SAMUEL 6:12–23; PSALM 96

How was it that Michal got to this place of hating David so much that it is said, "...she despised him in her heart"? Maybe his public display of unrestrained worship and affection for God embarrassed her, because she thought it "beneath the dignity" of the king to behave like this (2 Samuel 6:20). She might have been more concerned with appearances than with properly honoring God and celebrating him. A bit of jealousy could also be involved in her reaction. If she did not have the kind of intimate relationship with God that David had, it is very possible that his expression of joyful worship aroused in her a desire for what he had. Because she was either unaware of how to get it or simply unwilling, it is quite conceivable that this could have led her to lash out at David. Maybe other dynamics were occurring in their relationship that we don't even know about. Whatever the case, something about David's energetic worship set her off and that ultimately resulted in her barrenness.

Be very careful about how you regard others' relationship with God, and especially about their expressions of worship to him. It is so easy in this day to be cynical, to doubt someone's sincerity, or to criticize people for being different from us. But the fact is that we should always rejoice with those who rejoice in the Lord, and we must continually guard ourselves from rejecting expressions of worship solely on the basis of *our* dignity. Can you move beyond self-consciousness to God-consciousness as you worship him in prayer today?

PRAYER STARTER

Lord, help me to know when the "rules" of human propriety need to be pushed back to make room for extravagant worship. Grow me into a willing, unashamed participant in the flow of worship that continually comes before your throne.

DAY 115

Expressing His Greatness

SCRIPTURE READING: PSALM 105;
2 SAMUEL 7; 1 CHRONICLES 17

David had a constant and lifelong need to glorify the name of God. He expressed this inspiration in his private prayer life: "How great you are, O Sovereign Lord! There is no one like you, and there is no God but you, as we have heard with our own ears.... Do as you promised, so that your name will be great forever" (2 Samuel 7). He also expressed this impulse in his interaction with other people: "Make known among the nations what he has done" (Psalm 105).

How committed are you to glorifying his name? Make it a point today and this week to tell him *and* others of his greatness and the mighty things he has done!

PRAYER STARTER

Lord, unloose my lips to speak of your greatness and mighty deeds. You are the King, both of this universe and of my life. There is truly none like you.

Let this begin in private—may I be quick to confess your greatness in my prayers. Give me a heart of praise. May I likewise be quick to speak of your goodness to me in my conversations with others, that they might somehow see you through me.

DAY 116

Showing His Kindness

SCRIPTURE READING: 2 SAMUEL 8–10;
1 CHRONICLES 18–19; PSALM 60

In 2 Samuel 9, David emphatically asks if there is anyone left of Saul's family "to whom I can show God's kindness?" What a question! Granted, David had a special relationship to Saul's family and he was particularly motivated to honor them in some way; however, I believe this question typifies the heart God wants to develop in each of us regarding other people. As we grow toward spiritual maturity, followers of Jesus should be asking more and more, "To whom can I show God's kindness today?" No one can serve everyone or meet every need, but there are likely many times when showing God's kindness would cost us very little, but our consciousness is not raised—we simply aren't asking the question.

Our questions seem to typically be about how we can get more, feel better, achieve higher, or be more highly regarded by others. It seems all too rare for us in today's world to ask the question David asked, and even (shameful as it is) sometimes in today's church. Why not ask in sincerity today, "To whom can I show God's kindness?" We never know how God may choose to use our efforts.

PRAYER STARTER

Lord, you have shown such kindness to me ... help me be eager to show your kindness to others. Sometimes I don't know how, and often I don't particularly feel like it, but I ask you to help me overcome this and offer kindness to someone today.

DAY 117

Dealing with Temptation

SCRIPTURE READING: 2 SAMUEL 11–12;
1 CHRONICLES 20:1–3; PSALM 51

TEMPTATION IS A REALITY FOR EVERY ONE OF US. Even a man "after God's own heart" is fully capable of being enticed away from the path of purity in a moment of weakness. David's sin with Bathsheba becomes the one notable black spot on his years of service as Israel's king, and it has devastating consequences in later years within his family. The agony of his reckoning with this sin is portrayed vividly in both Nathan's confrontation and David's writing in Psalm 51, but the psalm also serves as a model of the proper mind-set with which to approach repentance and restoration.

Let us be warned that the strategy of the enemy is not all that different today. He still places the enticement in front of us and then takes us further than we want to go, keeps us longer than we want to stay, and costs us more than we want to pay. If there are sins you have committed and need to bring before God for cleansing, why not do it right now? Don't face another day living halfway for him. Certainly, we all must be on our guard, recognize temptation, and say "no" *early.*

PRAYER STARTER

I AM A SINNER, PRONE TO WANDER FROM YOU. Accept my repentance right now from the paths I've chosen that were not of you. Restore and renew me, even as you did your servant David. Renew a rightness of spirit within me, that I may glorify you at full speed all day today!

DAY 118

Saying No Early

SCRIPTURE READING: 2 SAMUEL 13–14

The rape of Tamar is in some ways a dramatic picture of what often happens when we give in to sin and turn away from God's way. Although Amnon's sin was sexual in nature, the picture it provides holds true of all different kinds of temptation. We can be enticed to the point of obsession, just as Amnon was about Tamar. Then, if we give in to the temptation as Amnon did, we come to realize that whatever captivated us does not truly satisfy us as we thought it would. At the same time, we experience the added weight of guilt. This situation often results in the kind of hatred Amnon then showed to Tamar. We hate the thought of our transgressions for not satisfying us, because sin always promises more than it can deliver. Sin is always a perverted attempt to achieve happiness, comfort, security, and so forth, apart from God.

What we truly need is to recognize on the front end the emptiness of sin's promises, and then stand strong against the enticement, realizing it is a lie. Commands and encouragements to resist in this way are found throughout scripture. How serious are you about turning from sin in your life?

PRAYER STARTER

Lord, I know that I cannot truly turn from temptation in my own power, but I want badly to see sin for what it is *before* I allow it to captivate my heart. Help me today to recognize the enticements of the evil one, and then to have the wisdom, courage, and power to turn away, so that my life can glorify you more fully.

DAY 119

Willing to Be Offended

SCRIPTURE READING: 2 SAMUEL 15–17

David's maturity—evidenced by both his humility and his ability to rightly discern priorities—is remarkable and is exhibited in the episode with Shimei in 2 Samuel 16. Shimei is cursing David and throwing rocks, and instead of reacting with self-defense and vengeance, as some of his men want to, David refuses to make a big deal out of the incident. He is willing to absorb some personal humiliation and injury without becoming consumed by a prideful desire to "save face." David rightly discerns that bigger issues are at stake than what this guy thinks, says, or does to him. How rare this mode of operation is among the leaders (and followers) of our day, in both small venues and large!

Our society is so sensitive to any kind of "affront," "being taken advantage of," "damage to reputation," or "violation of rights." Why are we so afraid of what another person can say about us or do to us? Do we really believe, as David did, that God is our strength, our fortress, our shield, and our defender? Allow God to grow in you the same kind of maturity that David displays. Focus on what is truly important, and go against the cultural tide of being either shattered or enraged by every "offense!"

PRAYER STARTER

Lord, help me grow to maturity, especially when it comes to the issues of personal injury and insult. Help me not to escalate every such situation into a crisis or even to the level of requiring a response. You are my defender, and while I know there are appropriate boundaries to avoid situations of real abuse, I choose to forsake the hypersensitivity of this culture. I trust you to ultimately protect me.

DAY 120

He Is Greater

SCRIPTURE READING: PSALM 3; 2 SAMUEL 18–19

The words of Psalm 3 recount David's signature themes of finding security in God and trusting him even amid overwhelming opposition. Although it is later in his life, David finds himself right back at the place of desperation that he was in so often when hiding from Saul. Even though he's in a completely different stage of life, the ultimate answer for him remains the same—acknowledge God as your shield and deliverer and the One who lifts your head; then choose rest and trust in him, for he is greater than all the naysayers and all the opposition arrayed against you.

When you are pursued, harassed, misunderstood, and attacked, realize what David realized. It does not matter what stage of life you are in or how much experience, education, wisdom, power, fame, or respect you have. At times in this life, we come face to face with the reality of our ultimate helplessness, and it is at those times that we desperately need to draw close to God, find his perspective, and access his power. Of course, it is during the meantime that we must be pursuing a relationship with God that will sustain us when the "bottom drops out."

PRAYER STARTER

Lord, I know that no matter what I face, you are greater. I will look to you for strength. Show me how to be closer and closer to you, so that when storms come my way, you are not a stranger to me. Build my faith!

DAY 121

With God Through the Sloppiness

SCRIPTURE READING: 2 SAMUEL 20–21; 23:8–23;
1 CHRONICLES 20:4–8; 11:10–25

It is increasingly evident from today's reading that there was virtually no end to conflict and rebellion throughout the reign of David. Part of this was simply the nature of the sociopolitical climate of the times—being a king meant that one would spend a lot of time at war and defending the throne from pretenders. Another reason for this severe reality in David's life was the result of David's sin with Bathsheba and its consequences: "Now, therefore, the sword will never depart from your house, because you despised me and took the wife of Uriah the Hittite to be your own" (2 Samuel 12:10).

Despite this constant climate of wars and rebellion, and whatever its cause, David was still able to walk with God and ultimately build a successful kingdom that honored him. In our lives, we need to realize that amid the frustrations, pains, conflicts, and confusions, God still has great purposes he wants to work out in and through us. Although we may not be earthly kings in the same way David was, God still desires that we keep our eyes on him through life's hardships and ugliness, so that he can use us for purposes beyond ourselves.

PRAYER STARTER

Lord, it's so easy to get discouraged by life's ugliness and sloppiness. Please show me how to live for your glory today. Whatever part of my trials I have brought on myself, please deliver me from wallowing in guilt and failure—let me learn the lessons and move along. Whatever part is simply living in a fallen world, let it not discourage me from continuing on until final victory!

DAY 122

Trusting in the Trappings

SCRIPTURE READING: 2 SAMUEL 23:24–24:25;
1 CHRONICLES 11:26–47; 21:1–30

What was so wrong about taking the census? This census basically amounted to an assessment of the military strength of the nation. It was like a conscription of sorts. The fact that David wanted so desperately to have this done, even during a time of relative peace, points to either a prideful desire to find glory in the strength of his armies *or* an attempt to find security in those numbers rather than in the Lord. Either way, it symbolizes a turning from the walk of faith and trust in God that the king of Israel was supposed to display.

Sometimes we can be tempted in the same way to become prideful about our money, power, possessions, or even the strength of our family, church, or nation. Be careful today not to take your eyes off of God. Allow him to be the One you glorify and the One you look to for protection and ultimate security.

PRAYER STARTER

Lord, I know you are my protection and my strength. Help me trust you with my security, not fretting about whether I have enough resources for victory—I know you do. Let me also be delivered from the pride that would lead me to trust in my own strength and glorify in my giftedness, accomplishments, or accumulations. You alone are worthy of glory. Quell my desire for it, and let my focus be your worthiness, not my own!

DAY 123

Planning and Preparing

SCRIPTURE READING: 1 CHRONICLES 22–24

Although David was not to be the one to build a temple for God, he was very careful to make full preparation for the work to be done by Solomon, his son. He did this for two simple reasons: he loved God and wanted to glorify his name as much as possible and he loved his son and wanted to be of as much help as possible in making him successful.

God wants us as his people to be planning and preparing for the future, too. There are certainly those who go to extremes and relentlessly prepare for any and every eventuality. This unhealthy obsession stems from a misguided desire to control the future and be God. Yet, to ignore the need for advance planning in our lives is foolish and will undercut our effectiveness in living for God and making the maximum impact for him. We need to periodically examine our direction in all areas of our lives—financial, relational, professional, parental, spiritual, emotional, physical, and so forth. There is nothing wrong with thinking about tomorrow and revising our "game plan" in whatever area we need to, so that we might better press toward the best future that God has in mind for us. In which area do you need to plan and prepare better?

PRAYER STARTER

Lord, without becoming obsessed by tomorrow, I desire to be faithful in planning and preparing for the future. Show me what I need to do today to make the future better for me, my family, and those that my life will touch in the coming years.

DAY 124

Finding Your Place

SCRIPTURE READING: PSALM 30;
1 CHRONICLES 25–26

It is clear from 1 Chronicles 25–26 that even in Old Testament times, the people of God were dedicated to different ministries according to their gifts. Three broad categories are listed in this passage.

First, the ministry of music was massive, which indicates that God's people have always placed a high value on celebration. Fully 288 men were committed to the ministry of music in the temple of the Lord! This was their vocation. A second ministry was that of gate keeping, which included many of the practical needs of the temple, such as the care of the equipment and furniture, food supplies for the priests and sacrifices, mixing the incense that was burned daily, and so forth. Finally, the duties of the ministry of the treasury are fairly self-evident.

In the body of Christ today, it is *imperative* for the maximum progress of the kingdom that *each* believer finds his or her place of service in the body. The three basic areas of service above still exist in the life of God's people, and there is still both the opportunity and the need for servants in each area. Many other areas of service exist in the church of today. It is not always instantaneous or easy to find the right place of service, but there is *something* that will use each person's abilities. No one can do everything, but we each can and should do something. Have you found your place of service? What can you do this week to move toward finding *or* being more effective in your place of service in the kingdom?

PRAYER STARTER

Lord, I pray for the local church of which I am a part, that each participant would be energized toward their place of service for your glory. I pray for wisdom for the leadership in using the gifts of the congregation. I pray above all that you would give me a servant's heart and guide me to my place of maximum effectiveness in service for this body.

DAY 125
The Triumphant Trifecta

SCRIPTURE READING: 1 CHRONICLES 27–29

THE WORDS OF ENCOURAGEMENT that David gives to Solomon just before his death can inspire us today. Although David was encouraging Solomon specifically in regard to the building of the temple, the qualities he encourages in Solomon are worthy of our focus. We need encouragement in the same areas today. He urges Solomon to be obedient (28:8), wholeheartedly devoted with pure motives (28:9), and strong, courageous, and unafraid (28:10, 20).

What a wonderful "trifecta" on which to set our sights! Imagine if all the believers in your church gave their attention to growth in these three simple areas. What wonderful progress the kingdom would make, regardless of church programs, plans, structures, and initiatives. These human efforts have their importance, but the kingdom's genuine advance in our lives and in this realm does not *primarily* depend on them. Instead, it depends in a much deeper way upon the obedience, motives, and courage of God's people, from the most prominent leader to the most obscure follower. Solomon could have had all the materials in the world and the best-laid plan, but without the qualities David encouraged in him, these things would have meant nothing.

PRAYER STARTER

LORD, I DESIRE TO BE OBEDIENT to you in everything. Guide me as you will. I long to be wholeheartedly devoted to you. Purify my motives as I seek you. I want to be free of fear and discouragement as I do the kingdom work to which I'm called each day. Give me your courage and strength.

DAY 126

Ultimate Justice

SCRIPTURE READING: PSALMS 5–7; 10; 11; 13; 17

THE PSALMS IN THIS SERIES are all about justice. They are a combination of cries for God to act in justice toward David's enemies and declarations of David's faith in God's justice. David is confident that the wicked—those who choose to do evil and/or oppose the mandate he's been given by God—will ultimately be punished. They will reap the fruit of their wickedness and learn in a dramatic way that God's way is always best.

Today, we can take comfort in the very same certainties that David did. God will ultimately triumph over evil. Sin is never worth it. Opposition to God and his purposes ultimately boomerang on those who choose it. These assurances should comfort us amid the opposition of this world and its people to our walk of faith. They should also serve to warn us when we are tempted to go the way of sin. God is a God of justice, and although He is merciful, gracious, loving, compassionate, and patient, the principle of sowing and reaping still holds true. Choosing to go against him is ultimately choosing defeat.

PRAYER STARTER

LORD, I KNOW THAT YOU ARE ULTIMATELY IN CONTROL, and that your justice will triumph in this realm. Give me patience when I feel tormented by others. Help me rest in the knowledge that your justice will make things right, and that I don't have to. When wrong begins to look right to me, remind me of the bitter fruit at its end.

DAY 127

My Shepherd

SCRIPTURE READING: PSALMS 23; 26; 28; 31; 35

These psalms of David all direct us to God's wonderful care over our lives. Psalm 23 is most poetic in this depiction, describing God as our shepherd. All these psalms reveal to us that God is our chief caretaker. He provides for our needs, protects us from enemies, establishes a secure place for us to rest, pours abundant blessings upon us, sustains us through the dark experiences of this life, and promises a secure future in his presence.

In prayer today, ask God to reveal himself to you personally as your shepherd. As you walk into this day, continually recognize all the ways He cares for you, and begin more and more to look to him for what you need. If you are in Christ, you are his precious sheep, and his care for you is profound. Like sheep, we sometimes don't have a clue just how extensive and amazing his care for us is, but if we will open our eyes he will reveal himself to us.

PRAYER STARTER

Lord, I need more than just the idea that you are my Shepherd—I need a Shepherd. I need your protection, your comfort, provision, encouragement, and promises about the future. Draw me close to you so I can truly know and experience these things.

DAY 128

The Dependable One

SCRIPTURE READING: PSALMS 41; 43; 46; 55; 61; 62; 64

One truth that runs throughout this group of psalms is that God alone can ultimately be depended upon. We cannot place our absolute trust in other people, because "the mind and heart of man are cunning" (64:6), and even friends are capable of being hurtful (Psalm 55). Our material possessions are not worthy of our ultimate trust: "though your riches increase, do not set your heart on them" (62:10).

No, the only absolutely, incontrovertibly dependable One is God. He is our refuge. He is the always strong and loving One. So if we will place our trust in him above all else, he will not let us be shamed in the end. Even though the earth will give way, the mountains will fall into the sea, and utter devastation will come upon the earth, we do not need to walk in fear if our hearts are set upon God!

PRAYER STARTER

Thank you that you are bigger, stronger, and more dependable than any other entity in which I am tempted to place my trust. Help me to put my hope in you, always seeing you for who you really are. Be my refuge and strength today and turn my heart toward you.

DAY 129

Honest to God

SCRIPTURE READING: PSALMS 69–71; 77

Consider today David's honesty before God. He does not hold back in these psalms from confessing his hurts, struggles, and weaknesses to God. It is funny how some of us so often seem to want to impress others, even God himself, with how we've "got it all together." David feels no such compulsion. He probably figures that God sees him as he is, so he might as well "own it" and ask for help. If more modern-day believers could just learn this lesson, it would be an absolutely freeing experience.

Look at everything David admits to God in these psalms. He admits, in one way or another, to being sinful, foolish, guilty, poor, needy, in danger, scorned, disgraced, shamed, troubled, helpless, and perplexed. Can you admit such things to God? If not, realize that new possibilities and vistas in your relationship with God will open up when you approach him with the level of bare-bones honesty that David had. Try today to be as honest as David as you pray!

PRAYER STARTER

Lord, I desperately want to have all the answers, have it all together, be pure and holy, be totally self-sufficient; and walk through this life "above the fray" of conflict and danger. But I (and you) know that I cannot. Help me get beyond my pride and admit my needs to you, and, when appropriate, to others. Help me learn to bare my soul to you as David did, so that I may truly find your help and healing.

DAY 130

Longing for His Honor

SCRIPTURE READING: PSALMS 83; 86; 88; 91; 95

Psalm 83 is an example of an imprecatory psalm, or a prayer for God's wrath upon the wicked. It is important to observe that these psalms are not just expressions of personal anger or rage, but instead are exhibitions of righteous indignation. The psalmist seeks retribution against his enemies, not just because they are hurting him personally, but even more because they have made themselves enemies of the Lord. He is concerned about the Lord's glory and his purposes, and he is pleading with God to make the situation right.

Do you ever think about God's honor? Does anything ever annoy you because it disgraces him? If so, then you have an inkling of what the psalmist was feeling. An important aspect of the walk toward spiritual maturity is an ever-increasing concern for God's reputation and his cause. Begin to pray for God's glory to be vindicated in specific circumstances and situations, and he will begin to change your heart and grow this desire in you even more.

PRAYER STARTER

Lord, I personally need your help in so many ways that I could spend all my prayer time asking you to intervene for me in numerous situations. While I am unashamed to beg for your help, I also want to grow in my zeal for your kingdom's victory. Teach me to pray in this way.

DAY 131

Reflecting His Righteousness

SCRIPTURE READING: PSALMS 108; 109;
120; 121; 140; 143; 144

THE PSALMS IN THIS GROUP, like so many psalms, draw a clear distinction between those who live righteously and those who live wickedly. There are reminders throughout that the ultimate end of a wicked way of life is judgment. Wickedness at times certainly seems like a shortcut to happiness, but let us be reminded today that this is only an illusion. Living in a way that pleases God is the only way to true contentment. The beautiful promises of Psalm 121 are only for those who follow the Lord's way and look to him for guidance and help.

Renew your commitment today to living a life that is pleasing to God. Perfection will never be ours in this lifetime; but we can, with God's help, progress in reflecting God's righteousness in our lives. We truly can be changed to have less selfishness, less pride, fewer destructive attitudes and actions, and fewer marks of unrighteousness in our lives.

PRAYER STARTER

LORD, I WANT TO BE ONE WHO LOVES YOU and your ways supremely. I want to be one who pleases you when you look into my heart. Change me however you need to, and help me reflect your righteousness more today than yesterday.

DAY 132

The Righteous Life

SCRIPTURE READING: PSALMS 1; 14; 15; 36; 37; 39

This group of psalms reinforces the contrast introduced in yesterday's reading between the wicked and the righteous. One can't help but be struck by the supreme worthiness of pursuing a godly world view and lifestyle. The man who delights in the Lord and his law is like a tree planted by streams of water, yielding fruit and prospering. He is watched over by the Lord. He is allowed the privilege of dwelling in the sanctuary of the Lord and living on his holy hill. He will never be shaken. He finds refuge in the shadow of God's wings. He feasts on the abundance of his house. He will have the desires of his heart. His righteousness will shine like the sun. He will inherit the land. His inheritance will endure forever. He will have plenty in a time of famine. He will be protected forever. His mouth will utter wisdom. His feet will not slip. He will be delivered from the wicked.

Now read back through these psalms again and see what is said of the wicked in contrast to these promises. Allow the truths here to impact your heart, and move you to a deeper love of righteousness.

PRAYER STARTER

Lord, I truly love your ways, but I know I could love them more. Build this love in me. Help me to live in the awareness of where wickedness leads today. Let it impact my words, my decisions, my actions, and my treatment of others.

DAY 133

In Times of Waiting

SCRIPTURE READING: PSALMS 40; 49; 50; 73

Waiting for the Lord is one of the most difficult, and yet most necessary, of all the aspects of the Christian life. David says in Psalm 40, "I waited patiently for the Lord; he turned to me and heard my cry." David found it necessary to wait for his deliverance many times throughout his life, but when deliverance came, it was always worth the wait, and he was always a stronger, better person for the experience! He responds with profound joy that he is out of the slimy pit, that he has a firm place to stand, and that he has a new song in his mouth. But he further states that because of his waiting and ultimate deliverance, others will develop a reverence for God and trust him!

Have you ever realized that your response to the silence or delayed answer of God could be a deciding factor in someone else's faith? Not to place a burden on us that no one can carry, but we really need to take this seriously. This life, our walk of faith, and even our experience of trials and suffering *are not just about us*. We should constantly consider how we are influencing others, not to the point of playacting or being ungenuine, but enough to turn our eyes outward as we consider our response. Waiting for God can build real "spiritual muscle" within us *and* profoundly encourage others *if* we approach it with the right attitude.

PRAYER STARTER

Lord, in times of waiting for you, let me bring you glory. Let me be able to say, as David said, "I waited patiently for the Lord." I ask you for answers, and I ask you to come quickly to save me. Give me true humility of heart, for I am poor and needy, but you are my help and my deliverer.

DAY 134

Valuing His Presence

SCRIPTURE READING: PSALMS 76; 82; 84; 90; 92; 112; 115

Have you learned to properly value the presence of God? The classic wisdom of Psalm 84:10 is quite profound: "Better is one day in your courts than a thousand elsewhere. I'd rather be a doorkeeper in the house of my God than dwell in the tents of the wicked." The psalmist is convinced that even a short period of time in the presence of God is better than unfathomable longevity cut off from him. The ratio suggested is 1000:1, and still the one day is better! Do we value his presence like this?

Furthermore, the psalmist says it is better to be in lowly servitude for God than walking away from him. Of course, there are many in our world who do not see it this way. They believe that power, money, pleasure, or independence are more worthy gods to serve. But the end of those roads is emptiness. We all serve something or someone, but the Lord God is the only master who will bring true and lasting blessings our way and crown our lives with ultimate purpose, no matter if we are kings or doorkeepers!

PRAYER STARTER

Lord, your presence is precious indeed. Help me crave it above all else that this world offers. Thank you that my time in your presence is not limited to one day, as precious as even that would be. Let me properly value your presence!

DAY 135

A Hunger to Be Righteous

SCRIPTURE READING: PSALMS 8; 9; 16; 19; 21; 24; 29

It is so tempting to fall into this present age's way of thinking, which says that punishment for sin is inconsistent with belief in a good and loving God. However, Psalm 9 gives some real insight into this issue. First, the psalmist acknowledges God's attribute of justice: "He will judge the world in righteousness; he will govern the peoples with justice" (v.8). Surely, in anyone's definition of a perfect government, the concept of justice has to appear. The idea of crimes going unpunished is repugnant to us when we consider civil governments, and yet so many are willing to forfeit the idea entirely when it comes to the government of the universe!

Next, he reiterates the personal responsibility the wicked bear for the punishments they will receive. He speaks of them as digging *their own* pit, being caught in *their own* net, and being ensnared by the work of *their own* hands. Many in this world want to absolve humans from any responsibility, but God's justice is such that the evil that springs from wrongdoers' lives ultimately "boomerangs" on them and becomes their undoing.

As God's people, it is time for us to fall in love with righteousness. Even though we will never attain it perfectly in this realm, it should awaken within us a strong sense of right and wrong and a discomfort with wickedness and compromise. God's way is best, and wickedness never pays.

PRAYER STARTER

God of righteousness, awaken within me a holy hunger to be righteous. You are the perfectly pure and just One. I adore your righteousness! You have the words of life for me; help me never settle for less and never believe I can excuse my disobedience because you are a God of love. Show me my wickedness and forgive me as I continually bring my sins to you.

DAY 136

Learning to Praise

SCRIPTURE READING: PSALMS 33; 65–68

Learning to praise the Lord is another one of those lifetime pursuits of the believer. For those of us who are not gifted musically, we can feel as though we are handicapped in this pursuit. We might feel unqualified to "play skillfully" (33:3). But the essence of true praise is not in instrumental prowess or vocal accomplishment. It comes from the heart and mind of the worshipper into the courts of the King. There is no exemption for the "unmusical." Psalm 33 says, "It is fitting for the upright to praise him."

True praise is simply telling God of his greatness. It can and should happen both in group worship settings and in "alone time" with God. Try devoting a solid minute to simply praise God today. Not counting preambles, confession, petition, intercession, or even thanksgiving, just fill a minute by telling God everything you can think of that is great about him. You can use these psalms as prompters, but allow the praise to come from your heart. It could change your day!

PRAYER STARTER

Lord, **teach me to praise you!**

DAY 137

Praised by His Creation

SCRIPTURE READING: PSALMS 75; 93–94; 97–100

REPEATEDLY THROUGHOUT THIS GROUP OF PSALMS, reference is made to the Lord receiving praise from all of creation—from the earth below, from the heavens above, and from the people who populate the earth. This concept informs and blesses us in a couple of ways.

First, we need to hear the sounds of creation literally declaring his praises, just as the psalmist did. Every wave that crashes on the shore, every sound of a rushing river, every clap of thunder, and every birdsong all join with the voices and instruments of humankind in declaring praise to the one who created them. The sounds nature makes are a constant testimony to his existence and his creative power.

Second, we also need to notice that scripture attributes to all of creation an awareness of the creator and actual desire to worship him. The level of nature's awareness does not enable the depth of relationship with him of which we are capable, but there is some kind of "groaning" for God that all of creation shares (see Romans 8:22). The question for us is this: if God is so great that even those parts of his creation without anything near the level of our consciousness can desire him, then how much more should those created in his image hunger and thirst to know him and give him praise?

PRAYER STARTER

LORD, I ASK YOU TODAY to increase my awareness of you through the testimony of your creation. Help me more and more to see your handiwork in the stars, your craftsmanship in the mountains, and your creativity at work in the animal kingdom. Also help me, Lord, to have an awareness of you and a desire for you that is worthy of my advanced design as a human being made in your image.

DAY 138

Hoping in His Power

SCRIPTURE READING: PSALMS 103; 104; 113; 114; 117

THESE PSALMS SPEAK OF the Lord's dominion over nature and all the nations. At times in this world, nature seems out of control, and quite untamed—think of tsunamis, earthquakes, avalanches, fires, global warming, etc. Moreover, there are certainly times when nations seem out of control and untamed—consider terrorism, communism, fascism, wars, international intrigue, international economic instability, etc. None of these circumstances can be totally controlled by a mortal or group of mortals, so our impulse to label them as "out of control" is valid, in a way. This state of affairs can give us a sense of helplessness and futility and can even discourage us toward hopelessness if we allow it.

There is great comfort, however, in the message of these psalms as they reaffirm the Lord's absolute sovereignty over both the creation he brought into existence *and* the affairs of the nations. No force of nature is mightier than he, and there is no issue of international import that is not ultimately under his control. There are plenty of things to be afraid of in the world of today, but as his followers we can take courage and comfort in the fact that *nothing* in this world happens outside his oversight, which means that even the bad and painful things somehow fit in his master plan for this universe. Have you come to grips with the almightiness of God?

PRAYER STARTER

LORD, GIVE ME A GLIMPSE of your almightiness today. Help me when I doubt it because of the chaos I see in this world. Even when it is hard, help me build my life on these two bedrock truths: you are almighty, and you are good.

DAY 139
The Word of Life

SCRIPTURE READING: PSALM 119:1–88

The power, beauty, and necessity of God's word in our lives cannot be overstated. Different words are used here for God's word. It is referred to variously as God's law, precepts, statutes, decrees, and commands. The point is quite clear. The truths of God's words give life, understanding, deliverance, joy, blessing, and righteousness. The psalmist has chosen to embrace his word and regard it as his very life's blood!

Is God's word precious to you? As we go through the massive undertaking of reading through the Bible, the task requires discipline and can even be monotonous. But your willingness to make and stick to this commitment (and catch up when you may get behind) is evidence that you grasp the importance of embracing his word. We will only be people after his own heart as we become people of his book. Select a verse from today's reading that speaks to you and reflect on it throughout your day. One choice is v. 32: "I run in the path of your commands, for you have set my heart free."

PRAYER STARTER

Lord, deepen my love for your word. Teach me to read it regularly, meditate upon it, memorize it, and share it, but teach me most of all to obey it!

DAY 140

Troubled by Evil

SCRIPTURE READING: PSALM 119:89–176

THE FERVOR OF THE PSALMIST IS REMARKABLE. He *so* loves the ways of the Lord and has *so* made the Lord's cause his own that he is moved to tears by the disobedience he sees around him. This is very different from the self-righteousness that smugly condemns others while ignoring one's own faults. The psalmist is very clear about his own weaknesses, his desperate need of the Lord, and his total dependence on God for light, wisdom, and guidance. But he is also very clear about his reaction to the evil around him: "Streams of tears flow from my eyes, for your law is not obeyed" (v.136), and "I look on the faithless with loathing, for they do not obey your word" (v.158). He loves God and his law so much that disobedience sickens him.

Do you love God that much? Does the evil around you trouble you, not because it scares you or worries you, but because it dishonors the One you love above all else? It is time for the Lord's people to return to this kind of passion for him. Why not ask him to increase your love of him and his ways today? Again, the aim is not a Pharisaic self-righteousness that throws rocks at others to feel holy, but a pure and simple love of God that affects us deeply in every aspect of our lives!

PRAYER STARTER

Lord, I am shamed by the fervor of this psalmist in his desire to see you glorified, honored, and obeyed. I confess that my fervor is often swallowed up in selfishness, pride, and apathy. At the same time, I am inspired by the words of this psalm, and I ask you to ignite this same kind of fervor in me, along with all my brothers and sisters in Christ, so that you might get great glory from this generation, beginning with me.

DAY 141

God's Enduring Love

SCRIPTURE READING: PSALMS 122; 124; 133–136

"His love endures forever." This repeating phrase of Psalm 136 is worthy of our consideration today. Herein is a profound truth—a truth that, if we should truly grasp it, could alter the way we view and deal with the majority of circumstances and issues in our lives. God's love will never end. It will never decrease. It will never wear thin or fade. It will never be exhausted.

The psalmist sets this up ingeniously. He recounts some of the mighty acts of God on Israel's behalf, and after each one he says, "His love endures forever." He is emphasizing that the great love that was exhibited in these mighty acts is still just as real and available today, and will always be. So whatever circumstances we are currently facing, and whatever tomorrow brings, the guarantee is that the God of the Bible is a God of love and goodwill, and he is always reaching out with a heart of love to meet us where we are! Reach out and meet him today.

PRAYER STARTER

Thank you, Lord, that I am incapable of stopping you from loving me. Help me believe, see, and experience your love in my life to a greater and greater degree. It is my greatest need in life. Help me consistently respond to your great love in the right way—by returning it to you and to others.

DAY 142

Nothing Hidden

SCRIPTURE READING: PSALMS 138; 139; 145; 148; 150

Psalm 139 confronts us with what can be a frightening truth or a supremely comforting truth, depending on how you look at it: God knows *everything* about us. He knows our actions, our thoughts, our words, and our whereabouts, even *before* we do! Whether this is comforting or troubling to us quite depends on our outlook and motives. If we seek to hide our lives, our thoughts, or who we are from him, living a life of darkness, then this truth is frightful. The psalm screams out that all our efforts to run from God or to deceive him have been futile. It tells us that no one outsmarts him, nothing escapes his gaze, and that all reality is ultimately accountable to him. This truly should be frightening for one who is walking in defiance of him.

However, this reality that is so troubling to the part of us that wants to be our own god can also bring us the most profound comfort imaginable. No trial or cloud that we will ever walk into can separate us from his presence! He knows every pain and challenge in your life and mine, and he cares deeply, refusing to leave us even at our very lowest points. Today, let the reality of his omniscience sober you and raise your consciousness that he sees all your ugliness, even what no other human can see. Let it also comfort you, in that despite this intimate knowledge, he *never* leaves his child!

PRAYER STARTER

Oh God, Who sees all that I do, say, think, and am, help me to live with a consciousness of your presence, especially when temptation comes my way. Let me believe more deeply and lean more heavily upon your ongoing presence of support, love, and guidance in my life.

DAY 143

A Daily Bath

SCRIPTURE READING: PSALMS 4; 12; 20; 25; 32; 38

MOST OF US TAKE SOME KIND OF PHYSICAL BATH every day because we value physical cleanliness. The words of Psalm 32 can help us to value spiritual cleanliness just as much. It tells us of the wonderful blessing it is to have our sins forgiven and be at peace with God. Let's consider this blessing today and make sure we are experiencing it to the fullest. We need to periodically turn our attention to spiritual cleanliness because we are prone to allow ourselves to become sullied by the world in which we live and never consider whether we are clean before God or not.

If we are in Christ, we have experienced the forgiveness of all our sins, past, present, and future, in an ultimate sense. They will not be held against us for judgment, because Christ has already served the sentence of death for them. So in this way, our sins are covered and our transgressions are forgiven; the Lord does not count our sins against us, as Psalms 32: 1–2 describe. There is, however, the need for ongoing cleansing as we walk through this life and on occasion "miss the mark" in our obedience to God. Today, ask the Lord to search you and reveal any act, word, or attitude of sin that you need to confess and turn away from, so you may enter back into undisturbed fellowship with him and so the words of this psalm will be your experience today, as well as for eternity!

PRAYER STARTER

As I confess my sins to you, Lord, help me turn from them and live to glorify you. Fill me with your spirit. Remind me how precious it is to have nothing between us.

DAY 144

Out from Under the Influence

SCRIPTURE READING: PSALMS 42; 53; 58; 81; 101; 111; 130; 131; 141; 146

The words of Psalm 101 challenge us to do all in our power to remove evil influences from our lives. The psalmist starts with what he sees with his eyes. He says he will guard what he lets his eyes see, and if there are wicked, vile things that could either cause him to stumble or steal his affection from God, he will not allow his eyes to feast on those things. Then he speaks of people he will avoid. He names the faithless, those with perverse hearts, slanderers, the haughty and proud, and the deceitful person. This can at first sound like an unloving, harsh, superior, and judgmental proclamation. Are we really supposed to reject other people? Aren't we supposed to love everyone? Even though our impulse may be to separate ourselves from people who are out of relationship with God, isn't this contrary to Christ's command for us to make disciples?

The key here is influence. When you really think about it, there is a lot of merit in buffering ourselves against the influence of what is ungodly in our lives. We must be very honest about how other people influence us in our Christian walk. Yes, we must be willing to rub shoulders, build relationships, and spend some of our time with people who are far from God, but we must always love our Lord and hate ways of life that are contrary to him. There is a difference between a relationship in which you try to help someone toward God and a relationship in which you allow that person to influence your life. We should always erect a dividing wall in our relationships, and those whose lives are marked by the kinds of wickedness the psalmist names should *never* be allowed to cross over into the depth of intimacy that involves true influence in our lives. This is not harsh, cold, judgmental, or unloving. It is wise!

PRAYER STARTER

Lord, show me the balance here. Help me to sincerely love other people, including those that do not know you as Lord and Savior *and* those who are unfaithful as believers at this point in their lives. But give me wisdom and courage to draw the line firmly concerning the influence I give them in my life.

DAY 145

Brutal Honesty

SCRIPTURE READING: PSALMS 2; 22; 27

The brutal honesty and feeling of disillusionment expressed in Psalm 22 can be shocking the first time we discover it on the pages of scripture. At the same time, it can be refreshing to us that even a "man after God's own heart," like David, could experience such a feeling of abandonment by God and still be considered among the heroes of the Old Testament. Surely we have all experienced times in our life when we've wanted to ask this kind of question. We want to know why God would "hang us out to dry" and allow such pain, frustration, and disappointment.

The beauty of this psalm, which Jesus actually quotes on the cross, is that it teaches us that God can handle our pain and frustration. David is not lashing out in an irreverent way; he is simply baring his soul to God, and sometimes that may not sound too pretty. What is your biggest pain and frustration right now? Have you expressed it to God? He really wants us to share our joys *and* struggles with him. Sometimes it is in the lowest times that we encounter God most profoundly. Share a pain with him today, so that he may help you bear it.

PRAYER STARTER

God, deliver me from a "spirit of complaint," but help me honestly share my struggles with you. You understand me like no one else, and you know all that lies within me anyway. Come alongside me and help me when my burdens are too big for me and save me from the pride that will not accept your help.

DAY 146

Being the Bride

SCRIPTURE READING: PSALMS 45; 47; 48; 87; 110

Psalms 45 and 110 are Messianic Psalms, which means that they point forward to Jesus, the promised Messiah of Israel. They also teach some great truths about him. Today, consider the words of Psalm 45 as they speak of him as a king, and the references in verses 10–17 to his wedding to his bride, the church. This is a picture of the eternal relationship between Jesus and those who follow him.

Does the idea of being a part of the bride of Christ trouble you at all? Is it threatening to you to consider such a relationship of intimacy with him? This is the relationship into which he is constantly calling us. The church, of course, is made up of all those who know Christ, but intimacy with him is something we must pursue and experience on an individual basis. The truth that we are the bride of Christ gives us several different affirmations that can encourage us mightily if we will embrace them. Being his bride means that he finds our companionship desirable and wants us to spend our lives with him. We are to be exclusively his and give him our deepest allegiance.

PRAYER STARTER

LORD, THANK YOU FOR CALLING YOUR CHURCH to be the "bride of Christ." Teach me what it means to be a part of your bride. Help me believe that you truly desire my companionship. This is sometimes hard for me to grasp when I consider that you know me inside and out and you are aware of all my weaknesses, sins, compromises, and hypocrisies. Thank you for your grace and forgiveness, which offer me the chance to draw close to the One who is so perfect and holy!

DAY 147

Taming My Ambition

SCRIPTURE READING: 1 KINGS 1:1–2:12;
2 SAMUEL 23:1–7

GODLESS AMBITION AND PRESUMPTION characterize the actions of Adonijah in this passage. He puts himself forth as the next king while his father is still on the throne, without the official sanction of his father or the priests and prophets of the royal court, and before his father has made any official pronouncement of succession. The consequences of his rash actions become clear as he is forced to plead for his life before the next true king, Solomon. He tastes complete humiliation because of his presumption, pride, and ambition.

The lesson for us is clear. We should seek to walk in humility and contentment and should refrain from grasping at glory, power, or possessions as if they are the key to fulfillment in this life. May God grant us the grace to truly be content and humble and never overstep our bounds in pride as Adonijah did.

PRAYER STARTER

LORD, MAKE ME HUMBLE, and help me to not grab for too much. Let nothing entice me to become so greedy, power hungry, or arrogant that I defy you. Let me be content to wait for your blessings in your timing.

DAY 148
The Heart of Solomon

SCRIPTURE READING: 1 KINGS 2:13–3:28;
2 CHRONICLES 1:1–13

THE VIRTUE OF SOLOMON is clearly seen as he asks for "a discerning heart to govern your people and to distinguish between right and wrong." When given a "blank check" from God, he chose to ask for this kind of wisdom instead of long life, wealth, honor, or the death of his enemies. Of course, his request pleased God, who then blessed him with all of the above. Solomon wanted to be the best king he could be for the benefit of his people. There was certainly a degree of self-interest in his request, but it is not blamable. He clearly made the godly choice by asking for a useful attribute rather than requesting a mere whim driven by greed, selfishness, security, or revenge.

What if you were given this kind of promise from God? Would you choose constructively like Solomon or selfishly, as most others probably would? What about in your prayer life now? What kind of requests are you making of God? We may certainly make our desires known to the Lord, but it is clear from this passage that there is a higher order of asking which pleases the heart of God. May we grow continually in our ability to make the constructive request of God, the kind that furthers his kingdom and the blessing of other people, not just our own whims and desires being satisfied.

PRAYER STARTER

Lord, give me the heart of Solomon, which sees what is really important and asks you for it. Change my desires where they are based on sheer selfishness. Help me make much room for others in my prayers and requests of you.

DAY 149

The Enthusiasm of Solomon

SCRIPTURE READING: 1 KINGS 5–6; 2 CHRONICLES 2–3

As we consider Solomon's building of a temple for the Lord, notice the enthusiasm he has for completing this important task for God and for Israel. He spares no expense, in terms of both labor and materials, to do something great for God. It seems he is excited to undertake this task left for him by his father, David.

Do you share this same enthusiasm for the assignments the Lord brings your way? Although "being" always comes first and is more important than "doing" in the Christian life, each of us has been appointed to do some work to further his kingdom. It is important that we embrace those assignments, whether they are witnessing, encouraging, teaching, serving, administrating, caring, or anything else. Solomon had fervor to see a house built for God in Jerusalem, and he led all of Israel to be consumed with the project for some seven years! May we share that fervor in building his kingdom here today!

PRAYER STARTER

I know that this massive temple project is an example of how fervently I should pursue the tasks you call me to do. Help me clearly understand what it is you want me to put my hand to and stop me from making excuses so that I will step up like Solomon to complete all the work you have entrusted to me.

DAY 150

The Precision of Solomon

SCRIPTURE READING: 1 KINGS 7; 2 CHRONICLES 4

IN THE BUILDING OF THE TEMPLE, and in the crafting of its furnishings, Solomon made sure the workmen followed God's specifications exactly (2 Chronicles 4:7). We must always be on guard against legalism (the worship of rules, especially human-made ones, or the belief that obeying them earns us favor with God), but when God does give specific instructions, we must follow them to the letter.

There are times to be creative, and God is glorified when we exercise our creativity. However, there is no room for creativity that adds to, alters, or contradicts any specific instructions God gives us in the Bible. We live in a world that is seemingly set on modifying the Bible's definitions of morality, sexuality, ethics, and in some cases, even God himself. Determine today that you will live without compromise or creativity when it comes to who God is and how He wants you to live.

PRAYER STARTER

DEAR LORD, IT IS SO EASY to take your instructions lightly or to pick and choose only the directives in _____ that I can follow easily. Help me to not fall into that kind _____ lay I always listen for your voice, hear you clearly, and _____ completely. Help me to obey you today!

DAY 151

God's Dwelling Place

SCRIPTURE READING: 1 KINGS 8;
2 CHRONICLES 5:1–7:10

Solomon declares that "The heavens, even the highest heavens, cannot contain you. How much less this temple I have built!" (1 Kings 8:27, 2 Chronicles 6:18). Yet God had the Israelites of earlier days carry the tabernacle with them and now has Solomon build a temple in Jerusalem as a special place where he can dwell among his people. This tells us something profound about God—that even though he is absolutely beyond us, unfathomable, and limitless, he values closeness with his people so much that he is willing to inhabit a paltry man-made structure in order to be with them. The further miracle of the new covenant is that he now is willing to live in the hearts of those who love him. May we never lose our awe and profound gratitude that the God of the universe takes up residence in his people.

PRAYER STARTER

Lord, raise my awareness of the wonder of your presence with me. You cannot be contained by this universe, and yet you live in me as a believer. You are the sovereign King of all creation, and yet you value fellowship with me. Let me never take this truth for granted or, God forbid, neglect it as an integral part of my life!

DAY 152

The Blessing of Good Leadership

SCRIPTURE READING: 1 KINGS 9:1–10:13;
2 CHRONICLES 7:11–9:12

Sometimes when we consider a great leader, we focus on the blessings he or she receives from being a leader. This would be particularly easy to do with Solomon because of his vast personal wealth and the great rewards he reaped from the period of progress that he initiated in Israel. But the queen of Sheba gives us another perspective from which to view the king. She puts forward that his leadership is a blessing for the nation of Israel that verifies God's love for them.

With the proliferation of dysfunctional leadership in our world today, we should easily appreciate the blessing that wise, solid leadership is for any nation or group of people. So as you consider the good leaders in your life today, instead of envying their position or the blessings that are theirs because of their good leadership, instead thank God for them as blessings to your life. And, if you are a leader in any sphere of influence, be sure you think of your leadership as a way to bless and enrich others' lives, and not as merely a way to attain advancement or blessing for yourself. Who can you bless with good leadership today?

PRAYER STARTER

Lord, please allow me to recognize, follow, and honor the good leaders in my life. Thank you for them. In venues where I lead, let it be said of me that my leadership is an unmixed blessing to those I lead. I could hope for no more; may I settle for no less!

DAY 153

The Priority of the Spiritual

SCRIPTURE READING: 1 KINGS 4; 10:14–29;
2 CHRONICLES 1:14–17; 2 CHRONICLES 9:13–28;
PSALM 72

THESE PASSAGES FOCUS ON THE WEALTH, power, and wisdom of Solomon. They are included to give historical information, to be sure, but also as testimony that God has fulfilled his promise to Solomon, to give him wisdom for governing his people *and* the blessings of wealth, power, and long life.

The larger truth here, and one that we often overlook, is that it is God who ultimately controls and distributes all such earthly blessings. What is the lesson for us? It is the consistent biblical proclamation that earthly blessings may ebb and flow in the lives of the wicked *and* the righteous and the Lord controls this current—but our wisest course is always to pursue spiritual blessings first and foremost, trusting him with other matters. As Jesus said, "... seek first his kingdom and his righteousness, and all these things will be given to you as well."

PRAYER STARTER

LORD, HELP ME TO NOT FIXATE to an unhealthy degree on what I have or have not been given in the physical realm. I know that life consists of so much more! Give me the clarity to pursue you above all else, giving due diligence to my earthly wellbeing, yet not being consumed by it.

DAY 154

The Beginning of Wisdom

SCRIPTURE READING: PROVERBS 1–3

As we begin Proverbs, a book dedicated to imparting wisdom for godly living, reflect today on one of the most famous phrases in the whole book, "The fear of the Lord is the beginning of wisdom, but fools despise wisdom and discipline." Solomon is saying that attitude is really the start of everything. The attitude of one's heart in relation to God is more important than intelligence, background, current life situation, education, or reputation. One who does not begin with a stance of humility, reverence, and willingness to learn has no shot whatsoever at the life wisdom can provide. Those who "know-it-all," or are determined to be their own God, need not apply.

What about you? Do you have a heart that fears God, stands in awe of who he is and profound humility about who you are? Because of this very issue, many in our world are tragically handicapped at just "getting out of the gate" to walk with God. Ask God today for continued reverence for him and continual thirst for his wisdom for life.

PRAYER STARTER

Dear God, so often I want to "go it" my own way, or at least figure life out for myself. Teach me the folly of this direction. Teach me my dependence on you, and help me to properly fear you and value wisdom and instruction. Push away my pride and replace it with a new teachability, starting today.

DAY 155

Saving My Sexuality

SCRIPTURE READING: PROVERBS 4–6

There are two separate passages of warning against adultery in today's reading, the first of multiple warnings throughout Proverbs. Solomon warns that when we are tempted by adultery, it can look so sweet, so harmless, and even so right, but its ultimate result is always destruction and ruin. His advice holds true for both men and women, and also with other temptations to misuse our sexuality. God has a plan for sex, and that is for it to be shared within a marriage and *nowhere else!* If you are currently struggling in this area, it is wise to heed the words of Proverbs and turn away from this path, with God's help.

When we are tempted to disobey what God says in any area, we need to remember that "a man's ways are in full view of the Lord, and he examines all his paths." Those things that might be hidden from the eyes of other people are never obscured from God's sight in the least. And he is the One that matters. May he grant us the strength to walk cleanly before him, and when we do not, the humility and wisdom to quickly seek his cleansing and renewal.

PRAYER STARTER

Lord, I know there is no area of my life that is obscured from your view. Guard me, so that I may use my sexuality only in a way that honors you. In a society where there seem to be few boundaries, keep all your children strong against the lie that adultery is acceptable.

DAY 156

Wisdom vs. Folly

SCRIPTURE READING: PROVERBS 7–9

There is much to ponder in this reading about the nature and value of wisdom, but consider today the contrast between wisdom and folly. They are both said to call out to us to come in and learn their ways, but their messages could not be more different. Wisdom advocates a life of submission to godly principles and a growing knowledge of God and his ways. Folly, on the other hand, encourages a life of stealing and deception to get ahead.

Which best describes your philosophy? Do you regularly bow to the hypnotic and intoxicating effect of wickedness, finding it more exciting to eat the stolen food of folly (9:16–17) than the wholesome banquet of wisdom (9:1–5)? Or do you see the enticements of folly for what they are, appreciating the true value of wisdom and seeking to live your life well? The voice of folly is loud in our world (9:13), and its enticements come to us all, in one form or another. It takes true courage, commitment, and clarity to choose the way of wisdom. May we be those who choose wisdom, in the big decisions and the little ones, even when all around us seem to be going the other way.

PRAYER STARTER

Lord, I know that without your wisdom guiding my life, I am as likely as anyone to fall into serious folly and to pay the price for it. Help me always listen for your wisdom and hear it clearly. Keep it fresh in my heart and mind that wickedness and folly lead to death.

DAY 157
Rootedness

SCRIPTURE READING: PROVERBS 10–12

Proverbs 12:3 says, "A man cannot be established through wickedness, but the righteous cannot be uprooted." The symbolism of a tree's "rootedness" is used to portray success in a person's life. If a plant never establishes a strong root system, it is very vulnerable to disease, weather, drought, and many other dangers. But a tree with a firmly established root system can withstand many more of these dangers without being harmed or uprooted.

So, in a person's life, real success that stands the test of time only comes to those who do what is right. They are developing "good roots." There may be temporary successes in the lives of the wicked that come at the expense of character (cheating on taxes or tests, scamming people out of money, etc.), but these will not endure. In the long run, evil behavior only leads to more evil behavior, not to success! It is interesting that so many people in today's world believe they can be established through wickedness. They think it is acceptable to do whatever they can to get ahead, no matter who it hurts. The message of this proverb is clear: the person who seeks power, money, popularity, or any other blessing through wicked means has no roots. He or she is building a life with no sure foundation and is therefore extremely vulnerable. But somehow, those who seek to live righteously become progressively more established, solid, and secure as they walk this way. How is your root system?

PRAYER STARTER

Lord, please help me develop strength of character that cannot be uprooted. I am so insecure when I choose the way of evil. Help me always say no to the lie that unrighteousness can in any way lead me toward true success.

DAY 158

Choosing Companions

SCRIPTURE READING: PROVERBS 13–15

It matters who we choose as close friends! Proverbs 13:20 says, "He who walks with the wise grows wise, but the companion of fools suffers harm." The teaching here is not that we should necessarily shun someone because he or she is foolish, but rather it is about who we choose to "walk with" in life. It addresses those with whom we choose to really share life. Remember that a fool is marked by a denial of God or a refusal to be taught wisdom for right living. It is good and necessary to at times be around such people. We should love them and seek to help them toward God and toward truth.

But trouble arises when we begin to be interdependent with such people to the point that they begin to have influence on us. When we become "companions" of the foolish, and when we begin to adopt their lifestyle and beliefs, we open ourselves to the very same consequences that are promised to fools throughout this book. In short, we will "suffer harm." Are you discerning in choosing with whom you share life? This is not about being elitist or "stuck up"; it is about guarding your mind, heart, and life from those who would pull you into destructive ways of thinking and living!

PRAYER STARTER

Thank you, Lord, for the godly and wise friends you have put in my life. Please increase their number, and deepen my relationships with them. Guard me from the influence of fools. Help me to love, serve, and positively influence everyone in my path, but make me wise in my choice of the companions I walk through life with.

DAY 159

Temper, Temper!

SCRIPTURE READING: PROVERBS 16–18

This reading contains a number of different themes, as do those for the next few days. Please be open to the Lord speaking to you on another matter if he wants, even if his words do not address the same themes explored here.

Proverbs 16:32 extols the value of patience, saying it is better to control one's temper than take a city in battle. This means that self-control is of even greater value than dramatic external successes. It is a great personal victory when we can exhibit patience in a hard situation or control our temper when we feel like exploding.

The Bible also teaches that patience is a part of the fruit of God's Spirit in a believer's life (Galatians 5:22). This means that he is the ultimate source of patience, and he can produce it in *any* life that is yielded to him. How are you doing at patience right now in your life? Do you have a "short fuse?" Even if you don't blow up easily, do you get tense, flustered, or resentful when things don't go your way, when people don't meet your expectations, or when things don't happen according to your timetable? Ask the Lord for patience and self-control today!

PRAYER STARTER

Lord, tame my temper. Make me a person who values patience more in my life, and give me your attribute of patience. Help me be patient with other people, with my circumstances, and with myself.

DAY 160

Treasuring Truthfulness

SCRIPTURE READING: PROVERBS 19–21

CONSIDER TODAY THE VALUE OF TRUTHFULNESS. We are told fully twice in Proverbs 19, "A false witness will not go unpunished." This is another theme that runs throughout the book (and throughout the Bible), but Solomon provides us with a very powerful, clear, and concise statement of it. When temptations to misrepresent the truth arise in your life, remember this promise. Truth may not be revealed immediately or even soon enough by human standards, but truth has a way of emerging.

Certainly at the end, when the Lord returns, everything that is in the dark will come into the light, but Solomon appears to also say that there are grave consequences for a deceptive mode of operation. My wife and I have tried to teach our kids that one of the very worst things they can do, the thing that will get them in more trouble with us than perhaps any other, is if they speak untruth to us. Trust is the basis for any healthy human relationship, and without it, the chances of a healthy relationship are severely undermined. Solomon says that "he who pours out lies will not go free." Think of someone you have known who habitually had a hard time speaking the truth. Did it seem to follow them around and catch up from time to time, causing them pain, loss, rejection, and so forth? Be mindful of this consequence as you choose your words today and every day.

PRAYER STARTER

LORD, I AM FULLY CAPABLE OF BEING A LIAR under certain conditions and circumstances. Grow in me the character to withstand this temptation, that I might more fully glorify you in my life, and that I may be spared the pain that always follows those who practice deception.

DAY 161

Maintaining Control and Clarity

SCRIPTURE READING: PROVERBS 22–24

THIS PASSAGE IS REPLETE WITH PRINCIPLES FOR WISE LIVING, from the value of a good reputation, to the importance of discipline for children, to the deceptiveness of wealth, to the importance of caring for the poor, and to the dangers of debt. But there is also a classic passage on the abuse of alcohol (23:29–35) that bears further examination.

Drunkenness is clearly forbidden throughout scripture as a sin, but this passage focuses more on its practical dangers and consequences. Woe, sorrow, strife, complaints, needless bruises, and bloodshot eyes are promised to those who "linger over wine." The influence of alcohol (or any other drug, for that matter) can cause us to lose control of our thoughts, attitudes, actions, and reactions. When we dabble with drunkenness, we exchange this control for the pleasurable feelings the drug supplies (or its anesthetic effects, if we are drinking to deaden pain). This trade is never wise. In addition to the negative results listed in this passage, there is also the shame and other consequences of what we may have done or said while under the influence. We live in a society that generally pays lip service to being concerned about alcoholism, but then is amused by and celebrates drunken revelry. Christ-followers are called to be different.

If you are convinced that the Lord has led you to abstain from alcohol, it is important that you live by your convictions, no matter the pressure to do otherwise. You must also be on guard against other areas of addiction and loss of self-control. If you have liberty before the Lord in regard to alcohol use, then it is imperative that you commit yourself to the utmost wisdom in the exercise of this liberty, with a firm commitment not to cross over to drunkenness (by which I mean *any* physical impairment).

PRAYER STARTER

DEAR LORD, YOU HAVE MADE ME A RATIONAL BEING, with the dignity of having been created in your own image. You have redeemed me for special purposes that can only be accomplished if I am living at my peak in body, mind, and spirit. Help me to not compromise this by the influence of, much less dependence on, any substance, activity, or involvement.

DAY 162

The Hard Truth

SCRIPTURE READING: PROVERBS 25–27

We all need people in our lives who love us enough to speak the truth to us, even when it is hard to hear. That is what Proverbs 27:6 means when it says, "Wounds from a friend can be trusted, but an enemy multiplies kisses." It seems we have a curious habit of gravitating toward those who say things that make life easy for us and who never really challenge us. But if we run from those who are genuinely speaking truth with our best interest at heart, this is just another way of running from God himself.

There is certainly a balance to be struck here. This concept is not about finding the most negative people you can and elevating them to the status of intimate friend and confidante. This would be suicide. It is all based on love. It is about finding those people whose love you trust, who know you best, and who will step up *when it is needed* and speak words of challenge or rebuke. We all need far more encouragement in our lives than negativity, but those who always and only speak coddling and ego-feeding words to us do us no favors. In fact, they actually prove to be our enemies by their "multiplying of kisses."

By the way, make sure of your own motives before you become the rebuker. Remember the speck and the mote in Jesus' teaching! Don't fall into the habit of some who use this principle as a pretext for beating others up with condemnation. Attitude is everything!

PRAYER STARTER

Lord, raise up those in my life who will love me enough to speak truth as well as consistently encourage my heart. Help me also to be this kind of friend to those you've placed in my life.

DAY 163

Softheartedness

SCRIPTURE READING: PROVERBS 28–29

Proverbs 28:13–14 says, "He who conceals his sins does not prosper, but whoever confesses and renounces them finds mercy. Blessed is the man who always fears the LORD, but he who hardens his heart falls into trouble."

This scripture reminds us of the importance of humility, honesty, and softheartedness before God. We must be open with him about our sins and remain in the habit of bringing them before him in repentance, so that he might renew us in our faith. We need to experience his mercy continually to stay on fire for him. It is only then that his blessings can flow uninterrupted into and through our lives. For this to happen, we have to maintain a reverential fear of God that allows us to turn away from pride and hardheartedness. It is so easy for our hearts to become hard toward him, even when no one around us would suspect this. Ask him today for a renewed softness of heart and sensitivity to sin, so that pride cannot harden you and make you fall into trouble. Especially if you have tried to hide or hold onto specific sins, bring them to him today.

PRAYER STARTER

Above all else, Lord, make me humble and softhearted before you. Help me never to hide or coddle my sin, but to always turn quickly toward you for healing and cleansing.

DAY 164

Material Wisdom

SCRIPTURE READING: PROVERBS 30–31; PSALM 127

In Proverbs 30:7–9, Agur advances the desirability of moderation. He warns that the danger of having too much is that we tend to forget the Lord and trust in our riches instead. The danger of having too little is that we might be tempted to steal to meet our needs. Hence, he asks for a moderate amount of provision for his daily needs.

What are we to do with these verses, then? Some of us have very little provision in comparison to others, while some of us have been blessed beyond measure. It is clearly not God's agenda to bless all people equally and moderately, so while we may wish and pray for this, as Agur did, this may not be our lot. So we have to take the warnings implied in these verses seriously.

No matter how much or how little wealth we have, we can be tempted to trust in our material provisions and forget the Lord. We need to realize that this tendency increases the more our wealth grows and we must guard our hearts against it. Likewise, no matter what our wealth is, we can become greedy for "a little bit more," and this can lead us into envy or even theft. We must also guard our hearts against these temptations. How is your attitude regarding wealth today? Have you found a place of contentment and humble reliance on the Lord?

PRAYER STARTER

Lord, guard me against these evils of pride and self-reliance on the one hand and envy and theft on the other. Help me see that they are equally insidious. Infuse me with wisdom regarding how I handle my material affairs so that I may not live in want, and yet may never be owned by the things I possess.

DAY 165
The Groom's Affection

SCRIPTURE READING: SONG OF SOLOMON

Perhaps you have previously missed the significance of the Song of Solomon. It is both an allegory of God's love for Israel and the church *and* a literal story about married love in which we learn much about love, marriage, and sex. It contains the most explicit statements on sex in the Bible.

Focus today on the power of this metaphor of Christ's love for his bride, the church—that's us! It is mind-boggling that he could adore us with the intensity of the love a man has for his bride, considering how frail and weak we often are in our attempts to follow him. However, one of the biggest keys to walking the walk he wants for us is realizing and embracing this very truth. Although we are weak and even hypocritical at times, he is passionate about pursuing us. He is crazy about us. He loves us more than we can imagine. Let this truth bring you comfort *and* inspire you to return his love today!

PRAYER STARTER

Lord, it is impossible for me, in and of myself, to really comprehend the depth, breadth, height, and strength of your love. But I long for a taste today. I need to realize your love and experience it deeply. It is only your love that can sustain me, heal me, and change me as I need. Help me move beyond talking about and believing in your love, all the way to experiencing it!

DAY 166

The Source of Meaning

SCRIPTURE READING: 1 KINGS 11:1–40; ECCLESIASTES 1–2

It is believed that Solomon wrote the book of Ecclesiastes late in his life, as he looked back on the significant portion of his life that he lived apart from God. His conclusion, reiterated again and again in these first two chapters, is that life apart from God is absolutely meaningless and empty. The rhythms of life on earth, all the wisdom of the ages, all the pleasures of the world, even the greatest vocational accomplishments, cannot truly bring satisfaction and meaning to the human soul.

Solomon speaks as one who knows. He had it all. He was given an unsurpassed gift of wisdom by God. He was able to afford all the pleasures the world of his time could offer. He even accomplished arguably the greatest construction projects in the history of Israel. And yet he gets to the end and finds it all meaningless. Where are you looking for fullness? What gives your life meaning? By this I don't just mean, can you give the "correct" answers? I mean do you truly find meaning and fullness in your life by living for God? If you are looking to anything or anyone less than him to fill your life and make it worthwhile, you will ultimately be disappointed!

PRAYER STARTER

Lord, let me truly pursue ultimate meaning, purpose, and fullness for my life in you. Let me never settle for less. I know that there is no amount of wisdom, pleasure, power, or accomplishment that can ever fill me up, but you can. Fill me, Lord, today!

DAY 167

Life's Rhythm

SCRIPTURE READING: ECCLESIASTES 3-7

In the midst of reinforcing his lament about the ultimate meaninglessness of all life and human activity, Solomon gives us some wise words about the reality of rhythm in our outlook on life. His famous verses at the beginning of Chapter 3 assure us that because there is a certain ebb and flow, or undulation, about life, we should not be surprised that it is a mixture of good and bad, pleasure and pain, gain and loss, silence and speech, killing and healing, and so forth. Those who expect life to be all good, all laughter, all blessing, all the time are deceived about the nature of life in this realm. They set themselves up for disappointment, disillusionment, and even anger at God as they buy into the "if-you-love-God-your-life-will-be-smooth" deception. Remember, everyone's life undulates, even those who are most godly—even the heroes of scripture!

Do you need to adopt a more realistic view about life? God promises to give us the strength to bear our burdens, not to always remove them. He promises to use our trials to build our character, not to keep us problem free. As American Christians, we are notoriously slow to learn this lesson. But the sooner we grasp it, the more quickly he can move us toward real maturity and effectiveness as his followers, and the sooner he can show us what victory in Christ really means!

PRAYER STARTER

Lord, I want to walk steadily with you through the ups and downs of this life. Teach me that the downs do not mean you have left me. Give me strength to bear up under the times to "die ... uproot ... kill ... tear down .... weep ... mourn ... scatter stones ... refrain ... give up ... throw away ... tear ... be silent ... hate ... and war" as well as to embrace and celebrate their opposites with all my might.

DAY 168

Sharpening the Axe

SCRIPTURE READING: ECCLESIASTES 8–12;
1 KINGS 11:41–43; 2 CHRONICLES 9:29–31

Solomon waits until the very end of the book of Ecclesiastes to talk about eternal and spiritual matters (12:13–14), but there is much profound wisdom in his observations about the nature of this life. Although his reflections are sometimes quite sobering and even pessimistic, he gives us some real jewels that can help us in our walk.

One such jewel is found in 10:10—"If the ax is dull and its edge unsharpened, more strength is needed but skill will bring success." Think of this as a metaphor about our talents and gifts. The message is that we need to develop ourselves to the fullest. We become "sharp axes" through a variety of means, such as formal education, focused learning experiences, spiritual disciplines, and plain old practice. If we are as "sharp" as we can possibly be, then we can be more effective in our homes, our jobs, our friendships, and especially in our service to God and his kingdom. As they say, "Even God can cut more wood with a sharp axe." Do you need to take steps toward personal development? Each one of us is responsible for developing our gifts and abilities to the fullest extent possible. So whether it is simply practicing more discipline and focus in what you are already doing, acquiring new skills, taking on a role of service or ministry to others, or engaging in a classroom somewhere, seriously seek God about the next step in your development as a person *and* as a follower of Christ.

PRAYER STARTER

Lord, it is so easy to believe there is a place in life where we stop developing, stop learning, and stop growing. Help me truly to always realize that place is a myth, and that I am called to become "sharper" throughout my life here. Show me what the next step is for me, and give me the courage to take it.

DAY 169

Using My Power to Serve

SCRIPTURE READING: 1 KINGS 12;
2 CHRONICLES 10:1–11:17

REHOBOAM'S FOOLISHNESS IN THIS PASSAGE is nothing short of remarkable. He literally loses his rule over the unified nation of Israel with one rash decision. His headstrong, arrogant, and power-hungry answer to the people of Israel when they come to ask for a lighter load of labor effectively alienates all the northern tribes. His attempt to "flex his muscles" and show them how tough he can be backfires in the most severe way possible.

Rehoboam actually makes two fatal mistakes that can instruct us how not to react to similar situations. First, he lets his pride rule him. Dismissing the idea of servant leadership, he decides that lording it over those who follow him is the way to ensure their loyalty. He could not be more wrong. His second error is in choosing the counsel of the young, foolish, inexperienced voices that are saying what he wants to hear, while ignoring the voice of experience and wisdom coming from the elders in his court. Let us determine to let neither our own pride nor the voices of unwise counselors turn us toward the way of Rehoboam!

PRAYER STARTER

LORD, I AM AS LIKELY AS ANYONE ELSE to abuse power instead of being a willing servant. Give me the grace to choose the latter. Also make me wise in choosing the counsel I receive. Help me hunger for true wisdom, even when it may seem like the harder way.

DAY 170

Hiding the Lord

SCRIPTURE READING: 1 KINGS 13–14;
2 CHRONICLES 11:18–12:16

NOW BEGINS THE TRULY TRAGIC PART of the story of the kings of Israel and Judah. Both Rehoboam and Jeroboam were displeasing to the Lord as kings, and they both ultimately fell under God's judgment. It is discouraging how quickly both these men turned away from God, despite his goodness to them. God took Jeroboam from relative obscurity and made him king over Israel, and he mercifully spared Rehoboam a part of the kingdom even after he proved unworthy and disobedient. Yet amazingly, neither man could find it in his heart to truly stand for and walk with God. They and their descendants reaped the consequences.

A phrase in 1 Kings 14:9 captures the essence of what both men did. God says that Jeroboam "... provoked me to anger and thrust me behind your back." What an awesome word picture. God is saying Jeroboam not only took his eyes off the Lord, but hid him behind his back, out of the sight of himself *and* others. He obscured all of Israel's view of God. It is easy for me to imagine a little boy hiding something behind his back because he is ashamed of it. Do we treat God like this at times? Isn't it time for the Lord to truly be our "banner," of whom we are not ashamed, and who we make every attempt to expose to others and not hide?

PRAYER STARTER

LORD, I WANT MY HEART to be radically different from those of Jeroboam and Rehoboam. Help me to not hide you or turn away from you, but boldly shine your light in the darkness around me!

DAY 171
Swift, Complete, and Consistent Obedience

SCRIPTURE READING: 1 KINGS 15:1–24;
2 CHRONICLES 13–16

ASA HAD THE POTENTIAL AND THE OPPORTUNITY to be one of Judah's greatest kings. He had a heart that wanted to follow God, a reasonable amount of courage, and he had a fairly long reign (40 years) that began with a period of peace. However, Asa had two overwhelming failures that kept him from true greatness as a king.

First, he did not go far enough with his reforms. Both 1 Kings and 2 Chronicles mention fairly early in their descriptions of his reign that "...he did not remove the high places from Israel." In other words, he left some of the venues of perverted and unacceptable worship operational, even though he did many good acts. This is clearly regarded as incomplete obedience in these passages.

Asa's second great shortcoming was his failure to trust in the Lord toward the end of his reign. He clearly turned an unhealthy degree to Aram (Syria) for help, and during his final years of illness he refused to seek God, choosing instead to seek only the help of his physicians. Guard against these two great lapses in your life. They can keep us from true greatness, just as they did Asa.

PRAYER STARTER

Lord, help me to always obey you swiftly and completely. Also enable me to keep my trust in you throughout my life, even in challenging times when it would be easy to turn to other people and rely on them instead of you. Teach me the right balance in seeking help from others when I need it. May I possess the strengths of Asa without succumbing to the weaknesses that limited his effectiveness.

DAY 172

The Blessings of Obedience

SCRIPTURE READING: 1 KINGS 15:25–16:34;
2 CHRONICLES 17; 1 KINGS 17

REWARDS FOR OBEDIENCE to God and consequences for disobedience do not usually happen as swiftly and precisely in our lives as they do in these passages, but the contrast presented here is worthy of consideration. The northern kingdom of Israel is subjected to a series of bad kings, each more wicked than the one before, and each dying by violence. Meanwhile, the southern kingdom, Judah, enjoys a period of relative prosperity as God's blessings come to the relatively good king, Asa, and the even better king, Jehoshaphat.

Again, events and circumstances do not usually flow so predictably. Many times we enjoy prosperity while being disobedient, and then walk obediently through times of want or suffering. But there is an important principle here. We need to understand that in the unseen spiritual realm, the destructiveness caused by our acts of disobedience is every bit as devastating, and often lasts just as long as that caused by these wicked kings. Likewise, just as the good kings brought tangible blessings upon themselves and their subjects by their obedience to the Lord, we always become blessed *and* we bless others in some way when we choose to follow his way.

PRAYER STARTER

LORD, GIVE ME THE STRENGTH to obey you throughout the day today, that I may not block blessings from my life or the lives of others. Let it be said of me, like Jehoshaphat, that my "heart was devoted to the ways of the LORD."

DAY 173

Never the Only One

SCRIPTURE READING: 1 KINGS 18–19

Elijah's discouragement in 1 Kings 19 is something we all have tasted if we have followed the Lord for any period of time at all. He thinks he is the only one in Israel interested in following the Lord, and he is tired. But the Lord's words of encouragement to him can also serve as powerful encouragement for us. First he gives Elijah his next assignment, and then he assures him he is indeed *not* alone. When you feel alone in your faith or when other believers let you down, know that throughout history God has always preserved a remnant that was truly faithful to him, and he still does today. Oh yes, and sometimes the best way to deal with discouragement and disillusionment is to get up and be proactive about the mission!

PRAYER STARTER

Lord, when I feel defeated and alone, come to me as you did to Elijah. Help me focus on your truth and be comforted that I am part of a much larger family, a family who lays claim to ultimate victory!

DAY 174

The God of Every Realm

SCRIPTURE READING: 1 KINGS 20–21

Where does God's kingdom and his realm of power end? The Arameans were mistaken about this, and it cost them dearly. After their first defeat at Ahab's hands, they gathered themselves together to fight with him on the plains because they thought, "Their gods are gods of the hills. That is why they were too strong for us. But if we fight them on the plains, surely we will be stronger than they." However, when they fought them on the plains, the same result was repeated. They learned in graphic fashion that the Lord is God on the plains as well as in the hills.

This episode may sound rather simplistic to you, but it communicates a powerful truth. This scripture tells us that wherever we go, whatever we face, however we feel, whoever opposes us, God is on the throne in every situation. This also means that God has dominion over our lives, plans, and actions, even though we may think otherwise. Today, ponder his absolute lordship and determine in your heart to trust him no matter the circumstance and to submit to him no matter the situation.

PRAYER STARTER

Lord, you are still the Lord of the plains as well as the hills. I know that I can never outrun your sovereignty, but I also know that I would not want to even if I could. Life, true and abundant life, is in you and nowhere else. Help me open every part of myself to your transforming presence.

DAY 175

Risking a Stand

SCRIPTURE READING: 1 KINGS 22:1–40;
2 CHRONICLES 18

THE DESIRE FOR A MEASURE OF POPULARITY *and* the desire to avoid injury *and* the desire to be successful can all work together at times to make us afraid to speak the truth. This was not a problem for Micaiah. He boldly proclaimed a message of truth in the face of 400 false prophets and the kings of two nations. He knew they would not be pleased with his truth telling, and that his actions could even result in some serious consequences for him. Yet he was bold and courageous in sharing what the Lord had truly said to him. He probably even had a good idea that his warnings would not be heeded, but he ended up choosing to tell the truth even though he would not meet with "success."

What about you? What does it take to make you compromise? How often do you fail to stand for what is right or share truth with someone who doesn't want to hear it? Yes, there are often immediate consequences when we decide to do so. And often our words will not be heeded. The eternal rewards, however, and the blessing intrinsic in obeying the Lord, far outweigh any such price!

PRAYER STARTER

LORD, HELP ME ALWAYS BE WILLING to stand for you. Transform me more and more into one who is unafraid to speak the truth in love when your spirit so leads.

DAY 176

When You Don't Know What to Do

SCRIPTURE READING: 1 KINGS 22:41–53;
2 KINGS 1; 2 CHRONICLES 19:1–21:3

WHY DOES GOD choose to tell Jehoshaphat and the people of Judah on the occasion of the impending battle with Moab and Ammon, "Do not be afraid or discouraged because of this vast army. For the battle is not yours, but God's"?

Consider the attitude the king displays in his plea for help: "... we have no power to face this vast army that is attacking us. We do not know what to do, but our eyes are upon you." Jehoshaphat speaks from a position of honesty and humility before God. We probably can't even imagine how difficult it is for a king to get to this state of mind and heart. But it is clear throughout scripture that the Lord is always attracted to this attitude and highly esteems it.

Our problem is that it is often *extremely* difficult for our hearts to get to this place. We find it hard to be honest about our limitations. "I don't know what to do" are the last words many of us want to say—to God or anyone else. So we let our pride keep us from the very posture that will invite God's most powerful help into our situation. When was the last time you said, "I don't know what to do"? Maybe God is waiting to fight battles for you if you can get to a place of humility and honesty. One of the sweetest sentences we can ever hear is, "Do not be afraid or discouraged ... for the battle is not yours, but God's."

PRAYER STARTER

LORD I BRING YOU MY BATTLES TODAY, and I acknowledge there are many times I don't quite know what to do. In those times, I desperately need you to say that the battle is yours. Grant that I may share all my battles with you, especially when they are decidedly bigger than my strength. Then meet me with your help in the midst of the battle.

DAY 177

Asking for a Double Portion

SCRIPTURE READING: 2 KINGS 2–4

Consider Elisha's request for "a double portion" of Elijah's spirit. He was asking here for twice the anointing, twice the power, and twice the presence of the Lord that had attended Elijah's ministry. Scripture is clear that his request was ultimately granted, because Elisha did see Elijah as he was taken up to heaven.

We might wonder about the appropriateness of Elisha's request. After all, isn't it strange for a servant of God to ask to be better or more powerful than Elijah himself? It may seem so, but we have to understand that Elisha's motives were judged to be pure in this situation. His main goal was clearly not power for himself or superiority over Elijah, but the ability to accomplish more for God. Are you willing to ask for great things from God? If we examine our motives and make sure we truly are not walking in selfishness, we need not be afraid to ask for great things from God. Get in the habit of asking God to do great things through you. You will come to see that this is not arrogance or selfishness, but a way of aligning yourself with the heart of God.

PRAYER STARTER

Lord, I ask you to do great things through my life. Whether or not these accomplishments are honored by men and women, I ask you to use me mightily for the purposes you desire.

DAY 178

The Simple Thing

SCRIPTURE READING: 2 KINGS 5–7

How are you with following God's directions in the "simple things"? Naaman was actually resentful because Elisha did not work a dramatic miracle or tell him to go to one of the rivers of Syria to wash, which he clearly would have preferred. He stumbled because of the simple, mundane, even menial directions the Lord gave him. He needed his servants to challenge him, "...if the prophet had told you to do some great thing, would you not have done it? How much more, then, when he tells you, 'Wash and be cleansed'!"

Sometimes it is easy for us to live for the dramatic and shun the mundane, even in our walk with the Lord. But the fact is that a faithful, God-honoring life is more about the multitude of small, simple, and "mundane" steps of obedience than it is about the few dramatic, larger-than-life events that may or may not come our way. It is about building a strong faith, a steadfast spiritual maturity, and a solid character through a lifetime of faithfulness in daily quiet times with the Lord; small group Bible studies in community with a few fellow-travelers; and group worship and teaching experiences with the larger body of Christ. It is about regular service in a ministry within the local church, which may or may not be broadly recognized or affirmed by other people. It is about day-by-day obedience to the Bible's teachings, when people are watching and when they are not. Don't fall to the same weakness as Naaman. He almost lost his healing because of his prideful demand for more than the "mundane."

PRAYER STARTER

Lord, keep me from the pride of thinking certain things are "beneath" me. I know that I, like Naaman, will forfeit many blessings if this is my mind-set. Let me not despise the small and common things, but remain faithful in them.

DAY 179

Living for What Lasts

SCRIPTURE READING: 2 KINGS 8–9;
2 CHRONICLES 21:4–22:9

THE REPORT OF THE END of Jezebel's life is a sobering one indeed. She was one of the wickedest women who ever lived and also one of the most powerful. However, the Bible reports that in the end all that remained of her evil life was her skull, feet, and hands (1 Kings 9:35). She had the power to turn Ahab's heart away from the Lord, and with him all of Israel. Her influence even spread to the southern kingdom, Judah, where her daughter married King Jehoram and helped turn his heart away from the Lord. However, all her power, her money, her prestige, and her life of luxury were ultimately stripped from her, and her legacy amounted to nothing.

While we are running this race called life, power, health, wealth, and even pleasure can make us feel like we will live forever. But the statistics are consistent—one hundred percent of people still die. Death has a way of stripping away all the external securities we have built up, no matter their extent. Ponder the course of your life today, and make adjustments where needed before your heart becomes hardened like that of Jezebel.

PRAYER STARTER

> LORD HELP ME TO RIGHTLY CONSIDER my direction in this life. I don't want to live for the momentary power, possessions, pleasures, and prestige this world offers. Help me to realize the utterly temporary nature of these things, and set my sights on that which is more lasting.

DAY 180

Incomplete Obedience

SCRIPTURE READING: 2 KINGS 10–11;
2 CHRONICLES 22:10–23:21

THE RETRIBUTION that Jehu wrought on the house of Ahab was sweeping—he basically went on a mission to destroy every last vestige. By these actions, he became the instrument of the Lord for the judgment on Ahab's house that had been prophesied. Jehu also instituted much needed reforms in the worship life of Israel, the most notable being the elimination of all the priests of Baal, effectively wiping out Baal worship in Israel.

However, even after all the reforms he instituted, this troubling synopsis appears in the description of his reign: "...Yet Jehu was not careful to keep the law of the LORD, the God of Israel, with all his heart. He did not turn away from the sins of Jeroboam, which he had caused Israel to commit." Jehu's shortcomings, much like those of some of the others that preceded him as king, amounted to an incomplete obedience that kept him from being and doing all that the Lord wanted. Guard yourself against the plague of incomplete obedience, the idea that you only have to do just enough good to outweigh the bad in your life, outperform others around you, and then you can stop obeying God. May he save us all from this lie!

PRAYER STARTER

LORD, MAKE MY SOUL DISCONTENT with *anything* short of absolute obedience to you. Although your grace surrounds me and covers my many faults, I wish to never excuse myself from listening to you and completely obeying. I know that only complete obedience will result in your maximum glory and my maximum good.

DAY 181

Tearing My Garments

SCRIPTURE READING: JOEL

This stirring prophecy of judgment on Judah, delivered between 835 and 796 BC, contains a strong teaching about the attitude of repentance God was requiring for Judah to be restored. In 2:12–13, Joel says, "'Even now,' declares the LORD, 'return to me with all your heart, with fasting and weeping and mourning. Rend your heart and not your garments. Return to the LORD your God, for he is gracious and compassionate, slow to anger and abounding in love, and he relents from sending calamity.'"

The tearing of garments was a symbol of deep remorse, but God makes it clear he is far more interested in true inward repentance than in an outward display of penitence. When he uses words such as "with all your heart," and "fasting and weeping and mourning," he is in essence proclaiming the need for extreme measures. Returning to God is serious business! But the assurance we have is that God's character is "gracious and compassionate, slow to anger and abounding in love."

Forgiveness always comes by turning from sin and turning toward God. If there are areas in your life you need to bring before him today, it is not too late for you to receive God's forgiveness. It is always his greatest desire that you come to him, but it requires deep remorse and sincere turning from sin within you.

PRAYER STARTER

Lord, please give me a continually repentant heart. May I never be satisfied to walk in sinfulness, but hunger with all my heart for your best in my life.

DAY 182

Repair Job

SCRIPTURE READING: 2 KINGS 12–13; 2 CHRONICLES 24

THE MASSIVE REPAIR OF THE TEMPLE recorded in 2 Kings 12 was only necessary because of the years of neglect under previous leaders. Notice the extent of the repairs. They included remortaring joints, cleaning out the filth, removing the idols, and polishing all the gold and bronze. The temple had been neglected because the worship of the Lord had been neglected. The people had strayed far from him.

When our hearts have strayed from God, there can be many outward signs of our neglect. We get angry easier, find it easier to yield to temptations, find it harder to get excited about God and what he wants to do in and through our lives, and we turn more prideful, cynical, and/or petty. Have you neglected the temple in your life? Maybe one or more areas in your life need a reclamation project. God is always ready to start this kind of work if we will just come back.

PRAYER STARTER

LORD I PRAY FOR ALL YOUR CHILDREN around the world who need repair work in their spiritual lives. Oh, what you could do if all your people would stay attentive to you! Let this process begin with me—show me what areas or issues I have neglected and begin a work of repair.

DAY 183

Accepting His Direction

SCRIPTURE READING: 2 KINGS 14;
2 CHRONICLES 25; JONAH

THE WHOLE FIRST TWO CHAPTERS of the Book of Jonah is the account of a man rejecting directions from the Lord and the consequences of that decision. Jonah was primarily motivated by the deep prejudice and hatred he had for the Ninevites, as we see clearly later in the book (4:2). However, other motivations could well have been behind his hesitancy. We certainly seem to have a plethora of reasons for running from God's directions. Sometimes it is fear, sometimes laziness, sometimes selfishness, and sometimes we are just stubborn and want to run the show ourselves.

The interesting thing is that God loves Jonah (and the Israelites) too much to leave him to this direction of rebellion. He brings a giant interruption in the form of a storm and a fish to break Jonah and turn him around. The fact of the matter is that God is willing to do what it takes to get the attention and the obedience of his children. Are you on the verge of telling God "no" about something he is telling you? Please examine your heart and consider the cost before you choose rebellion over obedience. Are you in the middle of a rebellion right now? Remember who God is! Do you wonder why life just isn't working out, you're running into walls, or you're walking through pain? *Maybe* God has sent an interruption in your life to work in you what he worked in Jonah. Why not go ahead and say "yes" to him?

PRAYER STARTER

LORD, MAKE AND KEEP MY HEART SOFT toward you, that I may always say "yes" to my King. Thank you for loving me enough to send pain to redirect my steps.

DAY 184

Chasing Other Loves

SCRIPTURE READING: HOSEA 1–7

Hosea's wedding to Gomer becomes a graphic picture of the sin of the nation of Israel. Just as she broke her marriage covenant by being unfaithful, the Israelites had broken covenant with God by following the wicked practices of the nations around them and by worshiping their gods. They united themselves with Assyria and Egypt in illicit relationships for military advantages. By these actions, they proved themselves unfaithful to God and broke his heart, just as an unfaithful wife breaks the heart of her husband.

This marriage is also a picture of our relationship with God today. It is so easy for us, like Gomer and Israel, to chase after other loves. We can be seduced by power hunger, greed, lust, dishonesty, hatred, pride, gluttony, drunkenness, or any other sin. It is very clear that when we do this, we are committing the same kind of adultery against God as the Israelites did. But he has a right to our faithfulness, just as it was Hosea's right to have a faithful wife. We sometimes act as if obedience to him is optional and we are doing him a big favor if we ever do what he says. But we are in a covenant relationship, and faithfulness to that covenant is *not* optional.

PRAYER STARTER

Lord, please forgive the times I have been unfaithful to you. Work faithfulness into my life, so that I may not let any other love take your rightful place.

DAY 185
God's Insane Love

SCRIPTURE READING: HOSEA 8–14

Hosea's relationship with Gomer is not only a picture of Israel's (and our) insane adultery against God, but is also a dynamic representation of God's extreme, even insane, love for them (and us). As 11:8 says, "How can I give you up, Ephraim? How can I hand you over, Israel? How can I treat you like Admah? How can I make you like Zeboiim? My heart is changed within me; all my compassion is aroused." The Lord has no intention of softening the reality of consequences for Israel's sin, as he makes clear in the preceding chapters. However, he is compelled by his almighty compassion and love to continue to reach out to Israel (and us). This compassion is not stirred by anything lovely in Israel (or us); it is an expression of his attribute of perfect love.

Are you truly thankful today for a God who keeps reaching out, wooing us home, even when we don't deserve it in the least? I know I am! Just as Hosea went and retrieved Gomer from her life of sin and restored her to the position of wife, God's deepest desire when we blow it and turn away from him is to "bring us home" and restore us. Do you need to come home today? God's love is absolute and he is ready to restore you!

PRAYER STARTER

Lord, heal my adultery and give me a faithful heart and a steadfast walk with you. I am no better than Gomer or Israel, because I have failed you just as greatly. Teach me to receive your love and prefer you to the others who would woo me away from you today.

DAY 186

The Pride of Success

SCRIPTURE READING: 2 KINGS 15:1–7;
2 CHRONICLES 26; AMOS 1–4

IT IS SO EASY FOR US TO FORGET who God is and who we are when things go well for us. Uzziah dealt with this very problem in his spiritual life. He started out as a good king, seeking God and learning from Zechariah himself to fear God. However, when success and power came his way, Uzziah proved unable to resist the pride that often results in such circumstances. He is called unfaithful because he became so puffed up that he presumed to perform worship functions that had been specifically designated for priests only. Indeed, "his pride led to his downfall," as he was chastened by his health being taken away through the horrible disease of leprosy.

The pride of success can be a horrible development in our lives, too. Like Uzziah, we can start out genuinely serving the Lord and end up serving ourselves. Ask the Lord to guard you from pride that could compromise your relationship with him, whether its source is success, intelligence, money, physical prowess, popularity, self-sufficiency, or something else. Allow the hard times in your life to make you truly humble, so that you can stay the course without falling into the pride trap that got Uzziah.

PRAYER STARTER

LORD, WHATEVER "SUCCESS" you might bring into my life, guard my heart against the pride that could short-circuit my very relationship with you. Thank you for the struggles in my life that have worked a measure of humility within me.

DAY 187

More than a Buddy

SCRIPTURE READING: AMOS 5–9;
2 KINGS 15:8–18

Read over Amos 5:18-24 once again. Amos points out a problem that had arisen in Israel from which we all need to guard our own hearts. It appears that the Israelites as a whole, and particularly the religious professionals, had fallen into the "God is my buddy" syndrome. The fear of the Lord had been forgotten, and the Israelites considered themselves well prepared to face God and spend time with him. They looked forward to the day of his visit as a day of blessing, prosperity, and reward. But God crushed their self-righteousness by saying the day of the Lord was something for them to dread, not to look forward to. He did not overlook their empty religion, their idol worship, and their utter lack of moral integrity.

So how are we to interpret this scripture today, in the age of grace? We need to understand that the Israelites who were under God's judgment were ones that took God's grace for granted and totally misunderstood their standing before him. This is a danger from which none of us is immune! We should trust completely in God's grace, love, and provision for us. But we should never presume that the state of our hearts does not matter to God. Eternal security does not mean that we "have it made" spiritually. It means we are in a place of ultimate safety in him, but we still are responsible to keep our worship pure, our religious acts real, and our integrity intact. We are to "work out our salvation with fear and trembling." Let us not presume on God's kindness and find ourselves with hard, cold, and self-righteous hearts.

PRAYER STARTER

Lord, break my heart where it is hard and presumptuous. Show me what a healthy fear of you looks like, and teach me the balance of a walk totally devoted to you. Give me joy, freedom, grace, love, and mercy, but also teach me the value of justice, righteousness, obedience, fear, and trembling.

DAY 188

His Cleansing Love

SCRIPTURE READING: ISAIAH 1–4

In the middle of this powerful passage about the severity of God's judgment on Judah and his hatred of their false worship, the Lord reveals the true desire of his heart. He says in 1:18–19, "Come now, let us reason together... Though your sins are like scarlet, they shall be as white as snow; though they are red as crimson, they shall be like wool. If you are willing and obedient, you will eat the best from the land;"

No matter the severity of the sin, God wants to cleanse, restore, and renew. Do you really believe this? His judgments are just, and in his righteousness God cannot abide sin—it must be punished. However, the deepest desire of his heart, even in the Old Testament, is always that people are set free and cleansed. We do not serve a God who gets some kind of glee out of judging our sin; he wants us to be liberated from it. See God for who he is today and be embraced by his cleansing, purifying love!

PRAYER STARTER

Lord, thank you that you are truly merciful and forgiving for those who will turn to you. Help me always be one of those. Thank you that I can be as white as snow in your sight, even though I have been the ugliest of the ugly. Show me how to release others in the same way you release me from past sins and offenses.

DAY 189

Walking Steadfastly

SCRIPTURE READING: 2 KINGS 15:19–38;
2 CHRONICLES 27; ISAIAH 5–6

Isaiah 6 stands out as a classic devotional passage, but my attention is drawn to a verse in 2 Chronicles 27. It is verse 6, "Jotham grew powerful because he walked steadfastly before the LORD his God." Jotham initiated spiritual reforms, military successes, and architectural achievements, and the reason given for these accomplishments is his steadfast walk with the Lord. We must not assume that this means all who are steadfast in their life of faith will necessarily reap similar types of blessings, or similar measures of blessings. However, this *was* the way God chose to reward Jotham, and throughout scripture blessings of one kind or another are repeatedly promised for obedience and faithfulness, from the multitude of promises to Israel in the Pentateuch, to Jesus' Beatitudes, and to the rewards foreseen in Revelation.

But what does "steadfastness" really mean? It means courage. Jotham was unmoved by the pressures of those who wished he would return Israel to the spiritual wasteland that existed before his father Uzziah's reforms. Steadfastness means contrition. He proved more obedient than his father because he resisted the kind of pride that Uzziah displayed by entering the temple and presuming to take on the role of the priests. Jotham remembered that the Lord was "his God." Steadfastness means consistency. Over time Jotham grew more and more powerful as he was consistent in his obedience to God. May God grant us the steadfastness to grow powerful for him!

PRAYER STARTER

Oh Lord, I want the steadfast kind of walk that Jotham had. Please grant me the courage, contrition, and consistency you look for in those you entrust with power for you.

DAY 190

Facing Depression

SCRIPTURE READING: MICAH 1–7

Micah 7 describes Israel's misery under the judgment of God, but it could also be describing the emotions of depression in an individual's life today. When we are caught in a downward spiral of depression, as was Micah, trouble seems to be all around us. There is rarely a simple answer to this kind of struggle, especially if it reaches a severe level, but God can bring us through such times of darkness so that we can again celebrate and glorify him.

We cannot pull ourselves out of a depressive cycle alone, no matter how hard we try. However, we have to muster enough faith to take a step forward, whether that means going to prayer, sharing with a trusted friend, or even seeking professional help from a Christian counselor. The reasons for our depression might be quite real, like disappointment with others, unfulfilling relationships, loneliness, fatigue, being criticized, a loss in our lives, an injury or injustice we've experienced, a genuine failure on our part, and so forth. However, no matter how legitimate our reasons are for being despondent, surrendering to this dejection is not legitimate for a child of God. Our dark times affect everyone around us, not just ourselves, and we have a responsibility to seek God's help so that we may ultimately say (and mean), "Though I have fallen, I will rise. Though I sit in darkness, the Lord will be my light."

PRAYER STARTER

God, there are many disturbing and distressing realities, both in the world at large and in my personal life, but I know your everlasting kingdom is bigger than all of them. Connect me to your positive truth through whatever resources you will. Help me also to help others rise, though they have fallen.

DAY 191

Turning to God in Troubled Times

SCRIPTURE READING: 2 KINGS 16;
2 CHRONICLES 28; ISAIAH 7–8

How do you respond when life's pressures mount up on you? Do hard times tend to turn you away from God, or toward him? In many ways, the choice is ours how we will respond in such circumstances. Ahaz certainly failed this test. In addition to turning to the king of Assyria for help when Pekah and Rezin were coming against him, the Bible says, "In his time of trouble King Ahaz became even more unfaithful to the Lord." What happens when you hit a time of trouble in your life? Do you get closer to God or begin to walk away from him?

God wants us to run to him, not only in the big, earth-shaking, tragic times of trial, but also amid the myriad pressures of everyday life. These, too, can either be opportunities for us to grow in our relationship with God or they can be the excuse for drifting away from him and becoming more unfaithful to the Lord, as Ahaz did.

PRAYER STARTER

WHATEVER THE TRIALS OF THIS DAY and this week, Lord, I want to turn to you and not away. Guard me from responding like Ahaz and looking everywhere else for answers except to the One who can really help.

DAY 192

Blind Arrogance

SCRIPTURE READING: ISAIAH 9–12

Isaiah predicts a mighty judgment that is to come upon Israel, and Assyria is to be the primary vessel of this judgment. But in 10:5–19, he speaks of judgment that will come on the Assyrians because of their wickedness, pride, and greed. Those who are used as the Lord's instrument of judgment will become the objects of his wrath! This speaks to us of the sovereignty of God. He uses even the acts of the wicked to carry out his purposes.

The Assyrians' blindness should give us pause today. Isaiah spends a good portion of this passage talking about their arrogance and their refusal to realize that the Lord is ultimately in control: "Does the axe raise himself above him who swings it, or the saw boast against him who uses it? As if a rod were to wield him who lifts it up, or a club brandish him who is not wood?" (v. 15). Let us not make the same mistake. Let us be quick to acknowledge the Lord's ultimate control of all things, especially any accomplishments, talents, or blessings that have come our way.

PRAYER STARTER

Lord, please help me to walk humbly before you. Let me be used by you knowingly and voluntarily, not in ignorance and rebellion like the Assyrians. Save me from haughtiness about what is accomplished through me, because I know that any power I have comes from you.

DAY 193

God of All Nations

SCRIPTURE READING: ISAIAH 13–16

THE SIGNIFICANCE OF THESE PROCLAMATIONS of judgment on the surrounding nations should not be overlooked. They tell us that the Lord is truly God over all the nations, even those that are unwilling to follow him or are dim in their understanding of him. It is sometimes tempting, even today, to believe that the God of the Bible is a "Jewish" God or a "Western" God, as if he were created by the imaginations of a nation or group of people, or as if his only concern were those peoples who are aware of him and predominately follow him. We sometimes provincialize God even further, to the point that we believe his primary concern is *our* church, race, denomination, family, or tax bracket. Jesus is the Light of the *World,* and that really does include every tribe and nation.

This does not mean that every nation is free to define God on its terms and according to its traditions and legends. It means just the opposite! It means that the God who is revealed in the Bible, including this passage in Isaiah, is truly the One with whom they have to do, whether they know him or not. Do you really believe that he is Lord of all nations? Does this belief affect your attitude and your actions toward those who are not of your "group"?

PRAYER STARTER

LORD, HELP ME SEE YOU TODAY not only as the high King of Heaven, but as the hope of all the nations of this earth. Guard my mind from the lie of this present age, which says that you are a creation of man, and not the Creator. May I never shrink you just to fit into the groups with which I identify, but may I likewise never broaden you beyond what scripture says, so that you become to me a nebulous, impersonal, unknowable concept, of which every nation is just struggling to understand a fraction. Finally, give me a heart that is concerned with the nations as you are, and not just with "me and mine."

DAY 194

Quick to Pray, Slow to Despair

SCRIPTURE READING: ISAIAH 17–22

In Chapter 22, the Lord turns his attention back to Judah, promising judgment on her for her sins. It must have been hard for the people of Judah to hear (or believe) themselves lumped in with all the other nations under God's judgment. However, the attitude of their hearts is clearly revealed in 22:8–14. They did everything they could to prepare for war, but they are rebuked because they never sought God's help in their crisis. Then, when they came under attack, they gave way to hopelessness, which then led them to self-indulgence: "'Let us eat and drink,' you say, 'for tomorrow we die!'"

Judah's real problem, revealed in both their refusal to seek God's help and their choice to feast when they should have repented, was that they did not trust God. They did not believe he had the power to help them (so they did not pray), and they did not believe his promises of an ultimately brighter day for his children (so they gave way to despair).

We must guard ourselves against both these expressions of faithlessness every day. We should be quick to pray to God when trials come our way and slow to give in to despair when things don't go "right" for us.

PRAYER STARTER

Thank you, Lord, that you stand with me through my trials and want to share them with me. Thank you that no matter how bad things seem for me now, as your child I have an indescribably bright future!

DAY 195
Pointing the Way to God

SCRIPTURE READING: ISAIAH 23–27

THE PURPOSE THE LORD INTENDED for the people of Israel was that they would be a blessing to all the nations of the earth, revealing to them the One who made them. The people, however, failed in this mission. They themselves had to be disciplined, as is evident in the preceding chapters. As Isaiah himself puts it, "We have not brought salvation to the earth; we have not given birth to the people of the world" (26:18). The church is the new Israel, and our purpose is clearly the same—to be a light to lead the people of this world to their King. What a tragedy that in many places this world-changing purpose of the church is not taken seriously, is totally ignored, or worst of all, is rendered completely ineffective because of conflict, hypocrisy, pettiness, selfishness, or worldliness among God's people!

Having said this, all you and I can do is look into our own hearts and lives to make certain we are truly committed to advancing this great purpose at all costs, then pray for others in today's church to be awakened to the extent that local churches all over our city, state, nation, and world become bright lights pointing the way to God, in much the same way as Israel was supposed to be.

PRAYER STARTER

LORD, PLEASE LET ME HELP, not hinder, people coming to know you. Help my church and the church universal to embrace our mission to this world seriously, tenaciously, and faithfully.

DAY 196

The Attitudes of This Age

SCRIPTURE READING: ISAIAH 28–30

Isaiah 29:13–16 is eerily relevant to our times. In fact, it is hard to imagine a time in human history to which this scripture speaks more directly. He speaks first of empty religious rituals that involve spoken words but no commitment of the heart. It is a temptation for believers in every age to say the right things to get by and yet have hearts that are truly unmoved, hard, and even resistant to the kinds of changes God wants to work.

Next, the prophet speaks of those who think they are wise or intelligent in their own strength. God specializes in exposing the folly of those who think they are smart. Then he talks about people who try to hide their wickedness from God and others, thinking they can get away with something in spite of his omniscience. Finally, he speaks of those who actually deny that God made them, thinking instead that he is a figment of the imagination which man has created in his ignorance. Do any of these attitudes sound familiar? We must continually turn away from *all* of them, despite the fact that they may seem to predominate in our culture.

PRAYER STARTER

Lord, please save me from the presumption of all the attitudes in this passage. Let my worship be real and heartfelt. Let me always grasp my ignorance compared to your omniscience. Let me never seek to hide from you, for it is impossible. And let me always remember that you are real and you are God.

DAY 197

A Vertical Life

SCRIPTURE READING: ISAIAH 31–35

Do you live life vertically or only horizontally? The rebuke to Judah in Chapter 31 is basically about the Israelites' refusal to see their "vertical" relationship with God as primary. They would not allow him to be the dominant presence in their decision making, and they would not turn to him as their first source of help in troubling times. Instead they chose to be driven by the physical circumstances surrounding them and looked to another nation—Egypt—as their source of help. They chose a "horizontal" approach to life, basically ignoring the God who had created them, chosen them as his special people, delivered them from Egypt, given them the land of Canaan, and provided for them within it. God was rightfully distressed and angry at their actions, for they were called to be people of faith, but lived as if he did not exist.

For those today who are limited to a horizontal mind-set, God is a non-factor. Even if they profess to know him, follow him, and love him, their lifestyle, values, decisions, and reactions to trouble are different than if he did not exist. Their faith is only theoretical, never practical. Again, what about you?

PRAYER STARTER

Lord, please help me genuinely live my life in a "vertical" way. I want to be totally aware of your presence, your power, and your purposes, and LIVE LIKE IT! Show me how to walk in faith, whether times are good or bad, and help me look to you as my primary authority, helper, and friend.

DAY 198

Unafraid to Stand Out

**SCRIPTURE READING: 2 KINGS 18:1–8;
2 CHRONICLES 29–31**

HEZEKIAH WAS NOT AFRAID TO STAND OUT. In fact, he is the king of Judah who *finally* did something about the "high places" of corrupt worship. The other "good kings" of Judah all have the same discouraging phrase in their biographical summaries: "The high places, however, were not removed; the people continued to offer sacrifices and burn incense there." But Hezekiah, on the other hand, "... removed the high places, smashed the sacred stones, and cut down the Asherah poles." He was not afraid to distinguish himself by going all out for God.

What about us? Sometimes it seems we hold back from devoting ourselves to God out of sheer timidity. Perhaps we are afraid we can't live up to a high level of commitment; or we may hesitate that others will see us as extreme. Maybe we don't believe God's word or love his ways enough to commit one hundred percent to him; or it could be that we simply prefer the path of least resistance, and real commitment to God is not always the easiest route. Whatever your reasons for holding back on God, why not make the decision, like Hezekiah, that you are not afraid to stand up for him? If you do this, it could very well be said of you, "There was no one like him (or her) ... He (or she) held fast to the Lord and did not cease to follow him."

PRAYER STARTER

LORD, I DESPERATELY WANT TO HOLD FAST TO YOU. Teach me the ways of real commitment, that I might live "full speed" for you today just as Hezekiah did.

DAY 199

Jesus Plus Nothing

SCRIPTURE READING: 2 KINGS 17; 18:9–37;
2 CHRONICLES 32:1–19; ISAIAH 36

2 KINGS 17 GIVES US AN EXPLANATION for the people known as the Samaritans during Jesus' time. The Samaritans were the result of the intermarriage of Israelites with the people of other cultures that came to Samaria as a result of the Assyrian occupation. They were known for their corrupt, confused worship practices that resulted from the melding of other religions with the worship of the Lord. This further dilution of the already corrupt worship of the northern kingdom, first reported in 2 Kings 17, had implication for numerous generations to come.

It is much the same for us when we dilute our worship of the Lord with other pursuits. Many considerations, even good ones, can ultimately corrupt our worship and sway our absolute allegiance from the Lord. C. S. Lewis called it "Jesus plus something else" religion. It is our tendency to elevate secondary concerns to the level of the sacred. So we can be for Jesus and pacifism, Jesus and war, Jesus and the Democratic Party, Jesus and the Republican Party, Jesus and the Baptist (or other) denomination, Jesus and home schooling, Jesus and private schooling, Jesus and public schooling, Jesus and capitalism, and so forth. You get the point. There are so many concerns that can distract us from absolute, primary devotion to Jesus! Not that we shouldn't have other involvements, beliefs, convictions, and priorities. The danger comes when these things become as important as the Lord in our lives. This is a sure recipe for spiritual corruption because our enemy, the devil, will take any and every opportunity to mix our devotion to Jesus with anything else!

PRAYER STARTER

LORD, HELP ME BE TOTALLY FOCUSED ON YOU, with nothing diluting or corrupting my devotion.

DAY 200

Hoping in His Might

SCRIPTURE READING: 2 KINGS 19;
2 CHRONICLES 32:20–23; ISAIAH 37

Much is revealed about the heart of Hezekiah in the happenings of 2 Kings 19 (and Isaiah 37). He is shown to be a man of true faith in the power of the living God. He does not tremble in fear at the threats of the field commander or give in to the threats of Sennacharib himself. Instead, he strengthens his resolve to seek God and cry out to him for deliverance. Even though he can see clearly the military might of Assyria and the devastation it wrought on other nations, he still believes in the Lord's ultimate sovereignty over the situation and that he, though unseen, is greater than even the greatest military might on the earth.

Today the Lord is looking for faith of this same ilk in his followers. He wants to use us and work through us to advance his kingdom. The questions to be reckoned with are only these: Will we be people of faith who will not cower even though we face overwhelming opposition? And will we, like Hezekiah, run urgently to prayer when such obstacles arise, and not merely to our own devices?

PRAYER STARTER

Lord, make me a person of prayer, who seeks your help first when trouble comes my way. Give me a steadfast hope in you that cannot be shaken by the appearance of the largest of armies, the most threatening of circumstances, or the most perplexing of problems.

DAY 201

Growth Through Suffering

SCRIPTURE READING: 2 KINGS 20;
2 CHRONICLES 32:24–33; ISAIAH 38–39

Hezekiah eventually attained a profound perspective on the value of pain and suffering in the midst of his illness. As he says in Isaiah 38:15, 17: "I will walk humbly all my years because of this anguish of my soul.... Surely it was for my benefit that I suffered such anguish." He understood that the pain and suffering in his life had helped him attain a state of humility, which was clearly needed in Hezekiah's life from time to time. He seems almost thankful for the hardship that he had earlier begged God to remove, saying it was all for his benefit.

This kind of perspective does not come easily to us—and usually does not come immediately, either. But at times, we can look back and clearly see how God has used a difficult or even crushing experience to help us see our limitations and strip away the pride that hinders his work in our lives. Whatever your heaviest burden or pain is today, God desires to draw you close to him as you deal with it and ultimately make you better because of it. Let him!

PRAYER STARTER

> Lord, the hurts in my life have too often discouraged me, closed my heart to you, and made me hopeless and bitter. But I know it does not have to be that way! I do desperately want you to liberate me from my trials, but I also want you to use them to strengthen my faith and break my self-sufficiency and pride, so that I can end up closer to you than I ever could have apart from the pain.

DAY 202

Soaring Like an Eagle

SCRIPTURE READING: 2 KINGS 21:1–18;
2 CHRONICLES 33:1–20; ISAIAH 40

It is an awesome truth that because of God's strength we can have strength amid the trials of this life! In Isaiah 40, Isaiah follows his proclamation of God's strength and sovereignty (vv. 21–28) with a classic promise of strength for our weariness: "He gives strength to the weary and increases the power of the weak. Even youths grow tired and weary, and young men stumble and fall; but those who hope in the LORD will renew their strength. They will soar on wings like eagles; they will run and not grow weary, they will walk and not be faint." Notice that the key to all these promises is hoping in the Lord. This means that instead of trusting our own strength (which easily runs out and gives way to weariness and weakness), we learn to lean on his strength.

For what do you need his strength today? Is there a problem that is bigger than you? Is there a need you cannot meet on your own? Is there a pain you cannot ease? Ask the Lord to help you learn to access his strength in such times of need.

PRAYER STARTER

> Lord, let me see you in your glory today, so that I might look to you for strength instead of trusting my own paltry resources!

DAY 203
Looking for the New Thing

SCRIPTURE READING: ISAIAH 41–43

The promise of the Lord in Isaiah 43:18-21 to Israel is a needed word today for his church. He urges his people not to dwell on things that are past, but look for the new thing he is doing. Because God is always at work around us, it is important that we constantly look for his handiwork instead of always dwelling on experiences we have been through, both good and bad. It is good to be aware of history, to be honest about it, and to learn all we can from it; however, we need to be even *more* fixated on what he is doing now and what he wants to do through us. After all, the purpose for his "water in the desert" is always "that they may proclaim my praise." "A new thing" does not necessarily mean a radical external change for you, such as a new home, job, location, and so forth. It simply means a fresh work of God, which can come either amid the trappings of a major life shift *or* in the everyday activities we have been doing the same way in the same place with the same people for years.

Could there be something new that God wants to do in and through you at this time in your life? Are you looking for the new plan God has for you? Are you willing to step out and do it, trusting God to meet your needs, no matter the desert you may have to pass through?

PRAYER STARTER

Lord, show me the "new thing" you are doing in these days upon the earth, in my nation, in my state, in my city, in my neighborhood, at my job, and in my home. May I be totally energized by your promise to do mighty things and provide for me!

DAY 204

The Absurdity of Idolatry

SCRIPTURE READING: ISAIAH 44–47

THE ABSURDITY OF IDOLATRY is blatantly put forward in this passage. How can someone worship an object he or she has made? How can one bow down to part of a piece of wood when the other part is thrown into the fire and burns up? As if the message is not clear enough, the Lord also continually says that he is God, and there is no other. He will bring his mighty judgment on all these false gods and their followers!

We, too, must grasp the absurdity of idolatry if we are to become the followers of Christ that he intends us to be. We must realize that there are tens and hundreds of things that would grab us away and steal our attention from the one true God. We need to see that money, career, social life, and all manner of other concerns will continually try to usurp God's place in our lives. When those times come, we need to keep our hearts set foremost on seeking the God of the Bible and count *all else* in our lives as secondary. It is easy to *say* this is how we operate, but in our hearts not begin to know how to go all out for him.

PRAYER STARTER

LORD, YOU ARE THE TRUE KING, and there is no other. Teach me to truly put you first in my heart and in my life today. Guard me against idolatry of any kind!

DAY 205

He Loves Us Anyway

SCRIPTURE READING: ISAIAH 48–51

WONDERFUL PROMISES OF RESTORATION for Judah follow the stinging rebuke of her stubbornness. We can truly see the hurt the people's actions have brought to the Lord in Chapter 48, as he basically calls them stiff-necked and hardheaded, both synonyms for extreme stubbornness. They have refused to follow him wholeheartedly, so he allows judgment to come upon them through Babylon's military superiority.

Even though their rebellion breaks his heart and offends his holiness, all the promises about restoration reveal something very special about God. Even after they have turned away from him, he is still committed to both revitalizing his relationship with them *and* transforming them into a people that will bring glory to his name. We need to realize that he has that same level of commitment to us; even though we, like Judah, have nothing in our attitudes or actions that would compel him to love us and save us, he does it anyway, out of his love for loving us and forgiving nature. This may seem irrational, but the fact is that God's grace is just as available to the worst of us as to the best of us, and it is just as available when we are at our worst personally as when we are at our best!

PRAYER STARTER

LORD, THANK YOU FOR YOUR WONDERFUL GRACE, which is greater than all my sin. Help me to not get bogged down in guilt, shame, and condemnation about things I have done. Help me see, know, and embrace your love above all else!

DAY 206

Appreciating the Suffering of the Servant

SCRIPTURE READING: ISAIAH 52–57

Isaiah 53 is perhaps the clearest of the "suffering servant" passages, which speak of the coming Messiah and which were fulfilled in the life, death, and resurrection of Jesus. This chapter quite simply puts forth the essence of the gospel story—that Jesus lived a perfect life, having no sin of his own that deserved the punishment of death. Yet he willfully took on our sins, the sins of the whole world, and died in our place on the cross. He was punished in our place.

The world of today says that this story is too barbaric, that it can't be the plan of an omnipotent, just, and loving God. Scripture tells us a different story, though. It asserts that this is the *only* viable plan. The wages of sin is death, as the book of Romans says. But Jesus loved you and me enough to take our wages, and to pay for our souls with his death. Does this reality move you anymore? If not, then ask God to show you once again, deep in your heart, how much he loves you. Even if so, ponder once again the price that Jesus paid for your salvation, and allow him to move you into an even more passionate desire to follow him in all things.

PRAYER STARTER

Lord, please move me to a deeper appreciation of your suffering in my place. And, Lord, don't just move me, but change me, so that my life may honor you in every way possible. I can never repay your grace, but I want to give myself to you because you gave yourself for me.

DAY 207

God's Chosen Fast

SCRIPTURE READING: ISAIAH 58–62

Isaiah 58 is all about true fasting – fasting that is acceptable to the Lord. He is very clear with his people that he is not just looking for them to go through the outward motions of religious ceremony. He is likewise very clear that he is not even satisfied with the genuine internal humility that comes from fasting. He is instead looking for the people to be moved to action as they fast. He wants them to rise up and begin to have a heart for justice. He wants them to seek to relieve the plight of the poor. He wants them to learn to truly walk in and practice love for others, not just talk about it.

The Lord wants no less from us today. Whatever the "ritual," he desires that it not be just an outward show and that it not be just something that moves us inside and makes us feel "holy." Instead, he wants all our spiritual practices and pursuits to be about the business of changing our hearts, values, affections, attitudes, and ultimately our actions. Whether it is attendance at church, Bible reading, prayer, fasting, giving, serving in a ministry, or some other religious pursuit, God clearly sees them as means to an end, not as ends in themselves. That end is always personal spiritual transformation that results in impact on the world around us!

PRAYER STARTER

Lord, please help me reflect the mind-set of the fast you choose. Help me, when I fast, to have open ears as to what you would have me do for the cause of justice and compassion for others. Let all the actions I take in the realm of spiritual practices bear fruit, not just in my knowledge, my character, and my intimacy with you, but also in my impact on this world!

DAY 208

Dependent on Grace

SCRIPTURE READING: ISAIAH 63–66

Isaiah 64:6 presses home a truth that is ever so hard for us to grasp: we can do no good thing that will impress God, earn forgiveness, or gain any credits from him whatsoever. The verse says it this way: "All of us have become like one who is unclean, and all our righteous acts are like filthy rags; we all shrivel up like a leaf, and like the wind our sins sweep us away." Yet it seems that we are still forever trying to earn our way with him! We may think that if we can just be a little bit better than "the next guy," that will be enough to satisfy him. Or maybe we believe that as long as the "good" we do outweighs the "bad," we will therefore earn his favor by making up for our failures.

In reality, these are just myths based on the assumption that we can do something about our own sin. But this verse is very clear and unrelenting in its assertion: even the best things we do in our own strength are tainted and ugly before God and can never make us right. We are fallen, and our best efforts still fall short and leave us just as far from his glory. This truth is the foundation for any understanding and response to the gospel of grace because it shows us our helplessness and absolute dependence on God's compassion, mercy, and kindness. Remember your position of dependence on his righteousness today, and allow this to humble you so that you truly lean on his righteousness. As long as we think of ourselves as righteous in any way, his righteousness cannot penetrate and change us!

PRAYER STARTER

Lord, you are my righteousness. In my own strength, I am as ugly and filthy as the lowliest of sinners. Help me to never kid myself that it is any different, but also give me courage to never back away from pursuing you because of my "unworthiness."

DAY 209

True Strength in Humility

SCRIPTURE READING: 2 KINGS 21:19–26;
2 CHRONICLES 33:21–34:7; ZEPHANIAH

As Zephaniah closes his word of prophetic warning to Judah, he puts forth an interesting assertion in 3:11–12. He says that in the day of hope, the meek and humble will be left within the city, while the prideful and haughty will be removed. This is interesting because it shows again how the Lord's economy is the polar opposite of the economy of this world. In God's kingdom, humility is the ultimate measure of strength and staying power. Of course, in this world, it is pride that often takes center stage and often wins the day. The question is, do we really believe this? It so often seems that the Lord's people are just as likely to walk in pride and presumption (if not more so) than people who don't know him at all! It's as if we don't grasp that we are denizens of a higher order now and that God's upside-down kingdom is for real!

Sadly, it also seems that among those who truly believe that humility is supreme in God's value system, many find it distasteful enough that they choose to play along with this world's system, even though they really do know better. They are willing to trade the true, solid, lasting power of a humble, dependent-on-God life for the rush of temporary power that comes with being consumed with one's own pride. Don't make the same mistake!

PRAYER STARTER

Please, Lord, help me not to be deceived by this world's power plays and its temporary form of glory that is marked by haughtiness and a sense of superiority over others. Teach me instead the path of humility, that I may have lasting power and impact because of your nearness to my life.

DAY 210

Excuse Making

SCRIPTURE READING: JEREMIAH 1–3

Jeremiah engages in a bit of Moses-like excuse making in the process of hearing God's call on his life: "I do not know how to speak; I am only a child," he says. To those of us who have ever sensed God telling us to do something, this line of argument surely sounds familiar. We often use this same "line of defense" whether it is something huge, like changing our vocation, or something relatively small, like helping out on a project at church, or speaking a kind word to a neighbor. Whenever we doubt our own ability to do something God is clearly telling us to do, we need to remember the words of God to Jeremiah: "You must.... Do not be afraid of them, for I am with you and will rescue you..."

Consciously turn from the excuse-making mind-set today as you spend time with God.

PRAYER STARTER

LORD, I WANT TO BE ONE WHO OBEYS YOU without question and without hesitation. Sometimes, though, it is easier to see my weakness than your strength. Open my eyes to who you are, so that I may obey you courageously despite my fears.

DAY 211

Guarding Against the Sin of Judah

SCRIPTURE READING: JEREMIAH 4–6

The spiritual complacency that often accompanies prosperity is clearly put forth in the words of Isaiah. It seems the people of Judah began to think of themselves as somehow invincible or at least immune to hardship. At the same time, they went to sleep spiritually. As Isaiah says in 5:11–14, "'The house of Israel and the house of Judah have been utterly unfaithful to me,' declares the LORD. They have lied about the LORD; they said, 'He will do nothing! No harm will come to us; we will never see sword or famine. The prophets are but wind and the word is not in them; so let what they say be done to them.'" In other words, in their material comfort and spiritual complacency, they began to live as if God did not exist.

How tragic it is when people begin to think this way! This is the beginning of being led completely away from allegiance to the Lord. We must guard our hearts against the very same lies that the people of Judah began to believe. We must keep strong our conviction that God is real, he rewards righteousness and punishes evil, and no person or group of people is beyond the reach of his justice or his discipline.

PRAYER STARTER

Lord, I too easily forget my place! Please guard me from the sin of Judah as described in this scripture. Make me more and more conscious of your presence and power and your willingness to intervene in human history, and let this keep me appropriately humble and mindful of my decisions and actions.

DAY 212

An Authentic Walk With God

SCRIPTURE READING: JEREMIAH 7–9

As Jeremiah continues relaying this message of judgment from the Lord, he addresses the hypocrisy of the people of Judah. He says that God is not only listening to the words his people say, he is watching how they live. He is aware that their religious practices are just a show and that they really don't love him the way they say. He sees their hearts and their attitudes and the acts committed in "secret," even though there really are no secrets from him. He tells the nation of Judah that he has now had enough of their wickedness and is about to exact a horrific judgment on them because of the games they have been playing.

We desperately need to hear the message of passages such as this. It is easy for us, in the age of grace, to play a similar game to that of the Judeans. We can believe it is all just a matter of saying the right words at the right times. Our walk with the Lord can rather quickly become shallow, artificial, and perfunctory if we don't guard the affections of our hearts and set them first and foremost on him. What God has always wanted is a love relationship. More than just jumping through religious hoops, he wants (and has always wanted) people who value him supremely, who choose him over all the other gods that vie for their attention, and who obey him whether or not they are being watched by other people.

PRAYER STARTER

Lord, please give me a more and more real walk with you. Help me, by your power, to overcome my tendency to play games and to think that it is enough to make people think I love you. I want to truly love you with all my heart, soul, mind, and strength!

DAY 213

Progressive Resistance

SCRIPTURE READING: JEREMIAH 10–13

In Jeremiah 12:4–5, God gives a profound answer to Jeremiah's question about the prosperity of the wicked. Jeremiah has asked God why he allows those who don't care about him to prosper, even though their sin has brought economic hardship on the land. Meanwhile, Jeremiah himself is constantly tested by the Lord, who doesn't let him get by with a thing! The answer from the Lord is instructive to us today. He basically says that Jeremiah has seen nothing yet; that things are going to get worse before they get better. His phrasing, however, is brilliant, and has become one of my favorite scriptures: "If you have raced with men on foot and they have worn you out, how can you compete with horses? If you stumble in safe country, how will you manage in the thickets by the Jordan?"

Don't miss this scripture's message for us—whatever problems you are dealing with right now, there seems to be a kind of "progressive resistance" that the Lord puts us through in our development. To refine and develop us as his children, he sometimes allows increasingly tougher challenges as our life moves along. This does not necessarily mean we are doing something wrong. In fact, it may mean we are doing something right! The next time you feel compelled to complain, blame God for your problems, and get discouraged by the general unfairness of life, take a moment to remember this lesson from Jeremiah. When "races with men" come, they often prepare us for tougher "races with horses"!

PRAYER STARTER

Lord, I desperately want to be strong for you. I want to develop into everything you want me to be. Help me not to be distressed or discouraged by the trials that I face because I know that they are often here to make me strong enough to face even tougher challenges for you later. Prepare me to "run with the horses."

DAY 214

Repentence, Then Restoration

SCRIPTURE READING: JEREMIAH 14–16

The Lord's directive to Jeremiah in 15:19 is worth examining today, because the principle involved still applies to us as followers of Christ: "If you repent, I will restore you that you may serve me; if you utter worthy, not worthless, words, you will be my spokesman." The requirement for restoration is still repentance. Many times we play games with God, as if we are waiting for him to overlook our sin, to say it's not so serious, or to inform us that the statute of limitations has run out and we are no longer considered guilty. But what a grand feeling of release when we do cross the line of repentance, see our sin as God does, and turn from it in our heart! It is part of the irony of the human condition that the one thing that could bring us cleansing, freedom, restored ministry, and true joy is often what we resist with all our might. If you have been fighting with God about something, isn't it time today to just say yes to him?

An important by-product of true repentance is that our words will become worthy, not worthless, so that God can begin to use us as his spokespersons. We kid ourselves if we imagine we are speaking for him and yet have hard or stubborn hearts toward him.

PRAYER STARTER

Lord, please make my life useful to you, both in actively serving and in effectively speaking. Shine your light on any way in me for which I need to repent, and grant me the strength, faith, and love for you which will enable me to truly repent.

DAY 215

The Potter and the Clay

SCRIPTURE READING: JEREMIAH 17–20

The Lord uses the image of a potter in Chapter 18 to describe his sovereignty over Judah in dramatic fashion. He basically says that just as a potter can crush a marred pot on the wheel and start over, so the Lord can remove Judah in its current state and start again, shaping a new pot to please himself. He can change his strategy with his vessel Israel, and just because the Israelites have been chosen as his people, they do not possess the immunity to sin and to follow false gods as they please. Through this symbolic lesson, he introduces the judgment that is about to come upon Judah.

Consider what God wants to say to us through this image of the potter. He is still the potter, and his people are still the clay. We need to recognize his sovereignty in our lives, just as Judah did. The question I'd like for us to focus on is not so much whether we are putting ourselves in line for a cataclysmic judgment when we resist his hand on our lives, although he surely still disciplines his children when they are disobedient, but whether or not we recognize that we are on a potter's wheel at all. We are apt to describe our lives and the events surrounding them in purely natural and scientific terms, but when we do this, we turn away from intimacy with him. If this passage teaches anything, it is that God constantly has his hands on us to make us something worthy, beautiful, and useful for him. Through the pains, pressures, problems, and pleasures of this life, he wants to teach us to rest in him and allow the shaping to progress!

PRAYER STARTER

God, keep shaping me and teach me how to trust you more. Give me enough faith to know your way is best and to stop being stiff-necked and hardhearted when you want to change something about me. Please make progress today, Lord, on the vessel you are making of me.

DAY 216

Responsive and Humble

SCRIPTURE READING: 2 KINGS 22:1–23:28;
2 CHRONICLES 34:8–35:19

Through the prophetess Huldah, the Lord said that because of two specific things about Josiah, he decided to relent from punishing Judah in the same way as Israel. Josiah was *responsive* to the Lord, and he was *humble* (2 Kings 22:19; 2 Chronicles 34:27). He of course acted out these two attitudes of the heart in all the reforms he brought about in the religious practices of Israel.

What two better things are there for us to ask the Lord to work into our lives? Frankly, most of the "short-circuiting" that takes place in my obedience to God has its roots in one or both of these areas. Either my heart is unresponsive to the Lord, and I find it easy to relegate him to a "shelf" in my life, or I am puffed up in pride, determined to handle life by myself, on my own terms, because deep down I am convinced I don't need him or that I have a better plan. May he deliver us from both these errors today, so that we may know him and serve him with maximum effectiveness!

PRAYER STARTER

Lord, please protect me from having an unresponsive heart. Help me to be sensitive to you all day long and move at the impulse of your word. Help me walk in humility, so I can clearly see and constantly admit my need for you.

DAY 217

A Brief Legacy

SCRIPTURE READING: NAHUM; 2 KINGS 23:29–37;
2 CHRONICLES 35:20–36:5; JEREMIAH 22:10–17

IT IS REMARKABLE THAT King Jehoahaz had such a brief reign in Judah (three months), and yet he still did enough evil in those three months to earn the same epithet as all the bad kings that preceded him: "He did evil in the eyes of the Lord, just as his father had done."

Remember today that it is not the longevity or brevity of your life that matters, but its quality and impact for the Lord. In the same way, it is not the length of your time at a given job (or any other opportunity in life) that ultimately matters, but whether you live for Christ there. Today, give God glory at "full-speed," as if your legacy were being established in the next three months!

PRAYER STARTER

JUST FOR TODAY, LORD, fill me with your power to live at full blast!

DAY 218

Praising in a Worst-Case Scenario

SCRIPTURE READING: JEREMIAH 26; HABAKKUK

Habakkuk 3:17–19 is one of the most powerful testimonies of hope in all of scripture. In the midst of a confession of his fear at the coming judgment of Judah at the hands of Babylon, the prophet breaks forth with determination to cling to the joy and strength of the Lord despite threatening, painful, and hopeless circumstances.

Take a moment to reread these three verses and let them speak to your heart about whatever could threaten your hope and peace today. The strength of the prophet's declaration is that it assures us that even if the very *worst* were to happen to us, we could still find God's resources in the midst of it and press on!

PRAYER STARTER

Lord, show me your great strength today amid my challenges. Fill me with your great joy amid my sorrows. Keep my eyes upon you over and above my circumstances.

DAY 219
Persistent Proclamation

SCRIPTURE READING: JEREMIAH 46–47;
2 KINGS 24:1–4, 7; 2 CHRONICLES 36:6–7;
JEREMIAH 25; 35

Observe today Jeremiah's perseverance in serving the Lord and proclaiming his message. He says in 25:3 that he has spoken the words God gave him to speak again and again for twenty-three years, with no real change happening in the behavior of the people! He had to have been disappointed again and again by the people he was sent to serve; but he was a faithful man, sticking to the task that was given to him, not allowing their response (or lack thereof) to affect him.

We all experience disappointment in our service to God and in our lives in general. We need to develop the kind of maturity that Jeremiah displayed in his ministry. We are conditioned by our society to want instant results from every effort we expend, and this is simply not realistic. Does this render our service useless? Does it give us a reason to "hang it up" out of frustration? *No!* Jeremiah would be considered a failure by many of today's standards, but was a resounding success in God's economy, despite having no notable success in turning his nation around. His success was due to faithfulness!

PRAYER STARTER

Lord, please develop perseverance in me. Help me not to be discouraged by the faithlessness of others or by the disappointments that occur in my service from time to time.

DAY 220

Keeping the Lines Open

SCRIPTURE READING: JEREMIAH 36; 45; 48

OBSERVE THE FOOLISHNESS OF JEHOIAKIM. He did not want to hear the word of the Lord, which demanded that he and the people of Judah turn away from the destructive path they had been moving down. He was so hardened that he actually had the gall to burn the words of Jeremiah in a fire so that he would not have to deal with them. He ultimately tried to have Jeremiah and Baruch arrested for saying the things the Lord had told them! Of course, when he did these things, he merely increased the judgment that was coming upon Judah (and himself).

Although it is fairly easy for us to see the rebellion in the heart and actions of Jehoiakim, we can easily resist the word of the Lord in much the same way ourselves. Have you ever pretended not to hear God, ignored him, or said "no" to him? Then don't throw too many rocks at Jehoiakim! Instead, learn from him how foolish and tragic it is to harden your heart against God, and ask him today to guard you from this error. Then he can speak more often and more clearly into your life, and blessing always follows when this happens.

PRAYER STARTER

LORD, PLEASE KEEP MY HEART SENSITIVE to your voice and ready to say "yes" to you. I know this is the only path to fulfilling your best plans for me, so guard me against hardness of heart!

DAY 221

Taking a Stand

SCRIPTURE READING: JEREMIAH 49:1–33;
DANIEL 1–2

As we read of Daniel's early training in Babylon, we see a truly great stand of courage by him and the other three trainees from Judah. They refuse to eat the foods and drinks that are brought to them, choosing instead to follow the dietary restrictions of the Torah. God honors their decision in a dramatic way. We need to see this decision as a precursor of the greater stands all four of these will take later. They had already made the ultimate decision that they were going to follow the Lord no matter the cost, so the rest of their time on earth was simply the fleshing out of that decision.

Have you made the same kind of decision for God? The starting point for a life of consistently courageous faith is a decision deep within the heart to choose God's way. Those who never really make this choice end up many times living a life wracked with compromise, indecision, and halfhearted obedience. They tend to waffle when things get tough. They have a pattern of holding back on God, because at the point of decision about their ultimate allegiance, they held back from absolute commitment. Is it time for you to choose God without reservation for your life today?

PRAYER STARTER

God, it is so easy to hold back from you. It is easy to make halfhearted commitments that I really don't have the resolve to keep. I decide now that you are worthy of my absolute allegiance, and I choose you now as my Lord. Help me to make courageous stands, just as these Hebrews did, starting today.

DAY 222

Promises of Intimacy

SCRIPTURE READING: JEREMIAH 22:18–30;
2 KINGS 24:5–20; 2 CHRONICLES 36:8–12;
JEREMIAH 37:1–2; 52:1–3; 24; 29

These passages portray for us more of the downward spiral of wickedness, which eventually leads to the complete downfall of Jerusalem. However, amid all the sadness of impending judgment, there are some great promises of ultimate redemption, in which God promises to sovereignly intervene to preserve a people for himself. One of these is in Jeremiah 24:4–7, in which he promises to watch over them, bring them back to the land, build them up and not tear them down, plant them and not uproot them, give them a heart to know him, be their God, let them be his people, and receive them when they return to him with all their heart.

Do you see that these beautiful promises all reveal God's heart for his new Israel, the church? His heart will watch over us, bring us back, build us up, and so forth. Read through these promises again with the realization that he desires these blessings for you. Allow this to encourage your heart today, and thank him for directing his mighty love toward you in these ways.

PRAYER STARTER

Lord, please show me your great heart of love for me today. Encourage me with your promises, and help me to believe them and cling to them with all my heart.

DAY 223
The Truth vs. Pretty Words

SCRIPTURE READING: JEREMIAH 27; 28; 23

JEREMIAH 27 AND 28 are about an argument between two prophets. Ironically, it is the more negative of the two—Jeremiah—who is truly speaking the word of the Lord, when he prophesies that Babylon will conquer Judah as part of the Lord's judgment. Hananiah, on the other hand, is basically saying that everything is going to be alright. He says that Judah will be free from captivity in two years. But all the pretty words and delusions of grandeur don't change the truth that Jerusalem is under judgment. Just as the king (and people) wanted to hear the good news but not the bad, we sometimes buy into the lie that the Christian life is supposed to be a cakewalk. But we know, deep down inside, that Christians are not immune to either struggle or suffering in this life. Beware of the tendency, very much alive today, to assume that a pain-free life is the highest good. God allowed the hard times under Babylon to build the character of his people and slow them down, and he still wants to use our times of pain to make us more useful

PRAYER STARTER

LORD, IT GOES WITHOUT SAYING that I don't ever want anything bad to happen in my life or those closest to me. But if I am asleep at the wheel and need a wake-up call, please allow me to be similarly tested.

DAY 224

Rumors

SCRIPTURE READING: JEREMIAH 50; 51

What do you do with rumors? There is some really good advice given to the exiles by Jeremiah in 51:46. He tells them to "not lose heart or be afraid" because of rumors that may circulate at any given time the next few years. He has given them a sure word about what will happen, and they don't need to waste their time and energy worrying about how things will develop.

In our lives, rumors can absolutely wreak havoc if we let them. Rumors can come from other people, our environment, society at large, or even within ourselves. Rumors are any groundless fears that threaten, disquiet, and distract us from being about our purpose for the Lord. Whatever rumors threaten you today, do not lose heart. We know that the kingdom of God is an unstoppable force, and in the end he will have perfect victory. We can run the race with confidence, just as the exiles did, and bring more glory to him!

PRAYER STARTER

Lord, help me to live with purpose today, unhindered by fearful rumors. Teach me to stake my life on your great promises and walk with unshakable faith.

DAY 225

No Better Way

SCRIPTURE READING: JEREMIAH 49:34–39; 34:1–22; EZEKIEL 1–3

Jeremiah 34 tells us of a terrible turn of events. After years of ignoring the Sabbath Year commands, Judah comes the closest to obedience as it ever will. Zedekiah makes a decree, and the people all release their Hebrew slaves. Then *they change their minds* and enslave them again. Of course, God's judgment follows their decision.

There are certainly times for all of us when we are tempted to rethink our commitments to the Lord and choose the way of disobedience in our lives. It is at these times when we must be strengthened in our resolve to obey. We should learn from Judah the utter folly of a choice to back away from our commitments to him. Today, whether in big or small matters, ask God for the strength to stand firm in your commitments, even when it costs something!

PRAYER STARTER

Lord, I want to steadfastly obey you, no matter what. Strengthen me against the enemy, who would make me think there is a better way than your way.

DAY 226

Forgetting God

SCRIPTURE READING: EZEKIEL 4–7

This tragedy that is predicted against Judah did not have to happen! The Lord says in Ezekiel 7:4, "...I will surely repay you for your conduct and the detestable practices among you. Then you will know that I am the Lord." The implication is that the root of Judah's problem is that they have forgotten who the Lord is. This forgetting has led them to pursue all manner of disobedience and vileness. Because of this, the Lord will now allow events so cataclysmic that they cannot escape being gripped by the reality of who he is.

Please take the time, today and every day, to remember that God is the Lord. This is the very place that we often start to get in trouble, just as the Jews did in our passage. When we forget his power, grace, and love, we open ourselves up to be caught in all manner of disobedience. But if we truly see who he is, we will continually bow in our hearts to his will.

PRAYER STARTER

Lord, you know how easy it is for me to forget who you are. Please guard my heart against it. Help me respond to your kindness so that I don't have to go to the level of responding to your discipline, as Israel did.

DAY 227

A Heart of Flesh

SCRIPTURE READING: EZEKIEL 8–11

Ezekiel speaks of the return of Israel to the land near the end of Chapter 11. He describes the kind of heart God will give them upon their return to the land, using the terms "undivided heart" and "heart of flesh." An undivided heart indicates a singleness of purpose. The people of God will find the Lord sufficient to their every need, so they will no longer chase after the many gods of the surrounding peoples. Their hearts will belong fully to the Lord!

When Ezekiel mentions a "heart of flesh" rather than a "heart of stone," he is really saying that God values tenderness of heart very much. He wants their hearts to be open, tender, receptive, and responsive toward him, rather than hard, deaf, and immovable.

Which kind of heart do you have?

PRAYER STARTER

Today, Lord, help me to have this kind of heart. Let my heart be clear and undivided in pursing you, as well as soft and tender to hear from you and respond.

DAY 228

Perhaps Today

SCRIPTURE READING: EZEKIEL 12–14

The warning at the end of Chapter 12 (in verses 21–28) is very apropos for our world today, and we need to heed its message. God tells Ezekiel that those who are left in Jerusalem are living in nonbelief and false security, because they are saying that the prophecies about the destruction of Jerusalem and subsequent exile of Zedekiah will never come true, or that it is for some time in the distant future. He promises, "... it will be fulfilled without delay." Sure enough, in less than six years time, it all comes true, down to the last detail.

We have many promises about Christ's return to wrap up human history. Just as in Ezekiel's day, there are many who have stopped believing it is true because it has not happened yet; or they believe it can't possibly happen in their lifetime—it must be a far distant event. We need the same type of wake-up call at times. Be ready! As the old hymn says, "What if it were today?"

PRAYER STARTER

Lord, teach me how to live with eternity in view, knowing that the end is closer now than it's ever been, and that it *could* be today! I choose to stay ready and walk with you one hundred percent, because I don't know how short the time is, either for this realm or for my own life.

DAY 229

Adultery Against God

SCRIPTURE READING: EZEKIEL 15–17

Chapter 16 presents an extended allegory of Judah as a harlot, comparing her many sins to the adultery and promiscuity of an unfaithful wife who turns to prostitution and gives herself to many lovers. The Lord is portrayed as a jealous husband, heartbroken and enraged to see his bride engaging in such scandalous behavior.

We who follow Christ, and are therefore a part of his church, really need to see our own sins in this light. We need to see that every time we choose to do the wrong thing, we are in essence committing adultery against our God. It breaks his great heart just as surely as any man's heart would be broken by the sight of his wife with another lover. May we never casually turn to any sin as if it doesn't matter or have consequence.

PRAYER STARTER

Lord, let me always choose the way of righteousness. If I should slip, please break my heart about my sin and let me see your broken heart of love as well.

DAY 230

Your Own Walk

SCRIPTURE READING: EZEKIEL 18–20

Ezekiel takes the people of Judah to task for a very common misconception. They believed that they were not being punished for their own sins, but for those of their ancestors. While it had been taught, even by Ezekiel himself, that the sins of previous generations can have grave consequences on those in the present and future, these people were using this truth as an excuse to live unrighteously. Because the people thought they were going to be punished no matter what they did, the people gave themselves free license to live how they wanted. But the Lord clearly states in this passage that they are responsible for their own sins.

The Bible is clear in its teaching that we are not punished for the sins of others. We might suffer from the effects of their sins, but God judges everyone individually. No one is condemned for the sins of their forefathers, and no one is deemed righteous because of the righteousness of their ancestors. Today, thank God that you are able to establish your own walk with God, regardless of your lineage.

PRAYER STARTER

Lord, I tremble at the fact that I stand individually accountable before you. But I am even more amazed at your grace, because you personally love me and wish to share life with me. Let me walk with you, not depending on the righteousness of my forebears, but neither living in condemnation because of their wickedness!

DAY 231

Humility's Value

SCRIPTURE READING: EZEKIEL 21–23

Two behaviors God emphatically values, and which were clearly forsaken by the Israelites and Judeans, are humility and the knowledge of the Lord. In 22:26, Ezekiel introduces a principle that is revisited in the New Testament: "The lowly will be exalted and the exalted will be brought low." It is later phrased this way: "God resists the proud, but gives grace to the humble." Israel and Judah started to get in trouble when they began to walk in pride. The inevitable result of this pattern, if unchecked, is a tendency to forget who God is. Once this happens, lawlessness, rebellion, and idolatry are the natural result. The desired result of all God's judgment on his people is clearly that they will remember who he is. As 22:16 says, "When you have been defiled in the eyes of the nations, you will know that I am the Lord."

Realize today the import of walking in humility before God and in acute awareness of who he is—the sovereign Lord of the universe.

PRAYER STARTER

Lord, tame my pride. It is easy to get puffed up, even without realizing it. Please grant me a humble spirit, and continually reveal yourself to me that I might never forget you.

DAY 232

Taking a Tough Step

SCRIPTURE READING: 2 KINGS 25:1;
2 CHRONICLES 36:13–16; JEREMIAH 39:1; 52:4;
EZEKIEL 24; JEREMIAH 21:1–22:9; 32:1–44

IN THE MIDST OF THE SIEGE OF JERUSALEM, God tells Jeremiah to buy a field outside the city (Jeremiah 32). This is land that the soldiers of Babylon are occupying, so it clearly is not a wise investment, in human terms. It is, however, a tangible illustration of faith in God's promise that the land will one day be restored.

This was undoubtedly a tough move for Jeremiah to make, just as every step of faith is tough. If it were easy, it would not be faith! Whatever risks or obstacles you believe lie before you, ask the Lord for courage and faith to step out and trust him, even when what he tells you seems illogical. If you know a message is from the Lord, obedience is really your only sensible option!

PRAYER STARTER

LORD, WHEN IT IS TOUGH TO DO WHAT YOU SAY, help me to remember the "all-in" faith of Jeremiah, who believed your promises even when there was nothing in the visible world to encourage him at the point of decision. I want to choose you like that.

DAY 233

Promises to the New Israel

SCRIPTURE READING: JEREMIAH 30; 31; 33

WITHOUT DISREGARDING THE IMPORTANCE of these prophecies of restoration for the literal nation of Israel, it is more than remarkable that almost six hundred years before the coming of Christ, this and other prophecies herald him clearly as the Messiah and Restorer of Israel. We know that the work Christ came to do was primarily spiritual, as opposed to political.

He came to establish a new people for the Lord, spiritually descended from Isaac and Jacob, of whom he says, "I will break the yoke off their necks and will tear off their bonds ... I will surely save you out of a distant place ... I am with you and will save you ... I will restore you to health and heal your wounds ... I will add to their numbers ... I will bring them honor ... I will punish all who oppress them ... I have loved you with an everlasting love ... I have drawn you with loving-kindness ... I will build you up again ... I will lead them beside streams of water ..." AND, "So you will be my people, and I will be your God."

We are that people! Let's live it!

PRAYER STARTER

I WANT TO BE YOURS, LORD. My hope for today and for the future is in your hands. Thank you for calling me to be a part of your new Israel, the church. May I walk with you today, conscious of all your great promises. Let me grasp the magnitude of what these words mean to me.

DAY 234

Realizing Who He Is

SCRIPTURE READING: EZEKIEL 25; 29:1–16; 30; 31

*I*N THIS ENTIRE SECTION OF THE BOOK, Ezekiel delivers God's message of judgment on the countries that surround Judah. It is important that we understand that these prophecies are uttered and fulfilled, not because these nations are the enemies of Israel, but because they have rejected the Lord, who is the only true God. Scan back through and notice how many times the phrase is repeated, "Then they will know that I am the Lord." The realization of people that he is God is apparently *very* high on the Lord's agenda.

Have you come to the realization in your own life that he is God, and you are not? How will the way you live today reflect that realization? Are you available for God to use you to help others come to that realization? Does your way of life help or hinder this process?

PRAYER STARTER

LORD, MAKE ME TOTALLY CONSCIOUS of your absolute omnipotence, omniscience, and omnipresence today. May the knowledge of you fill my heart, my family, my church, my neighborhood, my city, and ultimately the world. Show me my place in bringing this to realization.

DAY 235
Materialistic Pride

SCRIPTURE READING: EZEKIEL 26–28

THE PROPHECY AGAINST THE KING OF TYRE in Chapter 28 centers on his pride, and the reason for his pride is pinpointed as his great wealth (28:5). Tyre was known as a beautiful city, and it had grown wealthy because of its domination of the sea trading routes of the region. The Lord promised destruction on Tyre and its king, who had gone so far as to think of himself as a god.

We who live in the wealth of America should be very aware of this danger of materialistic pride. There is no doubt that a great disparity of wealth exists within this nation, but even those of us with more meager incomes by American standards are incredibly wealthy compared to the majority of the world. Wealth such as we possess can quite easily lead to pride, even if we don't intend it. The greater our wealth, the greater the opportunity is for pride to occur. There is no inherent wickedness in being wealthy, any more than there is goodness in being poor, for both bring with them their unique blessings and temptations. No matter what your income level is, ask God to guard your heart from materialistic pride. It is a spiritual killer!

PRAYER STARTER

LORD, HELP ME ALWAYS TO REALIZE that all I have has ultimately come from you. Help me remain humble, even if you should bless me with incredible riches. You are the one true God, and I will never be, no matter how much I accumulate. Keep this truth real to me!

DAY 236

The Courage of Jeremiah

SCRIPTURE READING: JEREMIAH 37:3–39:10; 52:5–30;
2 KINGS 25:2–21; 2 CHRONICLES 36:17–21

In Jeremiah 37 and 38, the contrast between the behavior of Jeremiah and King Zedekiah is striking. Zedekiah continually waffles as to how to treat Jeremiah. He sends for him secretly, wanting to hear a word from the Lord, and yet afraid to be caught talking to Jeremiah. Then he gives Jeremiah over to a group of officials who want to kill him. Finally, he rescues Jeremiah from his enemies and yet is still desperate to keep their conversations a secret.

Jeremiah, on the other hand, is a picture of courageous faith. He has spoken the word of the Lord boldly for forty years, and this has made him extremely unpopular. He has been beaten, jailed, and threatened repeatedly, and still he continues to prophesy the downfall of Jerusalem at the beginning of Chapter 38, even though this act could easily (and almost does) get him killed. Which of these two does your life most resemble? Are you more like the waffling, reactionary, and cowardly Zedekiah, or have you learned to stand for God and what's right, even when potential pain and loss is involved? The Lord looks for those with a faith like Jeremiah's, because it is these that he can use to his greatest glory.

PRAYER STARTER

Lord, please strengthen me today to live more like Jeremiah. Grow me to the point that I will not back down from walking with you one hundred percent, no matter what threats, fears, or pains come my way. I know that I don't have this kind of strength within myself, and that it can only come from your hand. Please grant it to me today.

DAY 237

Virtue that Attracts

SCRIPTURE READING: 2 KINGS 25:22;
JEREMIAH 39:11–40:6; LAMENTATIONS 1–3

It is ironic that the pagan officials of Babylon treat Jeremiah better than the officials of Judah, who represent God's chosen people. His own people have continuously rejected, criticized, and persecuted him, and yet the Babylonians set him free from prison and give him absolute personal liberty.

Granted, they may assume him to be a traitor to Israel because of his prophecies and his imprisonment, but this contrast in Jeremiah's treatment illustrates a very troubling reality that is sometimes true of modern-day Christians. Have you ever met a nonbeliever who is "nicer" or "better" than a lot of believers? I have. This is troubling to me, not because there may be virtue in someone outside of Christ—there are plenty of explanations for that. No, what is troubling is that so many "Christians" who, like the Judean officials, choose to ignore God and work at cross-purposes with him.

This is a troubling reality that you and I can perhaps do little to remedy in the big scheme of things. We can, however, guard our own hearts and make sure we are allowing the continual transformation of our lives that Christ wants, making us continually more like him.

PRAYER STARTER

Lord, please make me a virtuous person—not for the purpose of earning your favor, but to be a witness of your kingdom to a world in need. May I never be "outshone" by the pagan, who does not have your light in his or her heart.

DAY 238
Caring When Others Hurt

SCRIPTURE READING: LAMENTATIONS 4–5; OBADIAH

OBADIAH'S PROPHECY is all about the punishment that will come on the nation of Edom (Esau's descendents). Their greatest sin, as I read it, is that they rejoiced at the downfall of Judah, and even took advantage of Judah when it was weak.

Do you ever find yourself tempted to take some kind of pleasure in the difficulties of others? It is so easy to let a competitive mind-set rule our thinking, but living in love at the very least means we do not wish harm on others. This means that no matter how badly someone behaves toward me, and no matter how much rivalry there may be between me and another, as a follower of Christ I must allow the genuine pain of others to trouble me, not give me joy. Of course, this kind of supernatural mind-set is something only God can accomplish, but I have to allow the changes he wants to work in me.

PRAYER STARTER

LORD, PLEASE HELP ME LEARN THE WAY OF LOVE. Curb my impulse to laugh at or derive satisfaction from another's pain. Help me, instead, to care when others hurt, whether I feel they deserve it or not. Give me a truly Christian heart!

DAY 239

Don't Turn to Egypt

SCRIPTURE READING: JEREMIAH 40:7–44:30;
2 KINGS 25:23–26

When Gedaliah, the governor appointed by the Babylonians to rule in Jerusalem, was assassinated, the leaders and the people panicked and fled to Egypt. They did this even after promising they would obey Jeremiah's words (42:5–6) and after a very strong word of warning against going to Egypt (42:13–18). They allowed their concern that their numbers were depleted and their leader was gone to displace their commitment to do what God said. And God obviously was not pleased.

We often have essentially the same trouble. Obeying God can seem scarier than running for safety and security. However, if God has told us to persevere in a situation, whether it be work related, home related, relationship related, or something else, to bail out simply because of discomfort or discouragement is akin to Judah's decision to head for Egypt. God made it clear that his plan, which involved them staying in the land, would have a great and joyous outcome. On the other hand, although it looked like the path of safety, a trip to Egypt would ultimately result in multiplied pain for them. They did not believe him. Do you?

PRAYER STARTER

Lord, help me to persevere when things are tough for me personally, relationally, vocationally, or spiritually. "Egypt" looks comfortable and secure at times, but consistently remind me that this is only an illusion.

DAY 240
Acting on the Truth

SCRIPTURE READING: EZEKIEL 33:21–36:38

It is a dreadful disobedience to disregard the words of God, but this is exactly what the people of Judah had done. They were eager, it seems, to hear the words of the prophet, but they were content to just be entertained by him. They never even considered acting on his message; therefore we can question whether they believed it at all. God's words to Ezekiel in 33:32 sum it up perfectly: "Indeed, to them you are nothing more than one who sings love songs with a beautiful voice and plays an instrument well, for they hear your words but do not put them into practice."

To keep this same attitude from overtaking us, we must strengthen our resolve to truly value God's truth *enough to act on it!* What a travesty, to have exposure to God's message over and over again, but never respond. Sometimes we may believe that going to church to hear the Word is enough, or that opening our Bibles to read the Word is enough. However, we can love going to church, hearing biblical preaching, and even exploring and discussing biblical truth, and still find ourselves in the predicament of Judah—using our "religion" as a pastime that never really impacts who we are. May this never be!

PRAYER STARTER

Lord, help my spiritual life to be characterized by true obedience to and intimacy with you. I never want to just be fascinated by your truth, but transformed by it!

DAY 241
Can Dead Things Live?

SCRIPTURE READING: EZEKIEL 37–39

This vision of the valley of dry bones is one of the most powerful images in the book of Ezekiel. It is God's way of speaking hope to the nation of Israel amid the desolations they have suffered in the preceding years. The fact that life is breathed into the bones and they rise up and live signifies God resurrecting his chosen people to a bright and unified future.

The message to us is simple: God can make dead things live! Whenever situations seem most dead and hopeless, God is able to step in and bring a new start and a glorious future. Whatever is dead in or around your life today, offer it to God and ask for his life-giving touch to be upon it—whether it is a personal weakness or spiritual deadness within yourself, a crisis situation in your life, a relationship with which you struggle, or a profound need in the life of someone dear to you.

PRAYER STARTER

Lord, please take what is dead in and around me and breathe your new life into it. Let the bones come to life again by your great power.

DAY 242

Standing Under Pressure

SCRIPTURE READING: EZEKIEL 32:1–33:20; DANIEL 3

TODAY'S DEVOTION will be about the characteristics of the musical instrument known as the zither. Just kidding ... I had never seen the word "zither" in a devotional before, and decided to do something about it.

Seriously, the story of Shadrach, Meshach, and Abednego is a classic example of courageously standing up for what is right when the pressure to compromise and disobey is considerable. These three men knew that, in a sense, King Nebuchadnezzar held their lives in his hands, but they knew that in an even greater way, God held them in his hands. The pressures we face to compromise our walk are usually less severe than what they faced, and yet we sometimes come up short on the resolve to resist temptation, peer pressure, or pressure from "above."

The truth to remember today is that God still stands with those who stand for him! Ask God today for the strength to stand for what is right the next time you are pressured to "bow to an idol."

PRAYER STARTER

LORD, PLEASE FORGIVE ME for those times when I've compromised my faith because of pressure and/or fear. Strengthen my faith so that I may stand like these three, confident that you are ultimately greater than any force that could cause me harm—and that any harm incurred is a small price to pay in order to please you.

DAY 243

Walking With Him Into the Future

SCRIPTURE READING: EZEKIEL 40–42

The vision Ezekiel has in chapters 40–42 of the restored temple in Jerusalem is actually a promise of God for the restoration of the nation of Israel. God is essentially saying to Ezekiel (and through him to the Israelites) that what has been in Jerusalem will one day be again. The temple will indeed be restored to its former glory!

The beauty of this vision is that it is so real and tangible. As God points us toward the future in his service, we of course don't always see what is to come as clearly as Ezekiel did. However, it is always appropriate to be looking to God to clarify the future for us and even to ask him for a vision for our life and ministry that is so real it is almost tangible. The idea is not to ask God to be a fortune teller to give us an artificial advantage in preparing for the future, but rather for him to show us a clear and compelling picture of the purposes he has for us. This has a way of inspiring us and galvanizing our resolve to press forward fearlessly for him. Do you have a glimpse of what your future could look like in him?

PRAYER STARTER

Lord, please give me vision for what you want my future to be. However much or however little you show me about your future plans for me, help me be faithful to pursue it.

DAY 244

Taking God at His Word

SCRIPTURE READING: EZEKIEL 43–45

After the glory of the Lord refills the temple in Ezekiel's vision, he recites the rules of the priesthood, the care and use of the temple, the division of the land, and the observance of offerings and holy days. The remarkable aspect of this vision is that it is all given well before any return to the land has been attempted. The recitation of these details and instructions add dramatically to the air of certainty about the prophecy. In other words, Ezekiel's attitude is: "This is so surely going to come to pass that I'd better go ahead and give you instructions on what to do after it happens."

We need to realize that all the promises of God toward us are just as certain as this prophecy. When you find yourself susceptible to doubt, either about God's nature or his plan for the future, decide to take him at his word. Realize that all he has promised us is infinitely certain to come to pass.

PRAYER STARTER

Lord, give me increased courage and joy today as I count on the many wonderful things you have promised me, such as a home in heaven, provision for my needs, everything I need for life and godliness, and so forth.

DAY 245

The River of Life

SCRIPTURE READING: EZEKIEL 46–48

Water is often used in scripture to symbolize the life of God and the blessings that flow from obedience to God. The river spoken of in 47:1–12 is a case in point. Because there is no actual river that corresponds to this description, it must represent the life of God that will flow out of the restored Israel, bringing life to others. This explains the occurrence of these powerful descriptive phrases: "When it empties into the sea, the water there becomes fresh. Swarms of living creatures will live wherever the river flows ... this water flows there and makes the salt water fresh; so where the river flows everything will live.... Fruit trees of all kinds will grow on both banks of the river. Their leaves will not wither, nor will their fruit fail. Every month they will bear.... Their fruit will serve for food and their leaves for healing."

I believe this promise of fruitfulness applies to the church, the new Israel. It is God's purpose that we be a vessel of life to the world. He desires for the kind of fruitfulness described in this passage to mark each of our lives. And he is able to make it so! If we will just empty enough self-absorption from ourselves for him to fill us with his divine life, he can make it overflow in life to others! As the old camp song says, "I've got a river of life flowing out of me...."

PRAYER STARTER

Lord, thank you first that your river of life is an all-sufficient supply for me. As you did with Ezekiel, help me get in over my head! Then turn me into a vessel of your life, so that the river might not just flow to me, but through me.

DAY 246

Rooting Out Pride

SCRIPTURE READING: EZEKIEL 29:17–21; DANIEL 4; JEREMIAH 52:31–34; 2 KINGS 25:27–30; PSALM 44

In Daniel 4, God shows us how seriously he expects to be acknowledged as our ultimate King. King Nebuchadnezzar has become great among the kings of the earth. God warns him directly through a dream that it is essential that he acknowledge the Lord's role in providing the prosperity he has enjoyed. Instead, the king becomes even more proud and self-worshipful. The promised consequences then fall upon the king, and they remain until he repents of his arrogance and acknowledges God.

The nature of pride is the same today. It is extremely deceptive, and often goes unnoticed until it has all but taken over our hearts. It also still tends to blind us to our utter dependence on God and makes us think we are more self-sufficient, wonderful, smart, beautiful, and virtuous than we really are. Not only does pride still operate the same way, but God's attitude toward it is still the same. He still opposes the proud, but gives grace to the humble. Be on your guard against the pride that so easily removes our eyes from God, even now. Courageously pray the prayer below!

PRAYER STARTER

God, please show me any pride that may be hindering my walk with you. May it never take the drastic measures Nebuchadnezzar required in order for you to get my attention. You are God, and I am not. Show me how to live this way.

DAY 247

In the Light of His Presence

SCRIPTURE READING: PSALMS 74; 79; 80; 89

Focus on Psalm 89:15 for a moment today: "Blessed are those who have learned to acclaim you, who walk in the light of your presence, O LORD."

This verse affirms two interrelated characteristics of a believer: learning to acclaim the Lord and walking in the light of his presence. The first is a definite action—worshiping God for who he is and praising him for all the good things he has done. We should continually acclaim him, which means to lift him up in our words, attitudes, and actions. This is something that must be learned. It does not come naturally or automatically to us.

The second characteristic the psalmist affirms is more of a continuous, ongoing attitude and perspective from which to operate in life. To "walk in the light of his presence" is to let him into every part of your life and to become increasingly aware of his presence in your daily experience. It is to live close to God, not just on Sundays, or when you're at church, but every day of the week. How far along are you in cultivating these two attitudes?

PRAYER STARTER

Lord, help me be a person who acclaims you. Teach me what I need to adjust to become this person. Help me also to live aware of your presence, walking continuously in your light!

DAY 248

Light in an Exilic Culture

SCRIPTURE READING: PSALMS 85; 102; 106; 123; 137

THE FIRST SIX VERSES OF PSALM 137 are a short lament about the Jews' experience of being in exile in Babylon. An interesting dynamic is revealed here: it appears that even as the Jews were weeping while they remembered Zion, the people of Babylon were asking them to sing the songs of their homeland.

I hope it's not too much of a stretch today to see the Jews' exile experience as a metaphor for the experience of the modern Christian in America. It can be very helpful to view ourselves as "exiled" in a culture that does not know God. As we grow to love God more and more it can feel very wrong to even be here, much less to engage with the people who are stained with the filth of this culture. However, we need to understand a truth that is hinted at here, one that was only grasped by a handful of faithful Jews during the years of exile: When the people of God experience exile, *God wants them to bring light into the other culture,* not simply to curse the darkness and long for home. There are probably those in your sphere of influence who have a level of genuine openness to the God you serve. Will you invest in them and invite them to him?

PRAYER STARTER

LORD, IT IS SO EASY TO WALK IN BITTERNESS and anger about the way you are dishonored in this culture. Help me to never lose or dilute my love for righteousness, but help me also to open up to those who are open to you, no matter how steeped in this "culture of Babylon" they may be.

DAY 249
Greater Than Wealth

SCRIPTURE READING: DANIEL 7; 8; 5

The indictment against King Belshazzar in Daniel 5 could be said of many in our day, even many who profess to follow Christ: "You praised the gods of silver and gold, of bronze, iron, wood and stone, which cannot see or hear or understand. But you did not honor the God who holds in his hand your life and all your ways."

It is tempting for us to be very harsh with our judgments as we read of Belshazzar's foolishness. Did he not realize the folly of worshipping physical elements and objects? However, in our current state of wealth in America, we need to constantly examine where our sense of security comes from, and in whom (or what) we are ultimately trusting. It is so easy to become entrapped by this material world! The power of money and worldly influence is plainly evident, while the power of true spirituality and relationship with God often remains hidden to us, although it is infinitely greater. It is clear that Daniel grasped this reality, as he refused to be impressed or swayed by the allure of material reward (5:17). May our eyes, as well, be clearly on the only God with real, eternal, life-giving power.

PRAYER STARTER

Lord, let me always see the wealth of this world for what it is—a tool for good or evil, nothing more. Guard my soul from being captured by the god of materialism. You are greater than any amount of wealth, prestige, or power I could ever possess. Help me keep whatever wealth you may (or may not) bless me with in proper perspective and worship you, not my possessions.

DAY 250

Confession

SCRIPTURE READING: DANIEL 9; 6

Daniel had a godly perspective on life, one that we would do well to acquire for ourselves. For instance, in his prayer in Chapter 9 there is no hint of excuse making or blame dodging in his confession, as is so often found in our "confessions." He courageously and straightforwardly (yet humbly) confesses the sin of his people and of himself, even adding, "We do not make requests of you because we are righteous, but because of your great mercy." This kind of honesty and humility is refreshing when we see it in others, but we often have trouble cultivating it in ourselves. He further exemplifies his godly perspective when he prays not for personal deliverance or divine favor for himself, but instead for the healing of Jerusalem and the restoration of the temple.

Ask God to give you the kind of humility, transparency, and vulnerability in prayer that Daniel experienced. After all, there is no need to strut or act before God; he sees right through our pretense anyway!

PRAYER STARTER

Thank you for being a God that I can trust. Thank you for inviting me to open up about my struggles and my sins. Teach me to pray kingdom prayers like that of Daniel!

DAY 251

More Than a Building

SCRIPTURE READING: 2 CHRONICLES 36:22-23;
EZRA 1:1-4:5

MANY TIMES WHEN WE THINK ABOUT the return of the exiles to Jerusalem, the feeling is that their singular focus was restoring the physical building, the temple that the invading Babylonians had destroyed. The exiles' actions upon arriving show this assumption to be distorted. They first rebuilt the altar and reinstituted the worship of the Lord. Even before temple walls were constructed, they worshipped God out in the open. The other peoples who inhabited the land saw what was happening and began to oppose the rebuilding project. The point is this: the Hebrews placed a high priority on offering worship to the Lord that was pleasing to him. This priority was so strong that they braved the elements and the opposition of other nations to make sure it was perpetuated.

It is still the same today. The Lord's deepest desire is not to have an imposing architectural structure built for his glory, but rather to have human hearts glorify him by the act of worship. His kingdom is never about the building as much as it is about human hearts being turned toward the God of Creation and truly giving him praise. This can take place in any building or without one!

PRAYER STARTER

OH LORD, I KNOW THAT THE CHURCH IS NOT A BUILDING, but a collection of people whose hearts are turned toward you. Help me to always value the spiritual over the physical and to regard pure, unfettered worship as more important and precious than any physical entity will ever be.

DAY 252

Esteemed in Heaven

SCRIPTURE READING: DANIEL 10–12

Daniel is twice called "highly esteemed" in Chapter 10. When the angel uses this description, he is saying that Daniel is highly esteemed in heaven. He has certainly earned this designation partially because of his constant and courageous stand for what is right. However, it is not primarily because of acts of heroism that he is heard in heaven. Rather it is primarily because of a decision Daniel made in his heart, and then followed: "Since the first day that you set your mind to gain understanding and to humble yourself before your God, your words were heard..."

There are two parts to Daniel's decison: he decided to gain understanding and he decided to humble himself before God. What two greater decisions can we make today?

PRAYER STARTER

Lord, increase my desire for understanding of the spiritual realm, and help my heart to be truly humble before you. I desire to be esteemed in heaven, not because I crave glory for myself, but because my effectiveness for the cause of Christ would be greatly enhanced.

DAY 253

Kingdom Concern

SCRIPTURE READING: EZRA 4:6–6:13; HAGGAI

THE WORDS OF THE PROPHET to the people in Haggai 1 were given to motivate them to zealously rebuild God's house: "Is it a time for you yourselves to be living in your paneled houses, while this house remains a ruin?" It was an invitation for them to step outside the pursuit of self-interest and begin to invest some of their possessions and their efforts toward the advancement of God's kingdom.

Have you heard such a call in your life? Have you said yes? Have you been faithful to "flesh out" that answer? The challenge from Haggai is very applicable in today's materialistic, consumerist, egocentric age. Jesus never shied away from asking his followers for their best and even for their all. He said we must lose our lives in order to find them. He told a man to sell all he had and give to the poor. Are you willing to settle for a cheap, easy, self-centered form of discipleship, or are you ready to answer his call with a joyful "yes"?

PRAYER STARTER

LORD, FORGIVE ME FOR BEING MORE CONCERNED about my own "kingdom" than yours. Show me how and empower me to invest in your kingdom's advance.

DAY 254

The Day of Small Things

SCRIPTURE READING: ZECHARIAH 1–6

In 4:10 Zechariah asks: "Who despises the day of small things?" His question relates to rebuilding the temple in Jerusalem. This is the Lord's way of encouraging the people of Jerusalem to not be dismayed that the temple was not yet completed, but rather to rejoice that Zerubbabel had made a start of it by laying the foundation.

The expression "despising the day of small things" equates to being discouraged, being angry, or giving up because everything in our lives is not smooth, all goals are not yet realized, or we have suffered setbacks along the way to fulfilling our dreams. We need to learn, just as the Israelites did, that victories worth winning are usually not instantaneous or easy. Sometimes in our walk of faith perseverance must kick in. If you are in the day of small things in any area of your life, determine right now to walk faithfully into the future with God. Don't even think about quitting on him, because in his kingdom a day of small things generally comes before a day of great things. Stop expecting to be the exception to this principle!

PRAYER STARTER

Lord, help me to be faithful and grow in every way you desire during the day of small things. Build my faith and my perseverance during such times, so that I may be trusted with greater purposes if it should please you.

DAY 255
An Authentic Faith

SCRIPTURE READING: ZECHARIAH 7–8; EZRA 6:14–22; PSALM 78

It seems to always be the tendency of God's people, even the most faithful and sincere, to want to substitute some kind of ritual observance for genuine, practical, around-the-clock obedience to God. That is the trap the Israelites had consistently fallen into, and Zechariah addressed the Lord's position in regard to their religious fasts in Chapter 7: "When you fasted and mourned in the fifth and seventh months for the past seventy years, was it really for me that you fasted? And when you were eating and drinking, were you not just feasting for yourselves?... Administer true justice; show mercy and compassion to one another. Do not oppress the widow or the fatherless, the alien or the poor. In your hearts do not think evil of each other." Do you see the emphasis on practical obedience? It appears that their rituals had no meaning if they were not truly and sincerely heartfelt and accompanied by a lifestyle of obedience.

It is easy for us to fall into the same trap as they did, although our "rituals" may be different, for example, attendance at church or a small group, giving a portion of our income to the Lord, having a daily quiet time of Bible reading and prayer, and so forth. However, the Lord's requirements are the same: genuineness of heart in our observances and a lifestyle of obedience to his commands and principles.

PRAYER STARTER

Lord, please grant me the kind of authentic faith you called for in your people so long ago. I turn from empty religious observances and toward a genuine walk of humble obedience to accompany my rituals.

DAY 256

Expressing My Thanks

SCRIPTURE READING: PSALMS 107; 116; 118

These are psalms of deliverance, which celebrate the Lord's provision for his people and their rescue from exile in Babylon. Notice how often in these three psalms the writer mentions *expressing* thanks and praise to God. The verb phrases used include "exalt," "give thanks," "rejoice," "proclaim what the Lord has done," "praise the Lord," "sacrifice thank offerings," and "tell of his works with songs of joy." The point is that the Lord wanted his people to *actively express* their praise and thanksgiving to him.

We are no different, really. It still pleases the Lord for his people to recognize who he is and the things he has done and then actively celebrate him. He wants us to speak praise and thanksgiving to him *and* tell others about his greatness and our gratitude. Do you make this a habit?

PRAYER STARTER

Lord, please help me to first recognize and truly be thankful for your blessings. Help me to then find ways to regularly and without shame express my gratitude, praise, and awe at your love and power.

DAY 257

Surrounded by His Presence

SCRIPTURE READING: PSALMS 125; 126; 128; 129; 132; 147; 149

Psalm 125:2 says, "As the mountains surround Jerusalem, so the LORD surrounds his people both now and forevermore." Consider the imagery here. Have you ever thought of the Lord surrounding you? This speaks to us of protection, intimacy, and watchfulness. Israel was asked to trust in the Lord's presence, even in the face of the difficult task of returning to and rebuilding their homeland and despite the threats of enemies and other obstacles.

The Lord asks us for the same kind of trust today. Instead of a life without obstacles, challenges, or enemies, which we would naturally prefer, he promises us a life *surrounded* by his presence. It is actually the presence of the difficulties and pressures of life that makes this promise so precious. Ask him today to increase your trust in his "surrounding love" as you face the challenges of your day.

PRAYER STARTER

LORD, I BELIEVE YOUR WORD when it says you surround me. Show me more of what this means for me, and increase my faith in your presence, especially when this world goes dark and cold for me.

DAY 258

Being His People

SCRIPTURE READING: ZECHARIAH 9–14

It is clear that this section of scripture has messianic overtones and verses 9–10 in Chapter 9 are direct references to Jesus. However, three additional realities that spring from this text deserve some meditation and prayer today:

The beauty which God finds in his redeemed people (9:16–17): Too often we are overcome by our shortcomings and failures to the point of discouragement. Notice that he describes us as sparkling jewels—attractive, beautiful, and filled with life. May it be so!

The grave sentence on the unfit, unfaithful shepherd (11:15–17): As an under-shepherd, I beg for your prayers for me and all of today's church leaders. We are certainly only human, and yet Rick Warren says the second biggest "giant" that victimizes the whole world today is self-centered leadership. I see judgment looming at every hand unless repentance and change come.

The names of the two staffs that are broken when God's judgment is released: Favor and union are essential elements for the people of God to move forward. Pray for God's favor and a spirit of unity to reign at your local church and for all that comes against God's blessing being poured out and his body having unity to be cast down.

PRAYER STARTER

Lord, please show me today how you see me—clean in Jesus and a beautiful, sparkling jewel. Bless my pastor(s) and all the pastors of your flock today. Keep them humble, faithful, and selfless in this role. Pour out your favor on my church. Advance my understanding of what this means, and in my church, bring great unity to your followers as we gather around your mission for us.

DAY 259
Risking for the Kingdom

SCRIPTURE READING: ESTHER 1–4

Mordecai's words of encouragement and challenge to Esther on the eve of her decision to approach the king serve as great encouragement to us. He is urging her to use the influence she has been granted to plead for her people, the Jews, to be spared: "And who knows but that you have come to royal position for such a time as this?" In the end, this famous utterance serves to motivate Esther to be willing to risk the displeasure of the king and make her request.

You and I have been given different forms of influence in others' lives. It may be influence on a grand scale, with many constituents, employees, children, congregants, and so forth. being affected by our conduct, actions, and decisions; or it may be influence on a smaller scale, with opportunities to sow into the lives of only a comparative few. Regardless of the particulars, the question comes to each of us from time to time when there is an opportunity to step out for God in a way that could profoundly impact others: "And who knows but that you have come to (your) position for such a time as this?"

PRAYER STARTER

Lord, give me the wisdom to discern when it is time to take some kind of risk for your kingdom. When it is time, give me the passion and the courage to use my influence for the reasons you have granted it to me.

DAY 260

Doing the Good Thing

SCRIPTURE READING: ESTHER 5–10

The action of Mordecai in the early part of the book of Esther, when he saved the king's life from the plot by his two officers, is rewarded in this passage. Imagine what the outcome of this story might have been if Mordecai had not acted with such virtue. He did not do it with the motive of getting something for himself, but his act set the stage for a later blessing, for both Mordecai and his people.

There is a principle of sowing and reaping in this life. We should not do good acts just so that we might be rewarded. We should do them because we love the Lord and he is working goodness into us. Having said that, we still never know, just as Mordecai did not know, what the future ramifications might be when we choose to do good to others. We should bless people when we can because it's the right thing to do, but we should also realize that we are, in a sense, planting a seed that in the future might just bear fruit in a greater blessing for ourselves and/or others. So *do* the good the Lord sets before you to do today!

PRAYER STARTER

Lord, I know there will be some opportunity for me to do good or bless someone today in some way. Whether it is dramatic or ordinary, give me eyes to see it and a heart to act on it!

DAY 261

Bigger Faith

SCRIPTURE READING: EZRA 7–8

How big is your faith? Ezra says that he was ashamed to ask the king for protection on the journey toward Jerusalem, because he and his group had told the king that God would be their protection. For Ezra, trusting in the Lord was not just lip service. He realized that if he confessed faith in God while deep down he was trusting in the protection of the king, this would undercut and invalidate his message, making his faith a sham.

What is it that you are tempted to trust in instead of God? Trusting God doesn't mean always looking for the "mystical" provision—sometimes God blesses and provides for us in very practical ways. However, there are times when trusting God does look a little crazy. Are you willing to trust him even when it does not make sense?

PRAYER STARTER

Lord, strengthen my faith, so that I don't always have to see before I'll believe! Let my trust in you be a testimony to others of your greatness, and never let my lack of faith discourage those around me.

DAY 262

Grieving Over Sin

SCRIPTURE READING: EZRA 9–10

THE EXTREME GRIEF AND MOURNING over their sin that both Ezra and the people display in this passage is truly remarkable. Ezra tears his clothes, pulls his hair out, sits in one place until evening, prays contritely, confesses, weeps, and throws himself down before the house of God. The people of Jerusalem assemble, weep bitterly, and ultimately take action to correct what they can of their disobedience. Their contrition is all the more striking to us, I'm afraid, because we live in a society that has forgotten how to blush.

Sometimes as followers of the Lord we are guilty of taking sin lightly ourselves. When we cease to take sin seriously, we begin to harden our hearts against the Lord; soon we are not troubled by the evil to which we used to be sensitive. The more ludicrous Ezra's reaction seems to us, the more we need to realize the serious nature of sin and deal with it accordingly in our lives.

PRAYER STARTER

LORD, MAKE ME SENSITIVE, first to the sin in my own heart and life, and then to the sin I observe around me. It is in being troubled by my own sinfulness that I turn to you for healing and restoration; and it is in seeing clearly the sin around me that I am able to avoid falling prey to it.

DAY 263

Committed to More Than Comfort

SCRIPTURE READING: NEHEMIAH 1–5

These first five chapters are, in many respects, a veritable textbook on the effective leadership of a project. We see Nehemiah get a burden for the rebuilding, spend extended time in prayer, petition the king for permission and resources for the project, inspect the walls, rally the team for the project, divide the labor among the participants, and deal with opposition effectively. However, let's focus on the great passion and courage that caused him to leave a "cushy job" as the king's cupbearer, risk rejection and punishment by the king, and embark on this incredibly difficult and perilous undertaking that is to be riddled throughout with opposition.

You see, without the kind of character that Nehemiah demonstrates, and without his assertiveness to actually pursue his plan of action, all the best laid plans and strategies in the world would have done absolutely no good. The wall would still lie in ruins. Is this kind of commitment to God's kingdom lacking in your life? What have you risked for God in your life? What have you risked for him lately?

PRAYER STARTER

Lord, please let my burden and passion for your work in this world grow to the point that I am actually willing to forego my own comfort and agenda in order to see your kingdom advance.

DAY 264

Total Commitment

SCRIPTURE READING: NEHEMIAH 6–7

In pressing through to the completion of the rebuilding, Nehemiah had to resist a lot of attempts to intimidate him. He had to remain focused on his project and on the glory of his God. They tried to scare him, bully him, discredit him, and discourage him. Nehemiah was able to stand strong and press forward in large part because he was simply sold out to the cause. There was nothing more important in life to him than rebuilding those walls.

A surprising amount of courage and resolve is waiting for us on the other side of total commitment to the advance of God's kingdom. Nehemiah did not fear what these bullies did because his mission was truly bigger to him than his own well-being. May we get to this same place in our walk of faith! May it happen today!

PRAYER STARTER

Lord, I want to live in that place of total commitment that Nehemiah found. Help me not live recklessly, but in total abandon to the calling and purposes you have for my life.

DAY 265

The Power of God's Word

SCRIPTURE READING: NEHEMIAH 8–10

The results of the rediscovery and reading of the law are nothing short of astounding. The people weep initially because they learn some of their history and specifically where they as a nation have fallen short of God's expectations. Then they celebrate at Nehemiah's command because of their great joy that they are hearing from God again. After this, they begin to obey the law in a practical way, beginning with the observance of the feast of booths. Finally they hold a large worship service, in which they confess their sin, read from the Word for extended periods, collectively praise the Lord, recite his historical dealings with their people, and craft a covenant of renewed commitment to serving the Lord. All this happens essentially because they read the Word!

Realize once again today the life-changing power of God's word. It is only through the truths contained in the Bible that any of us have been or will be genuinely changed. Thank God today for the access we enjoy to his written word, and commit yourself to continued regular exposure.

PRAYER STARTER

Thank you, Lord, that I am able to read your word at will. Bless those who don't have that privilege today, and please make a way for them soon. Also, let your word find expression through my life in increasing measure!

DAY 266

In God's Way

SCRIPTURE READING: NEHEMIAH 11–13

Nehemiah would not win many awards for political correctness today, would he? He was serious about physically taking care of the house of God, providing for those who served there, preserving the observance of rest on the Sabbath, and keeping the men of Judah from pagan wives. Nehemiah did not dream up these things to be passionate about—they had all been commanded by God. Nehemiah saw clearly what the compromises of these principles had done to the people of God and how they had continually fallen away from him (and paid the price for it). He was unwilling to silently allow spiritual death to creep back in among God's people.

What about us? Are we as serious about doing things God's way, even if other ways seem easier or more popular? I am not suggesting that we use force to convince others in God's family to obey him. We live under grace now, and we believe that God's Holy Spirit is more powerful than any compulsion we might bring on others to "behave." But the question this passage raises is this: Are we as grieved inside over being lukewarm, powerless, and compromised in the body of Christ as Nehemiah was about Israel? Ask God for a burden about this problem and for wisdom of how to be part of the solution.

PRAYER STARTER

Lord, give me a heart that is aflame for your glory. Let me hurt and care deeply when you are dishonored, especially by those who are part of your church. Show me what to do to contribute to revival and renewal among your people.

DAY 267

Robbing God

SCRIPTURE READING: MALACHI

The most well known passage in the book of Malachi has to do with the robbing of God. In 3:8–12, God accuses the Israelites of robbing him, basically because they were not materially giving to him what he required. Is it still possible to rob God materially? Is his method of funding the advance of his kingdom still to be the tithes and offerings of his people? Abundant New Testament scriptures testify that the answer to both of these questions is "yes."

Where are you in your personal stewardship of the possessions God has given you? Are you giving regularly and substantially to the advance of the kingdom through the local church? Ask the Lord today to show you any adjustments that need to be made in your approach to giving. Thank him for the material blessings he has provided that make it possible for you to materially participate in the kingdom's progress.

PRAYER STARTER

Lord, I know you own everything, even the things that have my name on them right now. Show me how to rightly manage my resources, and guide me to the level of giving to your work that is right for me at this time.

DAY 268

Part of a Heritage

SCRIPTURE READING: 1 CHRONICLES 1–2

Have you ever wondered why passages like this are in the Bible? The first two (and even the first nine) chapters of 1 Chronicles are easy to regard as boring and a hindrance to get "out of the way" so we can get on with our Bible reading plan. These genealogical passages, however, were very important to the people of Israel. As the Jews revisited these passages, they saw the names of their ancestors. They knew the tribe to which they belonged, so the genealogies gave them identity, connection, and renewed commitment to their nation.

We need to see ourselves as part of the historical movement of God in this realm, as well. This is a real challenge in today's world, because our day is different in so many ways from the bulk of human history. As believers, however, we have a heritage of godly forebears who have "handed the torch" to us, and we have a pivotal leg of the race to run! We not only have a heritage to uphold, we will leave a legacy as well. How is your leg of the race shaping up?

PRAYER STARTER

Lord, I know there have been so many godly, holy people who have run this race before me. Help me to learn what I can of them, but also to live in a way that gives honor to the way they lived and worked for you. Thank you for those who handed this faith down to me!

DAY 269

Praying for His Favor

SCRIPTURE READING: 1 CHRONICLES 3–5

WITHIN THIS EXTENDED GENEALOGICAL SECTION lies the prayer of Jabez (4:10), which has received a fair amount of notoriety in the past few years. Far from a mantra to repeat in order to merit blessings from God, it is actually a sound prayer that in principle can be prayed by any believer. It may sound like a rather self-centered prayer, especially from the NIV's rendering of the language. However, Bruce Wilkinson argues in his book on the passage that it is actually a prayer that Jabez will be blessed and kept from evil in order to be a blessing and have more influence for the good. This cannot be a bad thing for any of us to pray, both for ourselves and for others.

Try praying by this progression today, and make this a part of your prayers for the next few days, should the Lord so lead you.

PRAYER STARTER

"Oh, that You would bless me indeed,
and enlarge my territory,
that Your hand would be with me,
and that You would keep me from evil, that I may not cause pain."
(Chronicles 4:10 NKJ)

For further exploration of this passage and the principles contained herein, I recommend *The Prayer of Jabez*, a short book by Bruce Wilkinson that was first published in 2000 by Multnomah Publishers, Inc.

DAY 270

The Gift of Music

SCRIPTURE READING: 1 CHRONICLES 6

Music was an important part of the worship of Israel. There was a whole line of Levites whose life's work was the making of music in the temple (6:22–47). Music is still a powerful medium today. It is important that we allow the Lord to use music in our lives to bring us closer to him, whether it is participating in collective worship, listening to inspirational music with a biblical message, or singing in private to the Lord. It is equally important that we guard against a constant diet of music that reinforces unbiblical values or messages. Music can be a powerful force for evil as well as good. Of course, music does not have to be overtly biblical to be a blessing. But neither does it have to be overtly unbiblical to be a hindrance in our lives. Do you appreciate the power of this medium? Are you using it to grow closer to Christ, or away from him?

PRAYER STARTER

Lord, thank you for the gift of music! Make me wise in my use of music, and show me any way this needs to change to better glorify you.

DAY 271
Not Defined by the Past

SCRIPTURE READING: 1 CHRONICLES 7:1–8:27

Beriah got his name because there had been misfortune in Ephraim's family (7:23). Two of his sons were killed by Philistines ("Beriah" sounds like the Hebrew for "misfortune"). Despite his name, however, Beriah's legacy was determined by what happened after he was born, not before. The genealogy reports that not only did he have a great daughter responsible for building two cities, he also became the ancestor of Joshua himself!

We need to understand, as well, that events that happened before we were born—and even our own experiences up to this point—need not define us. As we surrender our lives to God regularly and allow him to change us, he can use each of us in ways we could not have previously dreamed. We just have to give our past to him, with all its hurts, bad decisions, and mistakes, and ask him to forgive, heal, and redeem it. Then we can be free to embrace the future he has for us as we keep walking with him.

PRAYER STARTER

Lord, there are things about where I come from, what I've done, or what's been done to me that could well limit me the rest of my life. Please free me to be all you want me to be and show me any steps I need to take to leave a positive legacy as Beriah did.

DAY 272

Laboring for Him

SCRIPTURE READING: 1 CHRONICLES 8:28–9:44

THIS IS A REMARKABLE PASSAGE describing the division of labor in keeping the House of God in order. Every priest and Levite had their specific job, dictated usually by their clan, and they were expected to execute these duties for the good of the place of worship and sustain and enrich the worship life of Israel. Notice how many people were involved in this enterprise in basically a full-time capacity: two hundred twelve gatekeepers! Incredible!

Today in his church, we are all to have some role of service. It is a tragedy when just a few are left the great work of advancing the kingdom, including caring for God's house, spreading the good news, nurturing the church's spiritual growth, caring for the hurting, and serving in various other roles. It is an unfortunate, often repeated axiom of modern church life that twenty percent of the people do eighty percent of the work. This leaves the twenty percent burned out and frustrated and leaves the eighty percent spiritually sleepy, paralyzed by a consumerist mind-set that blesses no one, not even ultimately themselves. This situation need not be. All it takes to reverse this situation is for every believer to find and faithfully fulfill the service role they fit. Where are you on the continuum? If you are in the twenty percent, pray for more workers to join the greatest enterprise on earth. If you are in the eighty percent, ask yourself why.

PRAYER STARTER

LORD, PUT ME IN TOUCH WITH THE GIFTS you have given me for ministry, and then place me in the most effective place for me to use those gifts for you. Forgive me for the times when selfishness has kept me from servanthood.

DAY 273

Receiving His Grace

SCRIPTURE READING: JOHN 1:1-18; MARK 1:1;
LUKE 1:1-4; 3:23-38; MATTHEW 1:1-17

As we begin the New Testament together today, focus on that phrase from John 1:17, "For the law was given through Moses; grace and truth came through Jesus Christ." In many ways this is a pronouncement of the difference between the Old Testament and the New Testament. The old covenant was based on the Law, which provided a clear delineation of what was right and wrong. The problem with law is that it cannot truly change people. It can make them aware of sin and can clarify the consequences of sin, bringing condemnation on those who fall short of its demands. But it takes grace to change a human heart, because in and of ourselves we are incapable of keeping the law. Jesus was the ultimate expression of truth, and as such He fulfilled the law in our place. What a wondrous thought—as the embodiment of truth, he lived a perfect life for us, and as the embodiment of grace, he died a sinner's death for us!

Are you living by law or by grace today? I'm not asking about your obedience—living by grace does not mean living in reckless disobedience to God. It means living in an obedient relationship with a grace-filled Person (Jesus Christ). But it also means living in freedom from trying to earn our way with God, realizing that the only way to begin with him is to receive from him freely.

PRAYER STARTER

Lord, I still need to receive from you today. I need to receive your grace, love, and forgiveness. Let me receive it all freely. I know I have nothing worthy to offer in return, so I thank you for your grace that says I don't have to.

DAY 274

Raising Up Fathers

SCRIPTURE READING: LUKE 1:5-80

John the Baptist's ministry was one of preparation—he was to prepare the people for the coming of Jesus, the Messiah. In the description of John's coming ministry, it is said that "...he will go on before the Lord, in the spirit and power of Elijah, to turn the hearts of the fathers to their children and the disobedient to the wisdom of the righteous—to make ready a people prepared for the Lord" (5:17). The two things mentioned here would truly be precursors of a mighty move of God in our day as well: the turning of the hearts of parents toward their children and the turning of the disobedient to the wisdom of the righteous.

Imagine our community, city, and nation if these two things happened on a massive scale. It's worth praying for!

PRAYER STARTER

Lord, start in my own life and family, but by all means, turn hearts of the parents of this nation to their children. Break the hearts of those who don't care about righteousness, so that we may be prepared for you to move in a mighty way.

DAY 275

Herod vs. Joseph

SCRIPTURE READING: MATTHEW 1:18–2:23; LUKE 2

NOTICE THE CONTRAST between the humility and love of Joseph and the pride and seething hatred of Herod. Joseph loves Mary and intends to deal as gently as possible with her when he suspects fornication. He then believes the incredible claim of the angel that this will be a virgin birth. He responds with immediate obedience when the Lord tells him to take Mary as his wife, to flee to Egypt, and then return to Israel. He is willing for his life as he has known it to be torn apart because of his love for Mary and his desire to obey the Lord.

On the contrary, Herod appears incapable of any selfless impulse whatsoever. His whole agenda in this passage is about protecting his turf and remaining in his position of power, and he proves willing to go to any length to accomplish this—even if it means the slaughter of innocent babies. Most of us usually live between these two extremes, but today is a good day to strengthen our resolve to be more like Joseph and less like Herod in all things!

PRAYER STARTER

LORD, HELP ME TO EXHIBIT the kind of selfless devotion in my life that I see in the actions of Joseph. Let my reputation, my convenience, and my predetermined plans no longer be my only grid work for decision making. I hate the times I've been more like Herod than Joseph. Help me so that fewer of those times occur.

DAY 276

Resisting Temptation

SCRIPTURE READING: MATTHEW 3:1–4:11;
MARK 1:2–13; LUKE 3:1–23; 4:1–13;
JOHN 1:19–34

The three temptations that Christ endures in the desert immediately before his public ministry sum up much, if not all, of the major temptation the enemy will seek to use upon us. Satan tempts Jesus first with bodily cravings, then with the allure of a spectacular testing of God's protection, and finally with the promise of immediate temporal dominion if Jesus will bow down and worship him. Jesus resists and defies all these temptations, powerful though they are, and is thus proven ready to embark upon his earthly mission.

Whenever you are tempted today, whether it be in one of these three areas or another that doesn't seem related, remember that it is Christ who truly has the power to stand against Satan, and that it is only through him that we can hope for victory over sin. Choose him!

PRAYER STARTER

Lord, please continually teach me how to access your great strength to resist the devil, so that he will flee from me. Help me to not be fooled by the allure of the things he holds in front of me, but to keep my eyes on you.

DAY 277
Faith to Follow

SCRIPTURE READING: JOHN 1:35–3:36

Believing, or placing our faith in Jesus, is arguably the dominant theme of this whole section of scripture. It is mentioned over and over, directly and indirectly, throughout. The reading starts out with Jesus' disciples believing in him enough to follow him, and it progresses to his discourse with Nicodemus about the nature and necessity of belief in him as the Son of God—capped off by the ultimate summary statement: "Whoever believes in the Son has eternal life, but whoever rejects the Son will not see life, for God's wrath remains on him."

Do you grasp the absolutely crucial nature of belief in Christ? Do you walk in that awareness daily? Realize today that there is a world full of people who *do not* believe in him—and it matters!

PRAYER STARTER

First, dear Lord, may my belief in you remain solid and be revived when necessary. Then, may I share your concern about the belief status of others. Help me do what I can to help them to you, realizing that it is *not* only someone else's job, but mine, too!

DAY 278

Spiritual Dullness

SCRIPTURE READING: JOHN 4; MATTHEW 4:12–17; MARK 1:14–15; LUKE 4:14–30

One striking thing about the story of Jesus and the woman at the well is the absolute dullness of the disciples to what is really going on here. They return to the well, find Jesus there talking to the woman, and immediately become concerned over whether he has eaten or not. They are oblivious to the kingdom activity that is going on right under their noses. As they dwell on the physical, Jesus tells them in so many words that doing the Father's will is more important to him than physical food. He refuses to be distracted from facilitating the advance of the kingdom, because he knows that God's working in this woman's life is more important than whether his stomach is full.

May we more and more adopt these same priorities. May we never be so concerned about our pleasure, comfort, or even our sustenance that these concerns overshadow the real ministry you wish to flow through us!

PRAYER STARTER

Oh Lord, show me what is really important in this life. Help me always be willing to postpone my own "needs" in order that your kingdom might move forward unhindered, especially when I see you at work in a powerful way.

DAY 279
Unworthy, but Called

SCRIPTURE READING: MARK 1:16–45;
MATTHEW 4:18–25; 8:2–4; 14–17;
LUKE 4:31–5:16

THE EXCHANGE BETWEEN Jesus and Peter in Luke 5:1–11 instructs us about the meaning of Jesus' call to discipleship. When Peter sees that Jesus has the kind of power that can result in a miraculous catch of fish, he is immediately filled with fear and tells Jesus to leave because he knows himself to be "a sinful man." He considers himself unworthy to even be in Jesus' presence, and yet Jesus utters the classic response, "Don't be afraid; from now on you will catch men."

Jesus is saying to Peter (and to us) that he is not hung up on what we have been until now and he is not looking for people who have always had it all figured out. He wants people who are humble enough, honest enough about their mistakes, and hungry enough for a better way that he can truly change and use them. He doesn't ask Peter to prove his worth, his giftedness, or even his sincerity—instead he already sees and declares what Peter will become if he follows the Master.

PRAYER STARTER

LORD, I KNOW SO WELL MY UTTER UNWORTHINESS to even be called your child. And yet you invite me to be changed into a fisher of men, into one who makes an eternal difference in people's lives. Help me say yes to that call today and follow you without fear!

DAY 280

Never a Pharisee

SCRIPTURE READING: MATTHEW 9:1–17; MARK 2:1–22; LUKE 5:17–39

These passages relate three notable occasions on which the Pharisees challenged Jesus. They challenge his authority to forgive sins, and he responds by healing the paralytic to validate his claim. They challenge his association with "sinners," and he responds by describing those he is with as spiritually sick people and himself as their doctor. They challenge his disciples' failure to fast as others do, and he responds by confronting their legalism with the radically new paradigm his coming ushers in.

We who know Christ must be continually on guard against the pharisaic spirit within us. We should walk in a kind of simplicity of faith that accepts Jesus unequivocally as Lord and Christ; loves those who are far from God, refusing to engage in religious snobbery; and pursues a life governed by a living faith in Jesus, not the ritualistic observance of the law.

PRAYER STARTER

Lord, change me where my attitudes and actions are like those of the Pharisees. Make me slow to judge, quick to love, and everything else it means to be a "new wineskin."

DAY 281

Joining in the Work of God

SCRIPTURE READING: JOHN 5; MATTHEW 12:1–21;
MARK 3:23-3:12; LUKE 6:1–11

This passage in John 5 is the very heart of the message of "Experiencing God," a study that the Lord used mightily in the 1990s, and which contains many dynamic principles for how to know and do God's will. Jesus says that the Father is always at work—this means he is constantly at work in this realm, all around us. It's just that often we don't recognize his work around us.

He then adds that "...the Son can do nothing by himself; he can do only what he sees his Father doing, because whatever the Father does the Son also does. For the Father loves the Son and shows him all he does" (John 5:19). This means that Jesus' approach to knowing and doing the will of God is to observe where the Father is at work, and then to "join" him in it. This approach would save us much confusion, doubt, and frustration, if we would just begin to operate by it ourselves. In other words, we are not charged to make good things happen, nor even to necessarily hear mystically from God about what we should be doing for him. We just need to find out where he is working and join him! May he give us grace to grow in our understanding of how to do this!

PRAYER STARTER

Lord, help me to walk in faith that you are constantly at work in this realm. Help me learn how to discern clearly where you are at work, and then have the courage to join you in it.

DAY 282

A Blessed Life

SCRIPTURE READING: MATTHEW 5; MARK 3:13–19; LUKE 6:12–36

THE VALUES ESPOUSED IN THESE PASSAGES in the Sermon on the Mount so often contrast with the values of this world, it is helpful from time to time to look at those values alongside our lives to be sure we are becoming people of the kingdom of Heaven and resembling less the people of this world. The beatitudes at the opening of Matthew 5 provide us a wonderful opportunity to do just this.

Is your life one that others would describe as poor in spirit? As one who mourns? Are you meek ... hungering and thirsting for righteousness ... merciful ... pure in heart ... a peacemaker? Are you willing to be persecuted because of righteousness or insulted and falsely accused of evil because you love Jesus? This may sound like an impossibly high standard, but the kingdom we are a part of demands no less of its citizens. It is, in fact, impossible in our own strength apart from Christ, but he never asks us to pursue it alone!

PRAYER STARTER

LORD, IT IS A PRIVILEGE to be a part of this kingdom you so richly describe. I love the virtues I see listed here and long for them in my own life in ever-increasing measure. Would you please press these qualities into my life, that I may truly be salt and light in this world?

DAY 283

An Eternal Perspective

SCRIPTURE READING: MATTHEW 6–7;
LUKE 6:37–49

Matthew 6 and 7 (and the corresponding section of Luke) are in large part about living our lives with an eternal perspective versus a purely temporal, earthly perspective. Jesus applies this contrast to the way we help others, the way we pray, the way we fast, our attitude toward worry, our judgments of others, our persistence in prayer, and the faithfulness by which we live our lives.

How is your journey shaping up by the standards of this passage? Is it all about the here and now for you—who you can impress, how comfortably you can live, or how conveniently your problems can be solved? Jesus teaches that his followers are called to a higher form of life—a life that is focused on God himself, on caring for others, and on eternity. Adopt an eternal mind-set now as you prepare to face the day.

PRAYER STARTER

Lord, help me today to "seek first your kingdom and righteousness," knowing that this is the all-important pursuit of my life and that "all these things" will surely be given to me as well.

DAY 284

Responding Rightly

SCRIPTURE READING: LUKE 7;
MATTHEW 8:1, 5–13; 11:2–30

CAN ANYTHING IMPRESS JESUS? These passages say that when he saw the faith of the centurion, who believed Jesus could heal his ailing servant without even going to him, Jesus was "amazed at him." Jesus takes notice when he finds a person of great faith!

Consider the contrast with the behavior that frustrates him later in the passage:

> To what, then, can I compare the people of this generation? What are they like? They are like children sitting in the marketplace and calling out to each other: "We played the flute for you, and you did not dance; we sang a dirge, and you did not cry." For John the Baptist came neither eating bread nor drinking wine, and you say, "He has a demon." The Son of Man came eating and drinking, and you say, "Here is a glutton and a drunkard, a friend of tax collectors and 'sinners.'"
>
> (Luke 7:31–34)

He is indicting the kind of cynicism that predetermines to reject God's revelation and therefore finds constant "reasons" to reject him, based on the form of the messenger or any other triviality. Each of us actually has the capacity for each of these responses. Which will you choose today?

PRAYER STARTER

LORD, I WANT DESPERATELY TO HAVE THE KIND OF FAITH you can affirm, not the cynicism that frustrates you. Help me today to walk as a child, so that I may believe you enough to act on your words and rest in you.

DAY 285

Good Soil in My Heart

SCRIPTURE READING: MATTHEW 12:22–50;
MARK 3:20–35; LUKE 8:1–21

Many times, when we look at the parable of the sower, we think of the seed as our own efforts to share the news of Christ with the world. This can provide us much comfort and encouragement when we meet hardened hearts, shallow faith, and temporary results in those we seek to help.

But it can be even more helpful for us to think of our own hearts and appreciate the value of making sure our own lives are places of good soil for the gospel. Examine your heart today and as you step out to serve him in whatever you do, and let it be soft and receptive to his word, so that it may go deep and grow strong in you.

PRAYER STARTER

Lord, grant that my heart may prove to be good soil today. Prevent the enemy from stealing your word from my heart; may my roots go deep, so that I may not fall away, even in times of testing. May life's worries, riches, and pleasures not be allowed to choke out my faith, but let me grow to maturity.

DAY 286

The Coming Separation

SCRIPTURE READING: MARK 4:1–34; MATTHEW 13:1–53

Two of the parables in today's reading, the separation of weeds from wheat and the separation of good fish from bad, show us two important realities that we need to carry with us today. One is that the good and the wicked are all mixed up together until the end. Our Father wills that we be in the world and among the people of this world, not separated and cloistered from it. It is easy to wish we only are supposed to be around people that are like us, but if that were his plan there would be no way to reach out to the others, to be strengthened by the trials of living among them, or to glorify him by living for his glory in a non-conducive environment.

The second reality is that a separation is surely coming, one that is permanent and irrevocable. This should motivate us all the more to live for him and be concerned for those who do not know him!

PRAYER STARTER

Help me today, Lord, even though I live among those who walk in darkness, to walk in your light. May the life I live have an impact on someone's eternity and your kingdom today!

DAY 287

Embracing Jesus and Change

SCRIPTURE READING: MARK 4:35–5:43;
MATTHEW 8:18, 23–24; MATTHEW 9:18–34;
LUKE 8:22–56

Matthew, Mark, and Luke all record that the people of the region of the Gerasenes begged Jesus to leave their region after he cast the demons into the herd of swine. Luke says it was because they were "overcome with fear." This has often troubled me. Why would you want someone who is capable of casting out demons and healing lives to leave your area?

I think it is more than a simple fear of the power Jesus had displayed. People fear change, and he had significantly changed the status quo of the region. Also, it is very possible they feared what he might ask of them. While they may not have understood the full implications of his mission, it must have been clear that he was more than an ordinary man—he had real spiritual authority. That can be scary.

We need to realize that Jesus is not someone for us to fear *unless* we turn away from him. Yes, he wants to change our world, to change us, and to ask great things of us, but this is wonderful, not fearsome!

PRAYER STARTER

Jesus, you are truly an amazing person to encounter. As I encounter you, help me not to react with the fear of the people in this passage. Help me to embrace you today, even when that means changes that make me uncomfortable at first.

DAY 288

Embracing Costly Obedience

SCRIPTURE READING: MARK 6:1–30;
MATTHEW 13:54–58; MATTHEW 9:35–11:1; 14:1–12;
LUKE 9:1–10

Jesus begins to raise the level of challenge to his followers with some relatively hard sayings in Matthew 10. He says he will acknowledge those who acknowledge him before men and disown those who disown him before men. He says he has come to turn people of the same household against one another. He says if anyone loves his family more than him, he is not worthy to be a follower of Jesus. Then he begins to talk about them taking up their crosses and following him.

How do these challenges strike you? It is clear that many of his early followers were troubled by these teachings, as scripture later records that many left off following when he brought the message of surrender, supreme allegiance, and potential conflict with loved ones. We need to understand, however, that he gives us the same type of challenge today. Will we love him supremely, above all the other relationships in our lives? Will we confess him before men rather than disown him? Will we take up our cross and follow him, even if it's hard, inconvenient, or conflict-ridden? Accept his challenge to go to the next level of discipleship, servanthood, selflessness, and even sacrifice!

PRAYER STARTER

Lord, I know that happiness, purpose, meaning, and fulfillment will be mine in proportion to how much you are the supreme love of my life. Let it be! Tame my reluctance to live full speed for you, and increase my level of intimacy with you.

DAY 289

Embracing Risky Faith

SCRIPTURE READING: MATTHEW 14:13–36;
MARK 6:31–56; LUKE 9: 11–17; JOHN 6:1–21

*I*F YOU WANT TO WALK ON WATER, you have to get out of the boat!" Perhaps you have heard this expression before, but the reason it's become cliché, as with most things, is because it is basically true. Jesus gives Peter a once-in-all-of-history opportunity by inviting him to walk on the water. But Peter is the one who must believe enough to take action and take risk. Even though his faith proves less than perfect, he is a man of faith to the degree that he takes that step.

This principle holds true in our lives, as well. However, it is often not so much that God is challenging us to do something totally radical and physically impossible as it is that he wants us to have enough faith to trust him and walk in obedience to him every day. Adopting this kind of lifestyle will undoubtedly lead to some specific opportunities for dramatic risk, but for us, getting out of the boat means making hundreds and thousands of less dramatic decisions to listen to God, do things his way, risk our popularity and standing with people, and forgo the short-lived pleasure of indulging in sin. Will you get out of your boat?

PRAYER STARTER

> LORD, HELP ME TRUST YOU AND YOUR POWER and love enough to get out of my boat. I don't want to be held back from doing your will because of my fear. Replace my fear with faith!

DAY 290

Embracing Authentic Worship

SCRIPTURE READING: JOHN 6:22–7:1;
MATTHEW 15:1–20; MARK 7:1–23

In Matthew 15 and Mark 7 we see again the Pharisees hung up on outward observances of "righteousness," and Jesus is again very hard on them for this. This time their attack centers on the ceremonial washing of hands before eating, but the interaction is in essence the same as when he healed on the Sabbath, plucked grain on the Sabbath, and declined to require his disciples to fast according to Jewish traditions. The problem with the mind-set of the Pharisees is that they are meticulous about matters that are quite trivial in God's economy, while missing what matters most—a heart that longs for God over and above some ceremony or ritual or rule keeping.

What are your rituals and rules? Do they spring from and support your pursuit of a living relationship with God, or have they, even on occasion, become substitutes for him? May it never be said of us, "These people honor Me with their lips, but their hearts are far from me. They worship Me in vain; their teachings are but rules taught by men."

PRAYER STARTER

Oh Lord, please let my worship of you be real and alive. Save me from degenerating into empty, vain observance of rules taught by men. Give me the wisdom, strength, and courage to seek you out in a real and personal way; keep me from mindlessly parroting the words and rituals handed down to me by others. Let my rituals and rules be alive with your mighty empowerment!

DAY 291

The Shallowness of Sign Seeking

SCRIPTURE READING: MATTHEW 15:21–16:20; MARK 7:24–8:30; LUKE 9:18–21

The Sadducees and Pharisees came to Jesus asking him for a sign from heaven to prove himself to them. While Jesus was a worker of miracles, and while he did not shy away from performing signs and wonders to corroborate his ministry and truth claims, he found something about their request deeply troubling. Most likely, he was concerned about the shallowness and cynicism that demands the dramatic, and says, "God, prove yourself to me." His miracles, by and large, are responses to the faith of those asking, not proof to overcome the skepticism of those who are demanding certain things from him. There is a world of difference.

Let us be on our guard about a "prove it, God" kind of attitude. Whether it be a demand for a dramatic miracle or sign before we will believe or obey; an expectation of a specific blessing of our choice when we have obeyed; or the anticipation that we should avoid trials, hurts, and heartaches because we follow God, Jesus characterizes the demand for a sign as the mark of "a wicked and adulterous generation." It does not take love for God or faith in God to demand a sign; in fact, the ones demanding a miracle here were filled with *hatred* for Jesus! Let's instead be a generation of faith, obedience, and humble service to the one we follow.

PRAYER STARTER

Lord, please help me today to believe you and your promises more deeply than ever before. Forgive me for the times I've been a "sign-seeker." Teach me instead to be a seeker of you yourself.

DAY 292

Handling Pain His Way

SCRIPTURE READING: MATTHEW 16:21–17:27; MARK 8:31–9:32; LUKE 9:22–45

When Jesus begins to explain his ultimate destination—Jerusalem, death, and resurrection, Peter immediately challenges him and is promptly rebuked as Satan! We might well wonder why Peter's concern would meet with such harshness from the Master. After all, it is surely out of concern for Jesus and grief over the prospect of losing him that Peter speaks. For an answer, we have to look more closely at Jesus' words: "Get behind me, Satan! You are a stumbling block to me; you do not have in mind the things of God, but the things of men." He is saying that Peter's words have the potential to trip him and possibly tempt him to abandon his mission. He also accuses Peter of holding earthly values as opposed to heavenly ones. By challenging Jesus' words here, Peter is kicking against the very thing that will secure eternity for all who believe.

Peter wanted a kingdom with no grief, loss, or real pain. He had his own agenda for how Jesus' ministry would turn out, and it did not involve suffering and death. How often we are guilty of the same kind of impulse as Peter: "No, thanks, Lord, I'll just have a life of comfort and uninterrupted joy and peace. No pain for me!"

The trouble is we don't get to make this choice. When pain comes into your life, whatever its form, scope, or severity, decide to trust God and humbly pursue him, even when it is hard.

PRAYER STARTER

Lord, help me never to try to impose my preferences, convenience, and comfort upon your mission. I know some things about this life are hard. I accept this and ask you for the courage to bear whatever losses are yet to come my way in this life with your dignity and grace.

DAY 293

A Kingdom for Children

SCRIPTURE READING: MATTHEW 18; 8:19–22;
MARK 9:33–50; LUKE 9:46–62; JOHN 7:2–10

JESUS VALUES CHILDREN *and* he values childlikeness in all of us. We should share his esteem and love for children because they are the leaders, citizens, and disciples of the future. Nurtured well, they can become the hope for a brighter tomorrow for this world. Look for opportunities to bless and add value to the children's lives to which you have access today.

We should also cultivate a childlike spirit of simplicity, wonder, and innocence before God. The more we can lose our arrogance, our control issues, and our pretensions, the more childlike (and therefore, God-pleasing) we become.

PRAYER STARTER

LORD, PLEASE GIVE ME A HEART TO BLESS, encourage, and help the children in my world today, and to see this as part of my positive contribution to making the world a better place tomorrow. Work in me the heart of a child, unafraid to bring you my fears, my needs, and my failures.

DAY 294

Water, Light, and Freedom!

SCRIPTURE READING: JOHN 7:11–8:59

THREE GREAT PROMISES FOR BELIEVERS stand out in today's reading. John 7:38–39: "'Whoever believes in me, as the scripture has said, streams of living water will flow from within him.' By this he meant the Spirit...." John 8:11: "I am the light of the world. Whoever follows me will never walk in darkness, but will have the light of life." And John 8:32: "...you will know the truth, and the truth will set you free."

Take some time today to meditate on these three promises, fulfilled in Christ. Living water will flow through us, touching the world around us and making things live! The light of life will rest upon us, keeping whatever darkness may be around from overcoming us! The truth is knowable and will set us free! Pray that these three promises find maximum fulfillment in your life today. God wants to give us these things; we simply have to receive them by faith and walk in them.

PRAYER STARTER

OVERFLOW MY LIFE WITH LIVING WATER, Lord, that I may be fully alive and help others to be. Let my life shine brightly for you, overcoming the darkness of this world. And lead me into truth, so that I might be free of the bondage that false beliefs, values, and actions have caused!

DAY 295
Practical Love

SCRIPTURE READING: LUKE 10:1–11:36

THE PARABLE OF THE GOOD SAMARITAN is a powerful urging for us to love our neighbors as ourselves *in practical ways*. The Samaritan saw a need and responded, without excusing himself as did the priest and the Levite. But the genesis of his action was that he "took pity on him." Many times, we really don't allow ourselves to be moved deeply by the pain of others, and this closes off any possibility of us being moved to actually *do* something.

It all starts with adopting the third of the three attitudes displayed in the parable: The thieves—"What's thine is mine, and I'll take it if I can." The priest and Levite—"What's mine is mine, and I'll keep it if I can." The Samaritan—"What's mine is thine, and you can have it if you need it." Ask the Lord to mold this attitude in you today.

PRAYER STARTER

LORD, PLEASE LET THE SAMARITAN become more of a role model for me. Help me not allow myself to constantly pass by on the other side, but show me the needs you would have me meet.

DAY 296

A Kingdom Mind-set

SCRIPTURE READING: LUKE 11:37–13:21

Beginning at a Pharisee's dinner party, Jesus plainly contrasts the mind-set of the kingdom of God with the mind-set of this world. He calls us as his followers to live on a higher plane than the pagan world around us. He speaks of taking off self-righteous, religious masks (11:37–12:3); of living free of fear about the physical consequences of following him (12:4–12:12); of shedding our preoccupation with material provision (12:13–12:34); of staying prepared for his return (12:35–13:9); of doing good without legalistic constraints (13:10–17); and of understanding the dynamic of God's kingdom's spread and growth (13:18–21).

God is looking for lives marked by these understandings and pursuits, and he clearly offers us the empowerment to live this way. What is it that holds you back from running full-speed toward a life like this? Whatever it is, give it to him today, and step into a full-speed God pursuit in your life.

PRAYER STARTER

God, please move me toward living this glorious blueprint of faith, contentment, love, genuineness, courage, and readiness. Reproduce your character in me, so that your kingdom can grow and spread through me!

DAY 297

The Good Shepherd

SCRIPTURE READING: JOHN 9–10

Jesus calls himself the Good Shepherd, who lays his life down for his sheep. He contrasts himself to the "thief," who comes only to steal and destroy the sheep, and the hired hand, who runs away when he sees the wolf coming after the sheep. In contrast to these, who are only about self-interest at one level or another, Jesus says he has come so "that they may have life, and have it to the full."

Rejoice today, that you have such a shepherd watching over your life and your soul. No matter the threat, he is *never* afraid and will *never* abandon us to walk through the trial alone. And not only is he the ultimate expression of courage, Jesus is also the perfect expression of tenderness and compassion toward us—he freely lays down his very life for us, so that we can live to the full!

PRAYER STARTER

Lord, thank you for being my Good Shepherd. I need your shepherding today. Teach me more about what it means to be your sheep, and help me to walk in this way today. Lead me to lay hold of the "life to the full" that you offer.

DAY 298

No Repayment Necessary

SCRIPTURE READING: LUKE 13:22–15:32

In 14:12–14, Jesus seems to say that his followers should not only do good to others and try to bless them, but that we should actually make it our goal to do things that *cannot* be repaid. What a radical departure from the normal value system of this world! This concept fits right in with his teaching in the Sermon on the Mount about those who do good works and religious acts for the eyes of other people. He says plainly that there is no eternal benefit to such behavior: "They have their reward."

Have you ever tried out this idea? Helping those who can do nothing for us is one way to purify our motives for doing good. It is so easy to become self-seeking or self-serving, even in our "benevolent" actions! If we look to help the helpless, in whatever venue, we become a little more like Christ, too. After all, what was his mission in coming to earth other than helping those who have no possibility of ever repaying him?

PRAYER STARTER

Lord, please make me more and more like you in every way. Show me someone I can bless who cannot "bless back." Use this exercise to purify all my motives in all my acts of giving or of service.

DAY 299

Material Seduction

SCRIPTURE READING: LUKE 16:1–17:10;
JOHN 11:1–54

THE STORY OF THE RICH MAN and Lazarus is a powerful reminder for us that the social structures of this world in no way define eternity (the selfish rich man ends up far worse than the beggar who has nothing). It shows us that the motives of our hearts and the actions they birth (or fail to birth) determine more about our ultimate destiny than our prestige or power in this world do. Notice also that the only character flaw even implied in the rich man is that he lives in obscene luxury with poverty he could alleviate in plain view every day.

Be reminded today not to be seduced by the material thrall of this world. It is nice to have more stuff, to be sure. Just be sure you guard and grow your heart and your character at least as much as your bank account.

PRAYER STARTER

LORD, GUARD MY HEART from the seduction of riches. I know I cannot serve two masters, and I choose you over money as my master today.

DAY 300

Owning My Need

SCRIPTURE READING: LUKE 17:11–18:17;
MATTHEW 19:1–15; MARK 10:1–16

THE PARABLE OF THE PHARISEE and the tax collector describes the stark contrast between pompous religious pride and genuine humility before God. The Pharisee makes the mistake of comparing his religious activity with that of another person. We can all look around and find someone we compare to favorably, if we only look long and hard enough. But God's kingdom does not work this way. Jesus makes the point that the tax collector has an advantage on the Pharisee only because he sees his true condition before God and responds accordingly. He is not susceptible to the sin of religious pride, primarily because he has not been religious about anything except cheating others and living selfishly.

Perhaps it troubles us sometimes, just as it did the Pharisees, to think of someone who has "been bad" receiving the grace and mercy of God, and perhaps worse, actually becoming pleasing to God without our "track record" of obedience and contribution to the kingdom. But the fact is that God looks primarily at our hearts. He always has, and he always will. So true contrition and awareness of our need of his mercy trumps religious activity designed to impress God, others, or ourselves. Do you see your need?

PRAYER STARTER

LORD, IT IS TRUE THAT BASED ON MY ACHIEVEMENT and merit, the only thing I've achieved and merited is eternity away from you. Help me live in a constant awareness of my utter dependence on you, and guard me from judgmentally looking down on those who appear to be behind me right now in this journey. Make me instead a loving encourager to them.

DAY 301

Priority Number One

SCRIPTURE READING: MATTHEW 19:16–20:28;
MARK 10:17–45; LUKE 18:18–34

Jesus saw clearly that the rich young ruler was being held back from true devotion to God by his love of riches. The young man went away sad because he had great wealth, and Jesus had told him to sell it all and follow him. He preferred his riches to a life of discipleship with Jesus. This might seem an extreme request for Jesus to make, but in reality, his call to discipleship is *always* an extreme request. He calls all of us to be willing to lay down whatever it is that stands between us and absolute commitment to him.

Is there something you can identify that holds you back today from an absolute devotion to Jesus? It could be anything that you have the tendency to value more than you value him. Ask the Lord to adjust your priorities to the point that there is nothing that would cause you to "go away sad" because you love material things more than him.

PRAYER STARTER

Father, I see that I am susceptible to the "rich young ruler syndrome." There are things in this life that I can be tempted to value too highly. Lord, become my supreme value in life!

DAY 302

Extravagant Love

SCRIPTURE READING: MATTHEW 20:29-34; 26:6–13; MARK 10:46-55; 14:3-9; LUKE 18:35–19:28; JOHN 11:55–12:11

Mary's anointing of Jesus at Bethany tells us much about the value of being extravagant for God. The argument was made even back then, "This is wasteful ... that money could have been used to help the poor." Today, we still hear vestiges of this same argument when the subject of doing great things for God's kingdom is raised. Even within our own hearts, the idea of "emptying it out" for God meets opposition from the practical argument: "God could not want me to do this radical, expensive, or risky thing ... there are so many other things that are constructive and would make more sense and cost far less!"

There are still times for "extravagance for God." And Jesus' commendation for those who obey at such times is still the same: "Why are you bothering (them)? (They) have done a beautiful thing for me."

PRAYER STARTER

Lord, make me willing to do the extravagant for you when you call me to. Help me believe and act on the belief that "emptying it out" for you is supremely pleasing in your sight. Show me how to empty myself today for your kingdom.

DAY 303

Firm, Not Fickle

SCRIPTURE READING: MATTHEW 21:1–22;
MARK 11:1–26; LUKE 19:29–48; JOHN 12:12–50

CONSIDER TODAY THE GREAT FICKLENESS OF MANKIND. There is doubtlessly great overlap between the crowd that here welcomes Jesus into Jerusalem with shouts and palm branches, and the crowd which just days later yells, "Crucify him!" This shows just how quickly the hearts of people can be turned from one course to another.

This passage also contains the account of some Jewish leaders who believed in Jesus, but who would not confess it publicly for fear of being thrown out of the synagogue ("... they loved praise from men more than praise from God.") We need to guard our hearts against such fickleness and to ask God for the courage and resolve to stand firm for him, no matter what the "crowd" near us does, and no matter what pressures are applied or implied from the power structures and institutions that surround us!

PRAYER STARTER

LORD, HELP ME LIVE RADICALLY and courageously for you, undaunted by the pull of the crowd and untroubled by any compulsion to please men over pleasing you.

DAY 304

More Than Talk

SCRIPTURE READING: MATTHEW 21:23–22:14; MARK 11:27–12:12; LUKE 20:1–19

THE PARABLE OF THE TWO SONS in Matthew 21:28–32 underscores the priority God places on what we actually do, not just what we say. In an ingeniously simple way, he depicts two sons, one of whom answers "no" to the father initially but later changes his mind and obeys, and one who says "yes" with his lips, but never does what he has promised. The message is clear ... all our big talk and stated commitments mean nothing unless we follow through in real life and actually *obey* God in the real world.

This means we will let him impact the way we talk, the way we treat others, the decisions we make, our priorities, and the way we react in different situations. May we never be like the second brother, professing belief in Christ as Lord and yet refusing to yield to his transforming power in our lives!

PRAYER STARTER

LORD, SHOW ME WHAT AREAS OF MY LIFE need your touch of transformation. Empower me to walk in true obedience to you, not just a "lip-service" that will get me by with other people.

DAY 305

Including Him

SCRIPTURE READING: MATTHEW 22:15–46;
MARK 12:13–37; LUKE 20:20–44

Sometimes it is easy to forget what is truly most important in life, especially in this age of complexity, hurry, and business. But Jesus sums it up well in these passages when he says love for God is the number one thing in all of life. Nothing else matters if we get this one wrong. Furthermore, if we get this one right, we really get it all right in the end.

If you had to measure your love for God today, where would you rank it? Would your answer change if I specified that the measure of your love is to be the way you live your life? Is God included on a day-by-day, hour-by-hour, and moment-by-moment basis? When we love someone, we include them. Ask God to show you how and help you to include him even more in your life, so that your love relationship with him might grow.

PRAYER STARTER

Lord, I know that loving you is the most important thing in life, and yet at times it seems one of the most difficult to do consistently. Help me, Lord, to love you with all of my heart, soul, mind, and strength. My desire is to love you more than anything or anyone else in this world. Help me do it!

DAY 306

Spiritual Ego

SCRIPTURE READING: MATTHEW 23; MARK 12:38–44; LUKE 20:45–21:4

Jesus's most fiery teaching is directed at the Pharisees, a sect of meticulous law keepers, who were known for their rigidity and judgmental ways and were continually at odds with him over his disregard for their religious traditions. He calls them "hypocrites" six times in this passage and "blind" five times, offering seven specific indictments against them. The majority of these indictments seems to hinge on their willingness to put on the outward effects of religion without being changed into truly godly men. They are content to play the game of looking "holy" to others, but inside they are full of pride, pretension, and self-righteousness.

Have you ever known anyone like this? Have you ever been like this yourself? The temptation as we grow in spiritual maturity (or just in religious experience) can be to become puffed up about the knowledge we've acquired, the character we've attained, or the works we've done. That is why we must always heed these words of Jesus as among his most important: "The greatest among you will be your servant. For whoever exalts himself will be humbled, and whoever humbles himself will be exalted" (Matthew 23:11–12).

PRAYER STARTER

Lord, I know that religious pride is perhaps the most deadly form of pride. Guard me from self-righteousness. Also protect me from the impulse to do good and live right just so others will see this behavior. May I live with an overwhelming sense of your presence, as this is the surest antidote to both these pitfalls.

DAY 307

Being Part of the Solution

SCRIPTURE READING: MATTHEW 24:1–31; MARK 13:1–27; LUKE 21:5–27

As Jesus talks about the last days, he says, "Because of the increase of wickedness, the love of most will grow cold, but he who stands firm to the end will be saved. (Matthew 24:12–13). Two points that really stand out are that most will grow cold in their love for God and this will result because of their discouragement at the proliferation of evil.

Let us *not* be discouraged by the presence of evil in our world, nation, state, city, or neighborhood—it is a fact of life in this world and all the more as the day of his coming draws nearer. Further, let us not even consider being discouraged because of others who fall away in frustration, but pray for them and resolve to be part of the solution, not the problem!

PRAYER STARTER

Help me, Lord, to not be discouraged by either the unbridled evil or the lukewarm spirituality I see around me. Empower me to rise above all this and be one who stands firm in your power and by your Spirit!

DAY 308

Being Found Ready

SCRIPTURE READING: MATTHEW 24:32–26:5, 14–16;
MARK 13:28–14:2, 10–11; LUKE 21:28–22:6

There are stern warnings here on three different fronts regarding the judgment that is coming at the end. First, stay prepared for his coming (the parable of the ten virgins). Second, invest all that has been entrusted to you wisely (the parable of the talents). Finally, do good to others as if you were helping Jesus in need (the sheep and the goats).

As you consider these powerful teachings today, resolve before God to live not just for today, not just as a consumer, and not just for yourself, but instead as one looking forward to another kingdom, as a giver and investor of blessings, and as a person marked by a deep compassion for others.

PRAYER STARTER

Lord, change me where I need to be changed so I'll be found ready when you come. Help me always seek a return for your kingdom with the time, talent, and treasure with which I've been blessed. Place in me a heart that truly cares about others enough to help them.

DAY 309

Being a Servant

SCRIPTURE READING: MATTHEW 26:17–29;
MARK 14:12–25; LUKE 22:7–38; JOHN 13

THE POWER OF JESUS' ACT OF SERVANTHOOD in washing his disciples' feet was so powerful that some Christian groups have elevated foot-washing to the status of an ordinance, akin to baptism and the Lord's Supper. The few foot-washing ceremonies I have been a part of have been utterly humiliating (both as "wash-er" and "wash-ee"), while at the same time deeply spiritually moving. I saw and experienced the tangible "fleshing out" of the attitudes we are to carry toward one another in our hearts. I have no doubt that in the faith traditions where this practice is observed regularly, it can devolve into a dry tradition, just as any ceremony or rite can—but it can definitely be a meaningful reminder of what it means to be true servants to one another. (And we don't even have the experiences of really dirty feet or the presence of the lowliest of servants regularly performing this task to cement the impact on us that it must have had on them!)

Whose feet do you need to wash today? Address in prayer today the pride that keeps you from being a servant, then go out and follow Jesus—"Now that you know these things, you will be blessed if you do them..."

PRAYER STARTER

LORD, TEACH ME TO BE MORE OF A SERVANT, beginning with those who are closest to me, then moving outward all the way to those who are far from you.

DAY 310

Being Rejected for Him

SCRIPTURE READING: JOHN 14–16

One of the major barriers to healthy discipleship is the desire to be liked and accepted by the world. However, Jesus says it plainly in "If the world hates you, keep in mind that it hated me first. If you belonged to the world, it would love you as its own. As it is, you do not belong to the world, but I have chosen you out of the world. That is why the world hates you" (Jn 15:18-29). When you really think about it, it is really rather absurd. We claim to be followers of one who was clearly not of this world, was summarily rejected, and eventually executed by the power structures and power brokers of this world, and yet somehow we expect it will be different for us. We even sometimes get to the state of mind that chooses the acceptance of the world over radical discipleship to Christ. Today, consider your willingness to be hated and hurt for him.

PRAYER STARTER

Lord, in my better moments, I want my life to be nothing but committed to you, no matter the cost. I do not care who accepts me or rejects me, and I don't care what the price may be for following you. Please let such moments increase.

DAY 311

Being Awake to God

SCRIPTURE READING: JOHN 17:1–18:1;
MATTHEW 26:30–46; MARK 14:26–42;
LUKE 22:39–46

Sometimes our trouble is the same as that of the disciples in the garden of Gethsemane, who seem to just not know the gravity of the situation facing them and Jesus at the time. They go to sleep while he is having the prayer struggle of his life. Jesus has predicted his death and gone through the elaborate ritual of the Last Supper—yet they do not seem to realize that his life is in the balance on this very night.

While the life of a Christ follower is to be filled with joy, and we should always guard against taking *ourselves* too seriously (another problem of the Pharisees), some things should certainly be taken very seriously. We should share Christ's burden for the lost of this world, to the point that we do something about it. We should share his hatred of wickedness and injustice, to the point that we allow him to change the evil impulses in our own lives and fight to make the world better. We should share his compassion for those who are hurting, to the point that we take some role in helping or healing others in need. We should share his love for the church enough that we pray for its mission to be accomplished and give a part of ourselves to the effort. And finally, we should love Christ himself enough that we pursue him daily in prayer, Bible reading, and obedience. May we never be like the disciples, who became blind to their situation!

PRAYER STARTER

Lord, thank you for your great and awesome love, which led you to the loneliness of Gethsemane and the agony of Calvary for me. May I and all your people live with great joy because of our deliverance, but help us also grasp the gravity of the serious pursuits you set before us.

DAY 312

Being Unashamed

SCRIPTURE READING: MATTHEW 26:47–75; MARK 14:43–72; LUKE 22:47–65; JOHN 18:2–27

Examining Peter's denial of Jesus gives us the occasion to examine our own hearts in the area of owning him before others. What does it take to make you deny Jesus? Just a little pressure or condescension from another person? The possibility of economic consequences? The likelihood of physical harm? Remember that Peter probably would have faced all of these pressures (and possibly worse) had he stepped up and done what we all know he should have. Instead, impulsive Peter finally displays the one impulse common to us all—self-preservation!

We know that Peter is later to become the "Rock" that Jesus promised in Matthew 16:18, but at this juncture, he shows himself to be a weak, reactionary, and insecure follower. In these passages he is an example of what we *don't* want to be. Ask God for the courage to not be ashamed of him before others. He won't work and move powerfully through a life of such paltry faith! He cannot give them life through us if we are ashamed to be his!

PRAYER STARTER

The thought of being ashamed of you sickens me! I want to live at full speed for you, no matter what others may think, say, or do about me. Give me the discipline to be with you enough to stay in love with you – to value you above anything that could threaten to make me ashamed.

DAY 313

A Kingdom Beyond Time

SCRIPTURE READING: MATTHEW 27:1–26;
MARK 15:1–15; LUKE 22:66–23:25;
JOHN 18:28–19:16

As you consider the trumped-up charges against Jesus and his undeserved condemnation, consider his words, "My kingdom is not of this world." No truer words have ever been spoken, and we need to remember this truth often if we are to truly be his followers. It was the perverted and imperfect system of justice of this world that sent Jesus to the cross! There are certainly necessary, noble, and worthy aspects of our criminal justice systems and many of the authority structures in our world. But they cannot be trusted for salvation, true meaning, or the ultimate bringing of righteousness and justice to the world. This is because even the best social systems are run by fallen people who will never get it all right. In the worst cases, they may even be controlled by downright wicked and selfish people who use them as instruments for evil instead of good.

Praise God today that his kingdom surpasses all this world may have to offer in the way of beauty, justice, righteousness, and purity. Also celebrate the fact that God has graciously allowed us to be a part of it in Christ!

PRAYER STARTER

Lord, thank you for your kingdom that is above and beyond the time-bound kingdom in which I currently find myself. Help me to live more and more as a citizen of that heavenly kingdom, as I become more of an agent of blessing and redemption in this earthly realm.

DAY 314

The Tearing of the Curtain

SCRIPTURE READING: MATTHEW 27:27–56;
MARK 15:16–41; LUKE 23:26–49;
JOHN 19:17–30

THE TEARING OF THE CURTAIN IN THE TEMPLE symbolizes the importance of the entire sequence of events recorded here. Until Jesus' death, there had never been an all-sufficient payment for the sin of mankind. Therefore, between man and God was a wall of separation that even the old sacrificial system could not totally overcome. The curtain in the temple was symbolic of that separation. Jesus' death solved this problem for all who will believe, giving us access to a personal relationship with God, because he paid our sin debt, taking on our sin and dying in our place!

Your debt is paid in full! Celebrate the wonder of this truth today and ask God to draw you close to himself and allow you to experience the intimacy he provided for on the cross. There is an old hymn that states:

> "Jesus paid it all;
> All to him I owe.
> Sin had left a crimson stain—
> He washed it white as snow."

PRAYER STARTER

LORD, LET ME GRASP ONCE AGAIN the import of this torn curtain. Thank you for giving me an access I could never earn or deserve. Come close to me today, by your Spirit, and fill me with the power of your presence. Help me not to squander this access, but to live in vital connection with you all day.

DAY 315

Spontaneous Service

SCRIPTURE READING: MATTHEW 27:57–28:8;
MARK 15:42–16:8; LUKE 23:50–24:12;
JOHN 19:31–20:10

PERHAPS, LIKE MANY, YOU HAVE NEVER THOUGHT much about Joseph of Arimathea. But today, consider his actions after the crucifixion. This was obviously an incredibly difficult time for him and all the other followers of Jesus, yet he steps out unselfishly to meet the glaring need of the moment. He is a classic illustration of someone who sees a need that he has the resources to meet. He was willing to step up and meet that need, even at great cost, and even at a very trying time.

As far as we know, Joseph did not have any religious authority structure, church program, Sunday school curriculum, or dynamic leadership skills pushing him to take this action—it was a spontaneous act of service that flowed from his personal faith walk with the Lord. What does it take to motivate you to service?

PRAYER STARTER

LORD, GIVE ME A HEART that spontaneously wants to serve you in creative ways. Bring to my attention the specific needs I am suited and called to meet today, and let me not shrink back into selfishness at the moment of truth. Let me instead boldly offer myself and my resources as Joseph did.

DAY 316

Risen Indeed!

SCRIPTURE READING: MATTHEW 28:9–20; MARK 16:9–20; LUKE 24:13–53; JOHN 20:11–21:25

Two themes recur repeatedly in these passages about the post-resurrection appearances of our Lord. He is indeed risen from the dead, and there is now a great mission for his followers to be about. The end of the gospels is not really the end of the story, but only the beginning.

Every one of us who follows Jesus needs to hear him again saying these two things to us personally: "I am risen indeed" and "There is a great mission for you to be about!" Jesus is still alive today, speaking to us, strengthening us, and working through us. We can count on him. From the famous commission of Matthew 28:18–20, to his reinstatement of Peter to feed his sheep, to your personal walk with him here in the twenty-first century, the purpose of his resurrection is to bring life to others and expand his kingdom on earth. Have you found your part in this great mission?

PRAYER STARTER

Thank you, Lord, that you are indeed alive, and that death is a conquered foe for me. Now that I have such a great salvation, show me my part in bringing it to others. Bless my efforts along with those of my church family to be true to your commission.

DAY 317

Waiting for His Blessing

SCRIPTURE READING: ACTS 1–2

It is significant that the Lord urges the disciples to wait for empowerment by the Spirit before launching the movement that will spread the gospel throughout the world: "Do not leave Jerusalem, but wait for the gift my Father promised, which you have heard me speak about . . . you will receive power when the Holy Spirit comes on you; and you will be my witnesses . . ." (Acts 1:4–8). So many times our impulse is to rush out and act, even if it means functioning in our own power and wisdom, with our own resources. The principle reinforced for us in this passage is that God wants us waiting for him to fill us and for him to be ready before we attempt to do his work.

How are you at waiting? Our world today does not encourage us much in this direction, but God's rhythm is much less frantic than the pace of this world. Always remember that God can do more in an instant than all our efforts can accomplish in a lifetime. Work at developing the discipline of waiting on God. This does not mean we do nothing at all, succumbing to a laziness of the flesh, but it *does* mean that constant activity is not the ultimate value, especially activity that is empty of spiritual power because it is hastily undertaken. Scripture is filled with stories of people who refused to wait for God, and they (and God's kingdom) always paid a price.

PRAYER STARTER

Lord, forgive me for the pride I have evidenced by my empty hurrying about, as if I could accomplish something of eternal value on my schedule, without a touch from you. Help me to not be afraid to wait upon you, because that is where true spiritual power comes from.

DAY 318

Bold and Effective for Him

SCRIPTURE READING: ACTS 3–5

THE PRAYER OF THE BELIEVERS near the end of Acts 4 (verses 24–31) is a truly remarkable phenomenon. These believers have just witnessed two of their prime leaders, Peter and John, hauled in before the Sanhedrin, questioned, and threatened. Instead of praying for an end to persecution, notice what they ask of the Lord: "Now, Lord, consider their threats and enable your servants to speak your word with great boldness. Stretch out your hand to heal and perform miraculous signs and wonders through the name of your holy servant Jesus." They prayed for boldness and effectiveness!

We are further told that the Lord responded positively to this prayer: "After they prayed, the place where they were meeting was shaken. And they were all filled with the Holy Spirit and spoke the word of God boldly." May he get us out of the twenty-first century church to the same place – so that instead of praying for comfort, ease, and the ending of trials, we would first be concerned about our boldness and effectiveness as ambassadors of Christ. This would require a monumental paradigm shift and adjustment of priorities of most of us. Do you have the courage to pray such a prayer?

PRAYER STARTER

LORD, ENABLE ME TO SPEAK YOUR WORD with great boldness. Perform whatever miracles you will through me, and let all of it bring glory to Jesus! Help me to be bold and effective in my impact for you, even if it doesn't mean all my trials will go away.

DAY 319

Finding My Place

SCRIPTURE READING: ACTS 6:1–8:1

Have you found your place of service in the local church? This is a bit of a pointed question, and certainly there are many needs to be met outside the church. However, the New Testament is clear about the importance of believers investing in some form of service to the local body of believers.

In Acts 6, we are told that seven men were set apart as deacons to address the very practical ministry of food distribution among the widows. It would not have been right for the apostles to invest significant time and effort to this matter, because their ministry of prayer and teaching would have suffered. Notice the outcome of this decision and action. After the account of the selection and installation of these men, we are told in 6:7, "So the word of God spread. The number of disciples in Jerusalem increased rapidly, and a large number of priests became obedient to the faith." The church grew and the kingdom advanced when God's people began to take their share of the work that was to be done!

PRAYER STARTER

Lord, help me find joy in serving you through my church. I know that Christianity is not a "spectator sport," so I pray that you will open up the exact right opportunities for service to me, and help me be courageous in pursuing them.

DAY 320

Seeing and Embracing His Work

SCRIPTURE READING: ACTS 8:2–9:43

This section of Acts shows us several examples of early believers obediently joining in where God is already at work. Philip goes to Samaria, shares the gospel, and heals many of the people's afflictions; then he obediently goes southward from Jerusalem, meets the Ethiopian eunuch who is reading Isaiah, and leads him to Christ. Peter and John go to Samaria, impart the Holy Spirit to the believers there, and boldly confront Simon the sorcerer. Ananias obediently goes to minister to Saul, the new convert, even though he fears and distrusts him. Saul begins to preach of Christ in both Damascus and Jerusalem, even amid great opposition by the Jews. Peter is used by God to heal Aeneas in Lydda, and then Dorcas in Joppa.

Are you ready to look for where God is at work around you and join him in what he is doing? This takes a willingness and obedience on our part, but it also requires us to allow him to change us and give us his character. We cannot very well join him in what he's doing unless we are learning to live as he lived.

PRAYER STARTER

Lord, I hunger to see you at work in dramatic ways in this world and to join you in what you are doing. Give me eyes to see, courage to act, and power to complete whatever task you assign to me. Make me more like you, Lord!

DAY 321

A Gospel for All

SCRIPTURE READING: ACTS 10–11

The impact of Peter's vision goes far beyond certain foods that were formerly forbidden being declared clean. It symbolizes the acceptance of those outside the Jewish religious tradition into the family of God on the basis of faith in Christ. At the same time, God is busy working in the heart of Cornelius the God fearer, opening him to the gospel and directing him to Peter as the one to share truth with him.

Praise God today that the gospel is for all people. Thank him for your own entrance into the kingdom of grace. After all, we are all "unclean" until we experience the grace and forgiveness of God through Christ. Pray for those who have not yet heard the gospel, that they would be exposed to Christ and open their hearts to him. Ask God to increase your burden for those who do not know him.

PRAYER STARTER

Thank you Lord, that you are the One who makes the unclean clean, regardless of race, language, or pedigree. Thank you for accepting me, although I am sinful, into your perfect kingdom of righteousness. Help me truly live as a citizen of your kingdom today, and broaden my heart for those you still wish to draw in.

DAY 322

Help My Unbelief!

SCRIPTURE READING: ACTS 12–13

THE REACTION OF THE BELIEVERS to Peter's deliverance from prison is so typical of how we sometimes struggle with unbelief. The passage says clearly that these folks are in the middle of a prayer meeting (talking to God). Peter shows up at the front door, miraculously delivered from prison by the hand of God, and what do they do? They tell Rhoda, the servant girl who announces his arrival, "You're out of your mind," and "It must be an angel."

We can assume that one of the things these believers have been praying for is the welfare of Peter, and even his deliverance; yet they cannot bring themselves to believe it could really be true that he is free. Are you looking for, and expecting answers to your prayers? Or have you given in to the cynical spirit of this age that cannot believe in a God of miracles? Imagine if God's children could start to really believe and act like there is a Father on the throne who really does answer the prayers of his children, and when it suits his purposes, the answer is yes! This type of faith could unleash a new day of effectiveness and power for the church.

PRAYER STARTER

Oh, Lord, I believe ... please help my unbelief! Help me be a person of faith who believes you for great things. I want to be a person of prayer, and I want to see and rejoice in your answers to prayer. Protect me from the cynicism that marks this age, and turn me into a true person of faith.

DAY 323
Finding Faithfulness

SCRIPTURE READING: ACTS 14–15

PEOPLE ARE CAPABLE OF INCREDIBLE FICKLENESS, as in the case of the crowd in Lystra. Our passage tells us that when the people saw Paul heal a man who had been lame since birth, their initial reaction was an attempt to offer sacrifices to Paul and Barnabas and bow in worship to them. They called them Zeus and Hermes, two of the classical Greek gods. Of course, Paul and Barnabas wanted nothing to do with this and told them about Christ. Then some Jews showed up and effectively turned the crowd against Paul to the point that they stoned him.

Notice the similarities with the crowd that welcomed Jesus into Jerusalem with palm branches and days later was yelling for his crucifixion. We must always remember this capacity for fickleness in men and women, and must place our ultimate trust in the only One in the whole universe who is ultimately incapable of fickleness.

PRAYER STARTER

LORD, CONSIDERING THIS PROPENSITY FOR FICKLENESS in people, I ask you to make me wise about what to entrust to whom. I also ask that you solidify my heart and remove the fickleness that is there, so that I may remain faithful to you and loyal to commitments I've made to others.

DAY 324

Living for the Living One

SCRIPTURE READING: GALATIANS 1–3

In some ways, Galatians 2:20 really says it all about the life we are called to live as believers in Christ: "I have been crucified with Christ and I no longer live, but Christ lives in me. The life I live in the body, I live by faith in the Son of God, who loved me and gave himself for me."

Paul speaks here not of a literal, physical crucifixion, but of the death of our old, sinful nature. The very life of Christ now resides within every believer, and we have the ability to allow him to live through us as we surrender to him moment by moment in our lives. When this happens, it is Christ's power and goodness that flows through us, causing us to live righteously, lovingly, and joyfully.

Of course, for this to happen, we do have to yield to him as he reveals himself to us in different parts of our lives. Today, allow him to crucify anything within you that holds you back from his will for your life, and open yourself up to him living through you in the various situations in which you find yourself. This is why he came and gave himself for you!

PRAYER STARTER

Lord, I hunger for your divine life to live dynamically through me. Teach me to live this life by faith in the One who loved me and gave Himself for me.

DAY 325

In with Both Feet

SCRIPTURE READING: GALATIANS 4–6

In addition to being a classic treatise on what it means to be free from the law now that we are in Christ, this section of Galatians contains valuable teachings on living in the Spirit as opposed to living according to the sinful nature (5:16–26). Paul says that these two natures are at war in the life of the believer, and he sets up a contrast that makes the two mutually exclusive. In others words, you cannot live for both at the same time.

Either you have a life that is marked by the Spirit's power (a life of love, joy, peace, and so on) or a life that is marked by all the ugliness of the sinful nature's dominance (sexual immorality, impurity, debauchery, and so on). Have you ever been guilty of having one foot in each of these worlds? This is a very unnatural position to be in. Why not commit to a total, one hundred percent walk in the Spirit, especially in the areas that are toughest for you?

PRAYER STARTER

Lord, please help me learn to walk in the Spirit and turn away from the service of my sinful nature. I want my life to count for you. Multiply my spiritual growth as I surrender to you, and help my life to reflect the glorious qualities of the fruit of your Spirit.

DAY 326

Controlling the Tongue

SCRIPTURE READING: JAMES

THE BOOK OF JAMES is all about practical Christianity. It shows us how to put action to our faith in several different areas of life. The use of our tongues is not the least of these areas. Reread James 3:1–12 and consider for a moment the power of the tongue. This passage says that this is arguably the most difficult area of our lives to control. James even goes so far as to say that if anyone masters this area, he or she is perfect (complete) and is able to control all the other wicked impulses of the body. At the same time, if one does not control the tongue, it "corrupts the whole person, sets the whole course of his life on fire, and is itself set on fire by hell."

Do a quick self check on your speech. Have you been able to control the language you use and ensure that it glorifies and honors the Lord? What about criticism of others? Bitter, angry, hurtful words? Gossip? Slander? Lies? Bragging?

PRAYER STARTER

LORD, I KNOW THAT I AM AT TIMES a person of unclean speech who lives among a people of unclean speech. Purify me where I have corrupted myself through the use of my tongue. Help me use it, instead, as an instrument for good today!

DAY 327

God's Wooing Work

SCRIPTURE READING: ACTS 16:1–18:11

THE REAL MEANING AND PURPOSE of the miraculous deliverance of Paul and Silas from prison (16:25–39) is often perhaps overlooked. It is not really as much about God protecting his servants and delivering them from prison as it is about God's creativity in finding ways to draw people to himself and ultimately get glory from a situation. Notice that the miracle God does in physically opening the doors and loosening the chains is *not* what results in their freedom from prison. It appears they were going to be freed *anyway*. The magistrates sent the order for their official release that very same morning. Paul did not even accept this release without condition, but was willing to stay until he got an apology for their treatment!

So if the miracle is not about the freedom of Paul and Silas, what is it about? It's about *the deliverance of the jailer!* Do you realize that a full eight of these fifteen verses are devoted to the process of this jailer coming to faith in Christ based on this miracle? The real importance of the doors being opened and the shackles being stripped away is that the Lord used the event to bring a Philippian jailer to new life in Christ.

If you've ever made the mistake of thinking that God's activity in this world is, or should be, about your temporal circumstances as a believer, please take the blinders off today and see the superior agenda of God in human history (including our time): to win hearts for the kingdom and glory for the Lord!

PRAYER STARTER

LORD, I KNOW DEEP DOWN THAT THE KINGDOM is a cause worth giving my best efforts to. I know also that you being glorified far surpasses me being comfortable as the grounds for your mighty works in this realm. Even so, I ask you to work mightily in my life, just as you did in that of Paul and Silas, so your kingdom can advance unhindered and you can get glory through me!

DAY 328

Thanking God for Others

SCRIPTURE READING: 1 THESSALONIANS

The first chapter of this book records Paul's musings about the believers in Thessalonica. He speaks of their work and labor, their endurance, their faith, their love, their hope, their chosen status, their imitation of his character, their hunger for truth amid great suffering, their joy at receiving the gospel, the widespread reputation of their faith, their turning from idols to God, and their eagerness for the second coming of Christ. In essence, he "fleshes out" his claim that "... We always thank God for you, mentioning you in our prayers."

Do you make a regular habit of remembering others in your prayers? I don't just mean praying for the needs of others; surely we are all doing that. I'd like to challenge you (and myself) to begin to thank God for specific attributes about others who are dear to you. Thankfulness of this kind expands—as you verbalize your gratitude to God, he will grow it even more. Pick someone today and begin to recite to God the things about him or her for which you are thankful.

PRAYER STARTER

Lord, I thank you for _____, and here's why...

DAY 329

Standing Firm

SCRIPTURE READING: 2 THESSALONIANS; ACTS 18:12–19:22

Paul emphasizes in 2 Thessalonians the importance of staying strong in the faith as we await the coming of the man of lawlessness and the final victory of the Lord Jesus. He encourages the Thessalonians to "stand firm." They are to do this by holding on to the teachings that were passed on to them and by the direct encouragement of the Lord Jesus.

The good news is that we have the same two sources of encouragement available to us today! We are able to tap into the sacred teachings of scripture on a regular basis, from which we get truth, life, and encouragement. Also, we are able to receive direct encouragement from the Lord himself, as the Holy Spirit fills, renews, and empowers us. On the other hand, if we are not absolutely committed to taking in the truth of Scripture and being constantly filled by the Holy Spirit in an intimate relationship, our chances of standing firm are virtually nil. What is your progress in these two practices?

PRAYER STARTER

Lord, please speak to me as I read your word, and please draw me close to you for strength day by day, so I may stand firm for your glory.

DAY 330

Too Smart for God?

SCRIPTURE READING: 1 CORINTHIANS 1-4

One of the most prevalent streams of thought in the world today is the idea that it's ignorant to believe in God. There is a kind of intellectual pride that wars against true faith and commitment to God. 1 Corinthians 1:18–31 is a fitting rebuttal of that mind-set because it stresses that God is not caught off guard at all by this attitude in people. In fact, he fully expects that those who think themselves intellectually elite will reject him. He knows that people have a tendency to think of themselves as "above and beyond" the realm of faith, because they're so smart. He has chosen to confront this dynamic, not by convincing and proving to the "wise" that he is real and his word is true, but by taking the humble, the faithful, and those "foolish" enough to believe, and making a world-changing force out of them.

We must always remember that this is a spiritual battle, and intellectual pride is a spiritual stronghold. It is not just a matter of convincing a rational being of God's existence, that Jesus is the Savior, and so forth. The war against this mind-set is really a confrontation of self-exaltation, self-importance, arrogance, and spiritual blindness. Those of us who believe in the Lord are not trying to convince people to be dumb. Instead, we (and God) are trying to take off the blinders that pride has put on, so that people can see themselves as they really are and God as he really is.

PRAYER STARTER

Lord, I pray against the spiritual stronghold of intellectualism. For all who think they are "too smart" for you, I pray that you will break into their hearts in a powerful way, break down their pride, and open them to the truth. Raise up within your body those who are equipped, called, and anointed to take your light to those in this prideful state of mind.

DAY 331

Enduring Loss for Him

SCRIPTURE READING: 1 CORINTHIANS 5–8

Are you willing to lose for Christ? As part of the conclusion to his teaching about the wrongness of believers taking one another to court publicly in front of nonbelievers, Paul pens these profound words in 1 Corinthians 6:7, "Why not rather be wronged? Why not rather be cheated?"

A large part of our problem in living out the Gospel in twenty-first century America is this: we have been inculcated in a cultural code that says the ultimate goal of this life is to *never* be taken advantage of, treated unjustly, or wounded by another. There is more recourse in our society for the "victim" than any other society in the history of the world. That is why it sounds a bit strange to us to hear someone saying that at times it may be better to be offended and never get justice, to be wounded and endure it quietly instead of seeking recourse. Yet that is exactly what this teaching of Paul urges us to do. Are you willing to "lose" for Christ? To what extent?

PRAYER STARTER

Lord, I know that your call on my life is a call of servanthood to you and of emptying my prideful and self-serving ways. It is a big step to be willing to forego my "rights" and lose for you and your glory, but I genuinely want to be willing, not because I love losing, but because I love you. Use this commitment to insulate me from those who discourage this level of commitment in my life.

DAY 332
Full Speed

SCRIPTURE READING: 1 CORINTHIANS 9–11

Paul uses a racing analogy at the end of Chapter 9 to describe the journey he is on with Christ, seeking to follow him and advance the gospel. He says strict training is involved in a physical race because everyone is working to get the "crown," the trophy given to the winner of a race, which often took the form of a garland worn on the head. Paul's point is that we need to regard ourselves as running in a spiritual race, and we should take a serious approach to our training regimen. The stakes are eternal, after all!

How are you doing in training for the mission into which he has called you? Have you abandoned yourself to becoming the disciple he wants you to be? Do you have a solid commitment to regular prayer, Bible study, and obedience to God? Do you share your faith, attend worship with others, and use your spiritual gifts to bless and serve others? Stop running aimlessly and beating the air—run in such a way as to get the prize!

PRAYER STARTER

Lord, make me a disciple! I want to train hard and make my body my slave, so that I can run at full speed for the prize to which you are calling me. Give me strength and perseverance in this. Let me always grasp its importance.

DAY 333

The Greatest of These

SCRIPTURE READING: 1 CORINTHIANS 12–14

1 Corinthians 13 tells us emphatically that love is necessary, especially in the life of a believer! Even in the church, there seems to be an alarming number of people who regard this truth to be of secondary importance. For example, spiritual power is more important to some than love is; "deep" spiritual truth is more important to some than love; right doctrine is more important to some than love; good works are more important to some than love; right conduct is more important to some than love. And of course, many lesser things outweigh love in the value system of many people—money, sex, pleasure, power, prestige, and so on.

We must guard ourselves from the tendency to think that love is optional. It is "the greatest of these." The world will see Jesus in us because of our love more than they will because of any other factor listed above. He is the only one who can remake our hearts and truly teach us to love. Resolve to surrender to this process!

PRAYER STARTER

Lord, I want to be a true reflector of your love for other people. Teach me how to love others in active, practical ways, that they may sense your love through me. Change me into a more loving person, and remove the things of self within me that block this process.

DAY 334

Giving Yourself Fully

SCRIPTURE READING: 1 CORINTHIANS 15–16

Paul spends the majority of Chapter 15 talking about the resurrection—the certainty of Christ's resurrection from the dead and our future hope of resurrection. He speaks of the resurrection body and of the contrast between this mortal life and the immortality to come. But he sums up the chapter with a double encouragement based on the hope of the coming resurrection: First, *stand firm* (which we explored a few days ago in 2 Thessalonians) and second, always give yourselves fully to the work of the Lord because you know your labor in the Lord is *not in vain*. It is wonderful to realize we can give ourselves *fully* to God in the here and now, because nothing we attempt, accomplish, or give up for him will ultimately be in vain.

Allow these truths to connect for you today. Because we are guaranteed a resurrection life that lasts infinitely longer and is infinitely better than this current existence, and because what we do here and now has a great bearing on how we will spend that eternity, the most reasonable, rational, fruitful thing we can do in this life is to live it "full speed" for the Lord! Sometimes we get duped into thinking that time and effort spent serving God, worshipping God, learning about God, praying, ministering to others, or sharing about him with others is wasted time. Sometimes it even happens very subtly, and we wake up one day with our values changed, even if we would never speak it. Stand against this shift in your own life today, and decide to give yourself fully to him. It is never in vain!

PRAYER STARTER

Lord, I believe that you and your kingdom are worthy of my very best affections, contemplations, and efforts. Empower me to resist the lie that it is somehow not worthwhile to serve you, or that there are more valuable things I can do with my time, talent, and treasure.

DAY 335

Pauline Courage

SCRIPTURE READING: ACTS 19:23–20:1;
2 CORINTHIANS 1–4

When Paul talks about the pressure he was under in Ephesus (2 Corinthians 1:8–11), he speaks of its severity and of its purpose. Of its severity, he says it was "...far beyond our ability to endure, so that we despaired even of life." This tells us how momentous it was that Paul actually wanted to address the mob in the theater. Although afraid for his life, he was willing, and even eager, to give an answer for the gospel he had proclaimed. May we have a portion of this same courage today! Let's ask God for this kind of courage to permeate the entire church of our day, so that the gospel may again spread like it did under the ministry of Paul!

Paul also addresses the purpose of the pressure that was put upon him in Ephesus, and in so doing gives us a principle that needs to reverberate constantly in our minds: "...this happened that we might not rely on ourselves but on God, who raises the dead." Perhaps many of the trials and pressures we endure are meant to teach us this very same thing. Imagine the impact if God were to work into us the kind of courage mentioned above mixed with the kind of faith and trust implied here. Ask him to build both of these in your life today.

PRAYER STARTER

God, please give to your church today the kind of courage I've seen in the life of Paul (and start with me), that he would risk death to bring glory to you and proclaim your gospel. Teach us also to rely on you and not ourselves as we press on toward excellence in our walk with you.

DAY 336

Making Many Rich

SCRIPTURE READING: 2 CORINTHIANS 5–9

THINGS ARE NOT ALWAYS AS THEY SEEM! After Paul speaks of the hardships he has gone through in the process of sharing the gospel message across the world, he lists in 2 Corinthians 6:8–10 a series of paradoxes that define the walk of faith: "...genuine, yet regarded as imposters; known, yet regarded as unknown; dying, yet we live on; beaten, yet not killed; sorrowful, yet always rejoicing; poor, yet making many rich; having nothing, yet possessing everything."

These paradoxes are powerful encouragement for us because they remind us that the physical circumstances in which we find ourselves do not define us. There is a spiritual realm that is even more important and more real than what we see, feel, taste, touch, and smell! In this realm, the believer has victory, and the second half of these paradoxes are true for us. Read back through this list, concentrating on the second part of each paradox and allowing God to sensitize you to its reality in your own experience today.

PRAYER STARTER

LORD, THANK YOU FOR THESE VICTORIES. Help me live with the reality of the spiritual realm before me, so that I can walk in victory even when things are difficult, just as Paul did. Especially help me to "make many rich" by the way I live, think, talk, and act.

DAY 337

The Thought Life

SCRIPTURE READING: 2 CORINTHIANS 10–13

There is a great deal of difference between "looking on the surface of things" (10:7) and looking at the true nature of the challenge of the Christian journey. Paul is emphatic in asserting that we should have a mind-set that transcends the physical realm. We have to realize the import of what goes on "behind the scenes". It helps us *immensely* in living for Christ to realize that our thought life is a prime spiritual battlefield. Paul says we should "take every thought captive to make it obedient to Christ." This means that we must be willing to intensely examine our thoughts, and then be willing to reject those thoughts and thought patterns that do not honor God.

Are you willing to do this on a moment-by-moment basis? Without moving into morbid introspection, begin to think about what you are thinking about today. When your mind begins to move in a direction that you know to be displeasing to God, stop and give it over to him, and ask him to help you change directions!

PRAYER STARTER

Lord, I want my thought life to please you, and I realize this is the starting point for many spiritual battles. Help me to progress today in bringing my thoughts under your dominion. Thank you for being concerned about even the thoughts that seem trivial to me and for being committed to making me like you.

DAY 338

Pervasive Fallenness

SCRIPTURE READING: ROMANS 1–3

In this introductory portion of Romans, Paul presents the tragedy of man's fallenness. His conclusion, stated several different times in several different ways, is that all of mankind stands guilty of sin and under just condemnation for this sin. It is this very simple proposition that many in our society find absolutely untenable. Romans 1–3 gives the most concise, plausible, and credible explanation of the current state of the world and the progression of human history thus far; but the pride of modern people will not allow them to admit their sinfulness or responsibility for this sin before an almighty, omniscient, and holy God. Of course this idea is threatening to those who have no intention of turning away from this prideful path to destruction, but it is essential for people to clearly see their need for Christ before they can come to him in a real way. We who believe must never be swayed from the message of life by those who have no life and don't realize it. That would be absurd!

Today, realize anew that you have no inherent righteousness aside from the righteousness of Christ which he has given to you. Pray for a spiritual breakthrough in your geographical area, beginning with an awareness of personal sin in the lives of those far from God.

PRAYER STARTER

Lord, I believe that "all have sinned and fall short of the glory of God." Help me to never forget the hopelessness from which you saved me. Bring conviction of sin to those in my neighborhood, area, and city, so that their hearts will be made ready to hear the gospel message when you send a messenger.

DAY 339

Dead to Sin

SCRIPTURE READING: ROMANS 4–6

In Romans 6, Paul explores the reality that we are dead to sin once we have accepted Christ as Savior. While Christ was in the flesh, although he never gave in to sin, he was fully human, which made him a target for Satan's temptations. So he was vulnerable and exposed to sin during his human life, just as we are. Furthermore, when he went to the cross he became sin for us, as we read just a few days ago in 2 Corinthians 5:21. When Christ died on the cross, however, he was no longer in any way subject to sin, because he died to it. Paul's point here is that when we come to Christ, he gives to us what he has attained, death to sin.

Our problem is that we are still tempted to sin, and we are fully capable of giving in to it. So the question arises, "How can I be dead to sin if I am still tempted, and still sometimes fall?" The answer lies in Paul's encouragement in verses 11–13: "... count yourselves dead to sin ... do not let sin reign in your mortal body.... Do not offer the parts of your body to sin ... offer the parts of your body to him as instruments of righteousness." Our death to sin is a reality that *we* still have to actualize. He has accomplished it and given it to us, but we must continually allow it to be real in our existence by an act of our will. It is as if he has given us a gift that we are to be continually unwrapping! Will you unwrap it today?

PRAYER STARTER

Lord, I know that I have at times taken the presence of sin in my life too casually. I know that I have many times accepted it as normal or something against which I am powerless. Forgive me for believing the lie and give me strength to truly walk in righteousness as I count myself dead to sin.

Continually break the sinful patterns within me that have been given to me by my inherited sin nature, my family's dysfunction, my culture's misconceptions, and my own selfish choices.

DAY 340

Coming Up Short

SCRIPTURE READING: ROMANS 7–8

In these two chapters, Paul gives us more insight into the struggle with sin after one becomes a Christian. Chapter 7 is about the frustration we all have felt at times when we have tried with all our might to do right and yet still come up short. Chapter 8 follows this up with a declaration of the victory we can have as we continually live by the power of the Holy Spirit within us. He caps off his encouragement with a classic paragraph (verses 31–39) in which he puts all our fears about being rejected by God or separated from him to rest.

Today, ponder the central truth of this concluding paragraph: *Nothing* in this universe can separate us from God's love in Christ. As you reflect on this wondrous truth, realize today that even your own "badness" is included. You cannot "unearn" God's love by your bad behavior any more than you can earn it by your good behavior. His love and our salvation *do not* depend on our deservedness. Shake off the weight of condemnation for your sin today and let his love embrace you. Then live in the Spirit!

PRAYER STARTER

Lord, I thank you that your grace is bigger than my sins and failures and that nothing can separate me from you, even when the struggle with sin is an oppressive burden in my life. Help me to live free from condemnation and experience your victory over sin today.

DAY 341

Free Choice And His Absolute Sovereignty

SCRIPTURE READING: ROMANS 9–11

As Paul begins to discuss the fate of Israel, he raises the issue of God's sovereignty in choosing to move beyond Israel as his uniquely chosen people and open the door for Gentiles to be "grafted in." Throughout these three chapters Paul continually refers to God's sovereign choice in such matters, e.g., 9:11–18, in which he mentions the choosing of Jacob over Esau—before they were born—for divine favor, and God's hardening of Pharoah's heart for his own purposes. At the same time, Paul also clearly asserts throughout the passage that Israel is responsible for its own rejection by God because of its people's nonbelief and that the Gentiles are accepted on the basis of their faith. So which is it, God is sovereign or humans are responsible? Any theologian worth his or her salt has to say that, paradoxical as it sounds, it is both.

Because we live in a humanistic age, the world around us has a lot of trouble accepting either of these concepts. God's sovereignty is distasteful to the humanist because he or she does not want to admit that there is a being higher than humankind that ultimately controls everything. The concept of human responsibility is only slightly more appealing; although it allows for humans' free choice, it also assumes they are responsible to someone other than themselves for the choices they make. Ask God today to guard you from the humanistic climate in which we live and work and to give you a deeper understanding of the relationship between our free choice and his absolute sovereignty.

PRAYER STARTER

Lord, I thank you that you are in control of human history. Thank you that you have chosen me as a recipient of your mercy. Help me to walk in faith instead of nonbelief today.

DAY 342

A Living Sacrifice

SCRIPTURE READING: ROMANS 12–15

Reflect today on the visualization of "living sacrifices." In Romans 12:1 this is how Paul says we are to present ourselves to God. The irony of this description is that sacrifices in the Jewish system were by definition dead, well before they even made it to the altar. There are even some detailed descriptions in Leviticus of how to carry out the killing of the animals to be sacrificed. The idea behind Paul's instruction is that although we retain our lives and are free from physical harm, we are to be like those animal sacrifices in every other way. They were to be totally dedicated and set apart to the Lord. Except for the waste and the parts set apart for the sustenance of the priests, they were to be totally and irrevocably consumed for his glory. We are to be the same way, except that our sacrifice is not the surrender of physical life, but the surrender of the reign of self. We are to learn how to empty ourselves, "giving ourselves up" regularly in worship, obedience, and service to God.

Do these descriptions fit your life? Is it the desire of your heart to be a living sacrifice? If not, then ask God to change your heart on this matter today. There should be nothing more attractive to a believer than surrender to Christ! If this is your desire, at least in your better moments, then ask God to teach you how to live it out more and more in practical ways.

PRAYER STARTER

Dear God, I know that my highest fulfillment comes as I surrender myself to you. I place myself on the altar now, as much as I know how to, and I ask you to take me and glorify yourself in my life.

DAY 343

Beware the Dividers

SCRIPTURE READING: ROMANS 16;
ACTS 20:2–21:16

In the midst of Paul's farewell to the Romans in Chapter 16, he gives them one warning. It concerns those who "... cause divisions and put obstacles in your way that are contrary to the teaching you have learned." He has thus identified two basic behaviors that concern him, especially within the church: causing divisions and advancing doctrines that undermine the gospel. Today, think about this matter of causing divisions. Paul takes this very seriously, as he advises the Roman Christians to "watch out" for them, and even to "keep away" from them. In other words, causing division within the body of Christ is a major "no-no."

Do you know those who are prone to cause divisions? These people are generally easy to identify and sometimes hard to resist. This is not so much about never disagreeing with one another, but about putting up walls and attitudes that effectively cut us off relationally from others within the body. There are countless ways to promote division in the body of Christ. It may be through the advancement of heresy or divisive doctrine, as described above. It may be through constant criticism of those with whom we disagree, especially about petty matters of no real import. It may be through a spirit of complaint against the Lord, the leadership, or a specific person or group within the church. It could be through an elitist, exclusive, or "cliquish" attitude that closes out all but our "inner circle" of friends. There are scores of other ways, both covert and overt, through which we can begin or feed divisions. May the Lord protect us and bring great unity to his church, within *and* among local fellowships worldwide.

PRAYER STARTER

Lord, I do not want to be a divider. Teach me how to turn away from patterns in my life that may contribute to divisions in my church, both intentionally and unintentionally. Teach me also how to heed Paul's warning to beware the "dividers" as I walk through this life.

DAY 344

Eagerness to Share

SCRIPTURE READING: ACTS 21:17–23:35

OBSERVE THE EAGERNESS OF PAUL to share his story of what Christ has done in his life. He is in the middle of a riot (begun by an attempt on his life), under arrest and bound by Roman soldiers, and being carried away for his own protection, and yet he begs to be allowed to address the crowd. He does not plead his own case to get a release from his predicament, but rather boldly presents his story of coming to Christ, in hopes of impacting some who are present to come to Christ as well.

How hotly does your desire to share Christ with others burn? Do you think about ways to share the gospel with your friends, family, and acquaintances? Do you have enough passion about the world being brought to Christ that you would take a risk, like Paul, in order to see it happen? Could it be God is leading you to some level of risk even today?

PRAYER STARTER

LORD, LIVING IN A SOCIETY in which the risks are so much less than what Paul faced, it seems absurd to even ask, but please give me the courage to risk so that your story gets out. Whether that means physical or social risks or risks that involve time or effort, may I be up to the challenge today!

DAY 345

Finding It Convenient

SCRIPTURE READING: ACTS 24–26

Have you ever put God off, expecting him to work in accordance with your own convenience? This is Governor Felix's problem in Acts 24. Paul has talked with him about "righteousness, self-control, and the judgment to come," and Felix, instead of pressing on and finding out how to get right with God, gets scared and sends Paul away. His parting words to Paul are, "When I find it convenient, I will send for you." Tragically, it appears he never found it more convenient to actually respond to what Paul was saying. It is reported that he sent for Paul frequently and talked with him, but there is every reason to believe that this never led to a conversion to Christ in his life.

Whether we are putting off an act of obedience to which he has called us, repentance from a sin by which we have been seduced, or the decision to place our faith in him as personal Lord and Savior, we run the same risk that Felix did—that of *never* really getting around to it. The irony is that it usually gets harder to respond to God over time, not easier. If God has been speaking to you about something specific, remember that procrastination is even more dangerous in the spiritual realm than in the business world or your personal life.

PRAYER STARTER

Lord, forgive me for times when I have put you off. Make me ever quicker to respond to your voice and not be so committed to my own convenience. Show me how to wait with grace when it is time for waiting, but to never wait once you've called me to action!

DAY 346

Prison Preaching

SCRIPTURE READING: ACTS 27–28

Paul again proves to be the ultimate example of determination and faithfulness in sharing the truth to whoever will listen. He takes great encouragement from the message of the angel in 27:24–25 that he and all with him will be saved so that he can go to Rome to stand trial. When he gets there, he finds a way to get the Jewish leaders together so he can share the gospel with them. He does all this while he is under house arrest. He manages to keep up his "prison preaching" in Rome for two years!

Ask God today for the same kind of passion and faithfulness that Paul had, so that you can be on the lookout for opportunities to share life with others even when your circumstances are less than ideal.

PRAYER STARTER

Lord, put the need for the spread of the gospel on my heart in a stronger way than ever before. Thank you for those who were bold and faithful enough to share with me. Help me to do my part today!

DAY 347

Prison Praying

SCRIPTURE READING: EPHESIANS 1–3

These chapters provide for us a wonderfully encouraging description of who we are in Christ, the glorious purposes he has prepared for us, and Paul's prayers for the spiritual welfare of the Ephesian Christians. Take a few moments today to consider the things he prays for them. He says he asks God to: give them the spirit of wisdom and revelation, so they might know him better; enlighten the eyes of their hearts so they can know the hope to which they are called in Christ and his power that works within them; strengthen them with power through his Spirit; let them grasp how wide and long and high and deep Christ's love is; and fill them to the measure of all the fullness of God.

Realize that these are things God desires for each of us, so it is okay for us to pray for them. More than that, these are great things to pray for one another, so take some time today to pray all these things for yourself and at least one other believer.

PRAYER STARTER

Lord, please grant to me the things Paul prays for the Ephesians . . . (pray through the list). Also, grant these things for my brother/sister in Christ, _____ (pray through the list for him or her).

DAY 348

Saying No

SCRIPTURE READING: EPHESIANS 4–6

These chapters are all about the new way of life we are to lead as those who are in Christ. Paul lists a plethora of things we are to avoid, including falsehood, inappropriate anger, stealing, unwholesome talk, bitterness, rage, brawling, slander, malice, sexual immorality, impurity, greed, obscenity, foolish talk, coarse joking, and drunkenness. Now, Christianity is *not* simply a religion of "don'ts"—it's truly all about grace and God's empowerment of us to become something different than we are. It is about the positive things God is doing in our lives and in this world.

However, sometimes the character change God is working in us *is* seen in some things we leave behind, such as the behaviors listed above. There really are some "don'ts." Are you truly serious about ridding your life of all the behaviors that displease God? Look back through this list and pick out at least one area in which you need a newer, deeper level of commitment and some new strength from the Lord to overcome.

PRAYER STARTER

Lord, I want to be more like you, and I realize that sometimes means taking some things out of my life. Give me the courage to truly say no to all the things listed above, that I might be a better reflection of you.

DAY 349

Struggling for Others

SCRIPTURE READING: COLOSSIANS

Have you ever "struggled" for someone else in the spiritual realm? Paul says he is struggling for the Colossians and for the Laodiceans, whom he has not yet met in person. He says that he has such a burden for them that when he prays, it is similar to a physical struggle—it is work! He is praying fervently that they will have encouragement, unity, and understanding. This kind of prayer is more than just a casual chat with God. Paul is expending effort in his pleadings with God.

God invites us to "struggle" in prayer as well. It may be for someone specific to come to personally know the Lord. It may be for another person's spiritual growth, healing, or even for a challenge they are facing. It may be for God to bless your church in some specific way, whether it be with numerical growth, spiritual depth, evangelistic results, unity, revival, joy, peace, wisdom, effectiveness, or any other thing that would advance God's kingdom. It may even be for an answer in your own life. Today, though, pick something outside yourself to "struggle" for in prayer and give it a try. Spend some time on one specific request and focus on it to the point of fervency in prayer.

PRAYER STARTER

Lord, I want to be one who struggles in prayer for things that are truly important. Please build this quality in me today as I struggle for _____.

DAY 350

Worthy of the Gospel

SCRIPTURE READING: PHILIPPIANS

PHILIPPIANS IS A REMARKABLE LETTER OF JOY, although Paul was in prison when he wrote it. His encouragement to the Philippian Christians in 1:27 is particularly applicable to the church of today: "Whatever happens, conduct yourselves in a manner worthy of the gospel." This means that regardless of the conditions around us, regardless of the pressures upon us, and regardless of the actions of other people, our overarching goal in this life is to be living in a worthy manner. The idea is not that we could ever merit salvation because of our conduct, but that because God has given us such a great salvation, our response should be a lifestyle that points others to him.

Is it a goal in your life to live in a manner that you would never be ashamed of before God? If not, why not dedicate yourself to this pursuit today? And if so, is there anything in your life that is not "worthy of the gospel"? Today would be a great day to confess that before God and get your life right with him!

PRAYER STARTER

LORD, I WANT TO LIVE A LIFE WORTHY OF THE GOSPEL. I want my life to count for you, and for there to be nothing in me that makes you ashamed. Draw me ever closer to this goal, and move me forward in it today!

DAY 351
Growth Through Sharing

SCRIPTURE READING: PHILEMON;
1 TIMOTHY 1–3

The sixth verse of Philemon shares a truth of which many are seemingly ignorant. It tells us that the sharing of our faith with others is inextricably linked up with our spiritual growth. Read it again: "I pray that you may be active in sharing your faith, so that you will have a full understanding of every good thing we have in Christ." Imagine that—we actually add to our understanding of Christ as we become active in sharing our faith! This is not the only place in which scripture links wisdom with sharing our faith. Proverbs 11:30 says, "... he who wins souls is wise."

Are you active in seeking opportunities to share your faith? God opens doors for each of us to share, no matter what our spiritual gifts are or what our maturity level is. Don't miss the opportunity to grow spiritually today by seeking chances to speak a word for Christ!

PRAYER STARTER

Lord, make me a faithful witness of your plan for the salvation of those far from you. Give me a genuine love for people that will not allow me to rest from the task of sharing my faith.

DAY 352
The Love of Money

SCRIPTURE READING: 1 TIMOTHY 4–6; TITUS

In 1 Timothy 6:6–10, Paul addresses one of the biggest snares for those seeking to follow Christ, especially in a materially wealthy society such as ours—the love of money. The passage is all about contentment versus greed. Paul describes the attitude that is free from this snare as "great gain" for the believer, and the life defined by a constant eagerness for money as "pierced ... with many griefs," including temptation, a trap, foolish and harmful desires, ruin and destruction.

How is your heart toward money today? Is it your first love? Is the number one pursuit of your life "to get rich"? Sure, none of us would mind more money, but we must guard our hearts against the love of it, about which Paul is warning us. The truth of the matter is that this kind of "money trap" in our attitude can sneak up on us. It can almost imperceptibly color our thinking to the point that all our decisions and all our priorities can begin to be driven by our thirst for wealth, without us really even recognizing it. This mind-set certainly won't ever be challenged by the greed-driven culture in which we live, so it is very important that we take time to examine our hearts periodically. As you do this today, be honest about the love and eagerness for money you may have and present it to God with a request for help to change.

PRAYER STARTER

LORD, PLEASE CLEANSE ME from improper greed or love of money, whether I have picked it up from this culture or just my own innate selfishness. Help me change into a more content and godly person. Tame my ambitions, so they may be pleasing to you!

DAY 353

Soldier, Athlete, and Farmer

SCRIPTURE READING: 2 TIMOTHY

In 2 Timothy 2:1–7, Paul encourages Timothy in developing spiritual strength by using three powerful metaphors: a soldier, an athlete, and a farmer. We can draw much insight for our own lives through these same metaphors. We should see ourselves as soldiers for Christ, enduring the hardships of battle and focusing on pleasing our commander. We should see ourselves as athletes, performing at full speed to win a race, and taking care to stay within the rules. We should see ourselves as farmers, working hard at our tasks to bring in a harvest at the proper time.

Ponder these three metaphors and allow the Lord to speak specifically through them to you. What changes need to be made in your life for you to be a better soldier, a better athlete, and a better farmer? Ask the Lord to work those changes in you so that you can progress in your spiritual strength and your effectiveness as his servant.

PRAYER STARTER

Lord, I know that you have called me to be a spiritual soldier, athlete, and farmer. Unlock the mystery of these metaphors for me, so that my life may be all that you intend for the advancement of your kingdom.

DAY 354

Resisting the Roaring Lion

SCRIPTURE READING: 1 PETER

We are not to give the devil more attention than he warrants, as some unfortunately seem to do. When there is a fixation on the enemy, it can become a distraction to truly following God and loving him with all our hearts. We can end up living "against Satan" rather than "for God." There is, however, an equal and opposite temptation to deny or ignore the presence and power of our adversary. He is said in 1 Peter 5:8 to be prowling around "like a roaring lion looking for someone to devour." This is serious business! This warning is written to believers, so the implication is that it is possible for the devil to do some real damage, even in the life of a believer.

Peter says we are to combat this guerilla-type warfare of the enemy of our souls by being self-controlled and alert, by resisting him, and by standing firm in the faith. The original recipients of this letter were likely undergoing some form of actual physical persecution, and the devil was using this to discourage some and turn them to apostasy. There are many other tools he can use on us to try to accomplish the same thing, but the plan of defense Peter outlines here is our most effective response, as well.

PRAYER STARTER

Lord, please help me understand better what it means to resist the devil when he comes to attack and to get better at consistently doing it. Help me develop more self-control and alertness, so that he cannot pull me away from you because of my selfish desires. Help me hold steadfastly to my faith, no matter the challenges that may arise to it!

DAY 355

The Corruption of the Kingdom

SCRIPTURE READING: JUDE; 2 PETER

Jude speaks frankly about negative influences that have sprung up among the people of God. As we examine what he says about these destructive people, it can be a reminder to us to guard ourselves from any of these qualities, and also to be aware of their presence in others in the church so that we can take appropriate actions, whether it is confrontation, separation, or focused prayer in a given situation.

He calls them godless men who use the gospel of grace as an excuse for immorality. He says they pollute their own bodies, reject authority, slander celestial beings, and speak abusively against whatever they do not understand. He calls them blemishes at love feasts; clouds without rain; trees without fruit and uprooted; wild waves of the sea, foaming up their shame; and wandering stars, for whom the blackest darkness has been reserved forever; grumblers; and fault finders. Finally, he says they follow their own evil desires, and they boast about themselves and flatter others for their own advantage. All these vices are traits we should have absolutely no patience for in ourselves (or in God's church). May he deliver us!

PRAYER STARTER

Lord, please flush any of the above attitudes or actions out of my life and heart, so I may more clearly represent you to everyone who crosses my path. Please deliver your church of today from these destructive elements, so your kingdom may advance undiluted, uncorrupted, and unhindered!

DAY 356

The Peace of Softheartedness

SCRIPTURE READING: HEBREWS 1:1–5:10

Hardening of the heart; rebelling against God, testing and trying God, letting the heart go astray, having a sinful and unbelieving heart, turning away from the living God—they all mean much the same thing, and they all receive stern warnings from the writer of Hebrews in Chapter 3. This kind of response to God inevitably leads to God's discipline, as well as to a profound lack of peace and rest in life. He quotes the Old Testament to back up this point: "Today, if you hear his voice, do not harden your hearts as you did in the rebellion.... So I declared on oath in my anger, 'They shall never enter my rest.'" In contrast, he says that a believing heart leads to the peace and rest of God being visited on that life.

So the question for each of us is really quite simple: will we walk in faith and belief, trusting God enough to obey him and reap the blessings of rest that accompany that lifestyle; or will we refuse to bow before him, allow our hearts to harden, and sign up for the futility, pain, unrest, and even discipline that *always* follows such a decision?

PRAYER STARTER

> Oh, God, I know my heart is very capable of hardness, rebellion, and nonbelief, but I also know that there is a "peace that passes understanding" available to me if I will keep my heart "soft" toward you. Help me walk in the kind of faith, obedience, and humility this passage advances, so that I might truly be at rest in you.

DAY 357

Still on Milk?

SCRIPTURE READING: HEBREWS 5:11–9:28

The writer of Hebrews makes an eloquent plea for maturity to be developed in the life of every believer, using the analogy of babies consuming only milk compared to those who are ready for solid food. He accuses the recipients of being "still on milk" because of their failure to progress in their walk with Christ beyond the basic truths of the faith, which they are in a cycle of consuming over and over again. He then uses these words to describe the mature: "...who by constant use have trained themselves to distinguish good from evil." In other words, maturity in the spiritual realm like many skills and abilities are honed in the physical realm, *by practice* (aka "constant use")!

Are you in the habit of practicing your spiritual walk throughout the week and throughout the day? Unfortunately, many are only committed to Christ to the level of being in a certain place at a certain time on Sunday morning (for some, not even that). The scripture makes it pretty clear, however, that true maturity and the discernment that goes along with it comes only as we relentlessly practice the "basics" in our lives, refusing to settle for just building vast reserves of "head-knowledge" about the things of God. Practice your faith today!

PRAYER STARTER

Lord, I want to be a mature believer, feeding on the meat of your word, no longer satisfied with just milk. Show me ways today in which I can practice my faith walk, so that I may grow to my maximum potential in you. Help me practice following you in everything I say, do, decide, and think—no matter what others do or don't do.

DAY 358

Living Aggressively for Him

SCRIPTURE READING: HEBREWS 10–11

Considering all that Christ has secured for us by his death, we should live our lives joyfully, hopefully, and aggressively for God! In Hebrews 10:19–25, the writer says that Jesus opened up access into the "Most Holy Place" by his blood. This is a place of fellowship with God that none could ever enter by their own merit, and which was truly closed to us until Jesus came and died for us. His very body is called the curtain into the true heavenly Most Holy Place. He has not only opened up access and intimacy with God for us, but he also acts now as our high priest, continually cleansing us.

Given these great realities, we are given four great encouragements in this passage: take advantage of this access and cleansing by continually drawing close to God; hold unswervingly to our faith; spur one another on toward love and good deeds; and be faithful in meeting together for worship and mutual encouragement.

Which of these do you need to pursue more faithfully today?

PRAYER STARTER

Lord, thank you for offering your body as a once-for-all sacrifice for me to gain access into the throne room in heaven. Let me be more bold to enter in, with increased faith in the sufficiency of Christ for my full acceptance, increased encouragement for my brothers and sisters to love and do good, and increased faithfulness in gathering with other Christians at appointed times.

DAY 359

Pain's Purposes

SCRIPTURE READING: HEBREWS 12–13;
2 JOHN; 3 JOHN

How different is the message of Hebrews 12 from some of the "prosperity gospel" messages that are so prevalent in parts of contemporary American Christendom! You know the message—if you just have enough faith, your life will be pain free and prosperous. You will not get sick, you will have wealth and success, your relationships will thrive, and nothing bad will ever happen to you. The writer of Hebrews, however, seems to assume that hardships will be a part of life, even for those who follow Christ. In 12:7–11, he gives fresh insight as to how to interpret the hardships of life. Instead of evidence that our faith is not what it should be, he says that the hardships a believer suffers are to be seen as the discipline of a loving father. The point seems to be that many times God allows pain in our lives to refine us. This is for the purpose of producing "a harvest of righteousness and peace for those who have been trained by it." There is certainly no harm in asking for deliverance from things that trouble us, but we do need to look beyond the pains and struggles when we can and realize that these pains can be evidence of God's love, not his rejection!

PRAYER STARTER

Lord, the pains and disappointments in my life are not easy, but I ask you today to use them to build the holiness, righteousness, and peace that you desire for me.

DAY 360

Fresh Forgiveness

SCRIPTURE READING: 1 JOHN

1 John 1:9 gives us one of the most precious promises of all scripture: "If we confess our sins, he is faithful and just and will forgive us our sins and purify us from all unrighteousness." There has been some debate among scholars as to whether this refers to our initial coming to faith in Christ or whether it means the continual cleansing from sin that is available to us as we walk through this life with all our stumbles and failures. I believe *both* realities are referenced here. The forgiveness we have through Christ is a truly indescribable gift. Thank the Lord for his forgiveness today. If you need a fresh taste of his mercy and grace, ask him now. Experience the wonder of his forgiveness anew as you bring your dirtiness and insufficiency to him in prayer.

PRAYER STARTER

Lord, thank you for your forgiveness. Help me to experience it fully and walk in it today, realizing that you freely forgive me for all my ugliness!

DAY 361

Lukewarmness

SCRIPTURE READING: REVELATION 1-3

The book of Revelation begins with seven letters from the Lord to seven churches. Although these were actual churches at the time of John's vision, the messages serve as powerful warnings to the church of today. The letter to the church of Laodicea is particularly applicable to the contemporary American church, and the essence of it is communicated in 1:15–17—" I know your deeds, that you are neither cold nor hot. I wish you were either one or the other. So, because you are lukewarm—neither hot nor cold – I am about to spit you out of my mouth. You say, 'I am rich; I have acquired wealth and do not need a thing.' But you do not realize that you are wretched, pitiful, poor, blind, and naked.

The two major accusations of this brief passage, "lukewarmness" and trust in riches, are two of the biggest threats to our walk of discipleship today in this culture. We should examine our own hearts and lives *frequently* for these twin cancers. Do you find your faith to be lukewarm, bland, and uninspired? Do you find yourself content with the material comforts of this life? If so, bring this to him today and ask him to change your heart. He can breathe new life into a dead faith, and he can certainly renew your sense of dependency on him. You must allow it, though!

PRAYER STARTER

LORD, RID MY HEART OF THE LUKEWARMNESS that constantly threatens to seep in from the world around me. Help me to be truly on fire for you, so you will never have cause to spew me out. Relieve me of the trust in riches that so often kills faith in you.

DAY 362

Learning to Worship

SCRIPTURE READING: REVELATION 4–9

Chapters four and five of Revelation give us a glimpse of the continual atmosphere of worship and praise in the throne room of God in heaven. This affirms the ultimate, eternal value of worship. The twenty-four elders, the four living creatures, and the multitude of angels are all consumed with praise for the One who sits on the throne and for the Lamb.

Does the worship of God ever take a "backseat" in your life? As you ponder this scene in heaven, let it remind you of the worthiness of *your* praise to God as you worship him privately and with others. When we adore him in our hearts and declare our praises to him, we are not striking out on our own, but are rather joining in the everlasting song of the twenty-four elders, the four living creatures, and the multitude of angels. Today, try declaring your own praise to God using the words of the eternal song in heaven that appears in Revelation 4 and 5.

PRAYER STARTER

> HOLY, HOLY, HOLY is the Lord God Almighty, who was, and is, and is to come ... You are worthy, our Lord and God, to receive glory and honor and power, for you created all things, and by your will they were created and have their being.... You are worthy to take the scroll and to open its seals, because you were slain, and with your blood you purchased men for God from every tribe and language and people and nation. You have made them to be a kingdom and priests to serve our God, and they will reign on the earth.... Worthy is the Lamb, who was slain, to receive power and wealth and wisdom and strength and honor and glory and praise!... To him who sits on the throne and to the Lamb be praise and honor and glory and power, for ever and ever!

DAY 363
A Martyr's Faith

SCRIPTURE READING: REVELATION 10–14

Whatever time frame you attach to it, the defeat of Satan recorded in Revelation 12 is a glorious event. His defeat comes not by the righteousness, good deeds, physical prowess, or wisdom of the saints, but by "...the blood of the Lamb and by the word of their testimony; they did not love their lives so much as to shrink from death" (Revelation 12:11).

In other words, the dragon is defeated by their willingness to face martyrdom for Jesus Christ. The saints are victorious in the same way in which Jesus the Lamb was victorious—through their deaths. This is notable for us in that it challenges the assumption that true spiritual victory in a person's life is accompanied by certain outward evidences of victory.

Many today subtly adopt this assumption, even those who do not hold to a radical "health and wealth" theology. It is a paradox to us that God would value martyrdom, which is easy for us to see as the biggest kind of waste. After all, once one is martyred, there is no more opportunity to live "the blessed life," or make an impact for Christ by "fulfilling his great purposes for your life." But God does not see it this way! Do you value the kind of faith that would cause someone to be willing to lay down his or her life? Do you possess this kind of faith?

PRAYER STARTER

Lord, it is impossible to know whether I possess a martyr's faith unless I am put in a position to find out, but I pray for this kind of faith. Please kill anything in me that holds me back from it. Help me get over my addiction to temporal victories, so that I may be used to accomplish eternal victories.

DAY 364

God Is Always Right

SCRIPTURE READING: REVELATION 15–18

As we read passages of judgment on mankind, such as the seven bowls of God's wrath that are poured out in Chapter 16, some of us begin to see God as cruel and unfair. We must not succumb to this way of thinking! Part of the very definition of God is that he is always right. He is entitled to judge his creation, no matter how uncomfortable this makes the intellectual elite, as well as the common sinner, of our day. As affirmed in Revelation 16:5–7:

> "You are just in these judgments,
> you who are and who were, the
> Holy One,
> because you have so judged;
>
> ...And I heard the altar respond:
> "Yes, Lord God Almighty, true and just are your judgments."

Thank God today that his character is unquestionably righteous and his decisions and actions are always right. Ask him for strength of conviction in this matter, as we live in a world that seems always ready to question every authority, including God, and to rely on its own perverted judgments concerning what is right and wrong, fair and unfair, and just and unjust.

PRAYER STARTER

Lord, please help me to never presume to sit in judgment of you. Help me to serve you with humility rather than listen to the battle cries of this world, which so often seek to challenge either your authority or your character. I am convinced of both—help me to be even more convinced.

DAY 365

God Wins — Eternally!

SCRIPTURE READING: REVELATION 19–22

These chapters contain the culmination of all the events that precede them. They record the return of the Lord Jesus, riding a white horse, to finally conquer the beast and the armies of the earth; Christ's thousand-year reign on the earth; the casting down of Satan into hell; the final judgment of humankind; and the ultimate renewal of everything, including a new, eternal Jerusalem.

Despite the uncertainty of how these events fit together chronologically and the details of their fruition, one thing is abundantly clear—in the end, God and his ways will win. And things will end well for all those who are in Christ! These graphic prophesies of victory for God's kingdom must have been a great encouragement to the first and second-century Christians who read the Bible. At times, these Christians endured great persecution and hardship, and in the midst of such times, the sure words of hope and victory provided just the encouragement they needed to stay the course.

Allow the coming realities of Jesus' victorious return and the beauty of a new heaven and a new earth with none of the pains of this present age to strengthen your heart today. Remember, Christ and those who are in him win!

PRAYER STARTER

Lord, as I prepare myself to walk forward into another day, help me to live in joyful anticipation of your return to make everything right. Thank you that you do have ultimate victory. Help me to live every minute in this today like I believe it.

ABOUT DEAN HILL

 DEAN HILL was raised in a Bible-centered church and a Bible-believing home in Commerce, Georgia. He came into a transforming relationship with Christ in 1985, and has been on a journey of growth in the Lord ever since. Dean committed his life to vocational ministry in 1985 as well, and has pastored three churches in South Carolina and Colorado. His passion is helping people toward true spiritual growth, and he believes that daily Bible reading is an integral part of that process for everyone.

Dean currently serves as the pastor of Stapleton Fellowship Church in Denver (formerly Cherry Creek Community Church). He lives in Aurora, Colorado, with Liz, his wife of 18 years, their two sons, Jake and Isaac, and their Sheltie, King Solomon the Great.